# DESIGNER'S GUIDE TO DIGITAL IMAGING

## CONTROLLING BLACK AND WHITE AND COLOR OUTPUT

## Carl Sesto

Wiley Computer Publishing

John Wiley & Sons, Inc.

New York • Chichester • Brisbane • Toronto • Singapore

*Publisher:* Katherine Schowalter
*Editor:* Phil Sutherland
*Managing Editor:* Mark Hayden
Text design and composition: Carl Sesto

*Library of Congress Cataloging-in-Publication Data:*
Sesto, Carl.
    The Macintosh designer's guide to digital imaging : controlling black and white and color output / Carl Sesto.
        p. cm.
    Includes index.
    ISBN 0-471-13750-2 (Paper : alk. paper)
    1. Computer graphics.  2. Macintosh (Computer)—Programming.
3. Image processing—Digital techniques.  I. Title.
T385.S373  1996
006.6—dc20                                                    95-49195
                                                                     CIP

Printed in the United States of America
10 9 8 7 6 5 4 3 2 1

# Acknowledgments

This book would not have been possible without the support and encouragement of my family, friends, colleagues, and students, to whom I wish to express my deepest appreciation. I especially wish to thank my wife, Cameron, who put up with more than I probably could have during the writing of the manuscript.

I'd like to thank Andrew Eisner at Radius for the use of their IntelliColor Display/20e and Precision Color Pro 24x video card, which made working on the text and illustrations a pleasure. Thanks also to Carol Maher at Agfa for providing an Arcus II flatbed scanner, which was used for most of the scans in the book and which renewed my confidence in desktop equipment. Thanks to Bob McCurdy at Graphic Technology, Inc., who generously loaned me one of their Soft-View D5000 Transparency/Print Viewer; the viewer was central to establishing a reliable color management system.

Without the efforts of Claudette Moore of Moore Literary Agency, and Phil Sutherland of John Wiley & Sons, Inc., this book would still be an idea floating around in my head.

I'd especially like to express my gratitude to Rob Day for his patient and thorough reading of the manuscript. His many suggestions and technical corrections have made this a far more user-friendly and accurate book.

Finally, my sincere gratitude to Alice, whose love and devotion never waiver.

# CONTENTS

# INTRODUCTION

## Aim and Approach

This book was written to help you scan, process pictures, and get the best results using inexpensive equipment. My goal is to provide you with a firm conceptual base and a sound strategy to work with regardless of how you plan to print the results. It is not about graphic design, page layout, or mastering specific software applications. Simplicity and accessibility are the key words to describe this book. It is a book in which you can easily access the important information you need to execute a variety of basic tasks. By following the detailed steps given, you will achieve results with a finesse that rivals that of someone who has worked hard for years to arrive at an accomplished skill level.

The advice and examples offered represent my particular biases, and while there are other ways to arrive at the same destination, they have usually been eliminated for the sake of simplicity. I have used as many illustrations as possible, as large as space permits.

## Organization

This book is organized in three parts: Part I: *Basics*, Part II: *Working*, and Part III: *Getting It Out*.

Part I runs down some important background material, including advice on how to set up your monitor. Even if you find you don't have time for the first four chapters, go over Chapter Five: *Setting Up Your Monitor* carefully. The quality and predictability of your output results depend heavily on your monitor setup.

Part II contains very specific advice on scanning and preparing your files for export to a page layout program if that's where they're headed. This part covers the basic manipulations that every file you print must undergo to assure optimum quality.

1

Part III covers critically important material on file formats, color management, color separations, duotones, and printing.

# Basic Assumptions

In order to infuse this book with the level of accessibility I think is essential for it to be of maximum value to readers, I have proceeded based on certain basic assumptions:

1. You have at least a rudimentary facility with the Macintosh environment. This means that you know how to launch applications, and how to create, open, and close files and folders, and that you know the difference between being in the Finder and in other applications you are running. In addition, you know the basic terminology of the windows environment: where the Close box, Zoom box, Size boxes, and scroll bars are and how to use them. If not, a few hours with a basic reference manual and your first intensive work sessions will get you on your way.

2. You are running Photoshop as your primary image processing application. While there are certainly other programs that will function well, Photoshop is currently the standard against which the others are judged.

3. Your goal is to take control of the scanning, image processing, color separating, and output file management yourself, on desktop equipment. This is in sharp contrast to leaving this work up to a service bureau or a printer. In the latter cases, you would typically be working with FPO (For Position Only) low-resolution images where the quality is irrelevant, and which would be swapped out for the real thing by the service bureau or printer.

4. You have a monitor that will display 24-bit color (millions of colors) if you are planning to work with color images. This capability usually requires an additional video card installed in your computer. If you are working in grayscale (black and white) only, an 8-bit monitor capable of displaying 256 levels of gray will do it. This is the usual capability of a monitor without upgrading. Monitor issues will be discussed in detail in Chapter Five: *Setting Up Your Monitor*.

# Strategy

Here is the basic strategy you will be using for getting pictures of any kind in and out of your computer:

1. Scan. There is more to it than clicking on the Scan button, and if you are using an inexpensive scanner, the original scan will usually leave something to be desired.

2. Adjust the image. This is an important part of the process which in many ways determines the ultimate quality of the result. Adjusting the image involves the following steps:

   - **Rotate and crop precisely.**
   - **Adjust size and resolution.**
   - **Adjust grayscale values or color correct.**
   - **Perform any stylistic modifications.**
   - **Apply Unsharp Masking.**
   - **Clean up dust or other defects.**
   - **Perform any local color or contrast adjustments.**

3. Create color separations or duotones when necessary.

4. Save in the appropriate format for export.

5. Place in a page layout program if the image is part of a book or larger project, or place in a program such as Illustrator if the image is part of a design with typographic elements.

This sequence of events will take more or less time and effort depending on your equipment, skill level, and the nature of the image, but must be performed on every picture you plan to print.

# Who This Book Is For

If you are confronting the challenge of getting optimum printed results from images created on or scanned into your computer, this book was written to help you. If you are planning to print on a desktop laser printer, color or black and white, offset, or any other type of output, you need to understand and be capable of controlling the variables that directly affect print quality.

If you are an artist, graphic design professional, production specialist, desktop publisher, or student, and output images of any kind in any output media—even black and white line work—you need to know what is explained and demonstrated in this book. Even if you are a seasoned graphics professional, with years of experience with FPOs, you may be faced with taking control of and responsibility for your picture files for the first time and find that you need help with the basic imaging concepts.

Armed with new skills, you can expect to get better results from your black and white laser printer, Canon Color Laser Printer, Iris Ink Jet, or die sublimation printer. In this case, better results means prints that more closely match your monitor. These digital proofs can be used as final presentation prints or as accurate digital proofs that will match subsequent proofs from film or offset printed results.

If invoking the Print command is an activity that you associate with crossing your fingers, prayers, mantras, or just fervent hopes because more often than not the results are a surprise, this book is for you.

# PHOTOSHOP ESSENTIALS 1

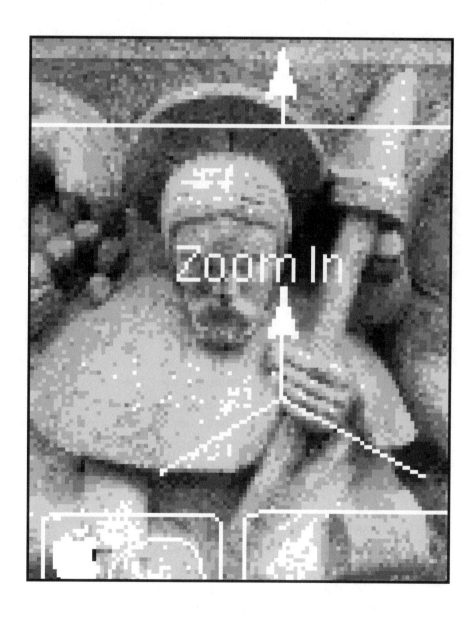

## Getting Around

To get the most out of Photoshop you need to operate the program with both hands. If you're right-handed, you'll use your right hand on the mouse and your left on the keyboard. If you're left-handed, I hope you have an extended keyboard with Command, Option, and Control on both sides of the spacebar. No professional worth her salt would be mousing her way all over the desktop clicking on tools or executing basic commands for which there are keyboard equivalents. Whenever you go to the main menu to execute a command, make a note of what the keyboard equivalent is and try to memorize it as quickly as possible.

### Three-Finger Rule

To begin with, there is a technique called the *three-finger rule (Figure 1.1)* as follows: put your ring finger on the Option key, your middle finger on the Command key, and your index finger on the spacebar. By using the three fingers of your left hand in conjunction with mouse clicks and drags, your work will be made considerably easier. These three keys work like this: when all three fingers are pressed you get the zoom-out icon. When you lift your ring finger, releasing the Option key, the zoom-in icon appears. When only your index finger is on the spacebar, you get the scroll hand. If you click when the zoom-in or zoom-out icon is displayed, Photoshop will respond appropriately. If you click and drag when the scroll hand is visible, you will scroll your image. This technique works exactly like selecting either the zoom or scroll hand tool from the toolbox except that you don't have to mouse your way up to the toolbox to select the tool—all you need are your fingers on the lower left of the keyboard. If you are using any other tool, such as the paint brush or the rubber stamp tool, when you use the three-finger rule, you

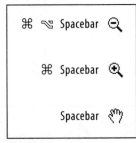

Figure 1.1
Three-finger rule.

⌘ Z     Undo

can instantly access the zoom and scroll hand tools without leaving the tool you are using. This technique is much quicker and easier than clicking on the tools in the toolbox.

⌘ C     Copy

## *Other Features*

When you have the zoom icon displayed, you can click and drag a marquee, instantly zooming way in or out. Double-clicking on the scroll hand tool in the toolbox fits the window to your screen. Double-clicking on the zoom tool brings you to a 1:1 ratio.

⌘ X     Cut

Two other important moves are:

> ⌘ **+ to increase window size**
>
> ⌘ **– to decrease window size**

⌘ V     Paste

These commands change the window size *and* the image size together and are a great way to get around. Try them out and notice how they work differently from the Zoom-in and Zoom-out commands, which change the image only, leaving the window size the same.

⌘ A     Select All

*If you have adjusted the window size with the Size box (lower right corner of the window), you need to click once on the Zoom box (upper right corner of the window) in order for these commands to work.*

⌘ S     Save

Added advantages to having your left hand on the keyboard are that many of the most commonly used keyboard shortcuts are also right there, and that they are the same in most applications *(Figure 1.2)*.

⌘ Q     Quit

If these advantages haven't convinced you, here's another benefit: in Photoshop, when you have a dialog box open such as Levels, Curves, or Unsharp Mask, using the three-finger rule is the *only way* to zoom in and out, and aside from using the scroll bars to get around, using the spacebar is the best way to scroll because you can't leave the dialog to select a tool until you click cancel or OK.

⌘ W

Close Window

Figure 1.2
Keyboard
shortcuts.

In addition to the commands above, Photoshop will move to any tool in the toolbox with the touch of a single key *(Figure 1.3)*.

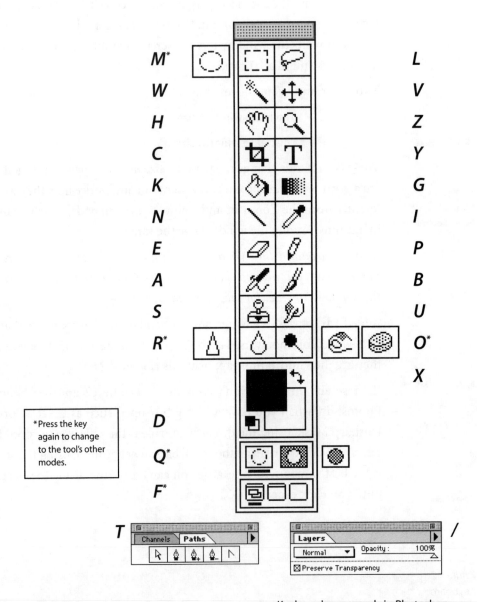

*Press the key again to change to the tool's other modes.

Figure 1.3                                              Keyboard commands in Photoshop.

# Selecting

Making, saving, and manipulating selections is one of the most fundamental concepts of working with Photoshop (as well as most other image manipulation programs). Selections are important for changing a specific area of your image without affecting the entire image. For example, to alter the color of a sky without changing the foreground of a picture, you need to first *select* the sky. This tells Photoshop that you want to change only the sky. Likewise, if you intend to apply a filter to an area without affecting the entire image, or paste something behind part of your image, you must begin by selecting it. Some selections can be made easily while others can take hours of careful work depending upon how distinct the outline is.

*A selected area is defined by the marching ants.*

Following is a brief rundown of the six tools used for selecting.

### *Rectangular/Elliptical Marquee Tool*

This is the top left tool in the toolbox. Option click on the tool to switch between Rectangular and Elliptical marquee or use the keyboard command M, which will toggle between marquee shapes by pressing it again.

The Marquee tools are used to directly select an area of your image by holding down the mouse button and dragging the size and shape marquee you want within the document window.

Important aspects of using the marquee tools:

1. You can constrain the selection area to a specific shape by changing the Style pop-up menu to Fixed, in the Marquee Options dialog box *(Figure 1.4)*.

   *Double-click on any tool to display its Options dialog box.*

2. You can feather the marquee selection as you draw it by first specifying a Feather Radius in the Options dialog box. This will give you a vignetted or soft edge selection *(Figure 1.12)*.

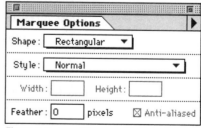

Figure 1.4        Marquee Options Palette.

3. By holding down the option key after you start to draw a marquee, the center of the marquee will be where you started to draw. Normally the marquee edge is where you start to draw, not the center.

4. By holding down the shift key after you start to draw, the marquee shape will be constrained to a perfect square if you are using the Rectangular Marquee tool, or a perfect circle if you are using the Elliptical Marquee tool.

## Lasso

The Lasso tool is used for making rough irregularly shaped selections. This tool is not useful for carefully drawn, detailed selections since you must complete drawing the marquee in a single stroke.

## Magic Wand

The Magic Wand is a great tool for making selections automatically where there is some brightness or color difference separating the area you intend to select.

Important aspects of using the Magic Wand tool:

1. Double click on the Magic Wand tool to display its Options palette *(Figure 1.5)*, and enter a value in the Tolerance field to make the pixels selected more or less specific.

   If there is not much difference between the area you want to select and the surrounding areas, enter a low number. To include a wider range of pixels, enter a higher number.

   The range available is from 0 to 255.

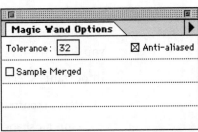

Figure 1.5    Magic Wand Options Palette.

2. Check the Anti-aliased box in the Magic Wand Options dialog box for a smoother edge on the selection. Anti-aliasing reduces the staircasing effect which is more apparent in low resolution files. Anti-aliased checked is the default (normal unless you change it) setting.

## Paint Bucket

The Paint Bucket tool works like the Magic Wand tool except that it adds a fill color or pattern after a selection is made. You can specify color (by changing the foreground color), Opacity, and Mode options for the fill.

## Quick Mask

The Quick Mask tool is a very sophisticated and powerful tool for creating selections. This feature allows you to create selections by painting with any of the paint tools such as the paintbrush, pencil, airbrush, or smudge tool. Using the Quick Mask tool, you can take your time and create highly detailed selections which include gradients (areas that gradually increase or decrease in selection strength) and soft edges.

1. **To use this tool click *once* on the Quick Mask icon on the right-hand side of the Quick Mask icon in the tool box.**

2. **Notice that the Title bar now says Quick Mask in parentheses *(Figure 1.6)*. It is very important to know when you are in the Quick Mask mode and when**

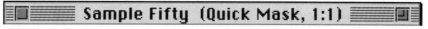

*Figure 1.6*                                                Quick Mask in Title bar.

**you are not, since you can't work normally in this mode. It is used only for creating selections.**

3. **If you double-click on the Quick Mask mode icon you will get the Quick Mask Options dialog box *(Figure 1.7)*, which will allow you to change the color and opacity of the mask. To change the mask color, click once on the Color icon and the Color Picker will open, allowing you to select a new color.**

4. **Type D to get the black and white default colors in the foreground and background.**

5. **Select the Paintbrush tool in the toolbox and paint a stroke on your image. Notice that the color you apply is a**

*Figure 1.7*                Quick Mask Options.

transparent red, but realize that you are painting a mask—not an actual color on your image.

Be sure to have the Brushes Palette open so you can change brush size easily and quickly.

6. Click once on the left-hand Quick Mask icon in the toolbox and notice that the area you painted has become a selection. That's the whole idea: whatever you paint in the Quick Mask mode *becomes* a selection when you return to the normal mode by clicking on the left-hand Quick Mask icon in the Toolbox.

8. Remember that you are painting a mask which will become a selection—you are not painting a color even though it looks like you are.

*If you happen to make a mistake and paint outside of the area you intended to paint, type X, which will reverse the background and foreground colors, allowing you to paint out the mistake.*

## Paths

Even more precise than the Quick Mask tool, the Paths feature allows you to create object-oriented paths (see Chapter Two: *Resolution and File Size*) in the same way that Illustrator and Freehand work. The clear advantages of this feature are that it will allow you to produce paths that you can save and that are *infinitely editable*, and it is the best way to create selections with gradual curves that would be impossible to draw freehand. Paths are not selections, but can be converted to selections at any point. Other advantages are that they can be exported to Adobe Illustrator, and saved paths do not increase the file size as saving a selection does by adding a new channel. The following steps will get you going, but to fully understand how this tool works, you will have to spend some time practicing with it along with some reference material such as the *Adobe Photoshop User Guide,* or a book on Illustrator, since paths work the same way in Photoshop as they do in Illustrator. Figure 1.9 illustrates a path with anchor points.

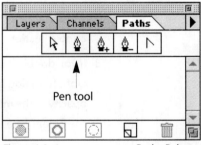

Figure 1.8                    Paths Palette.

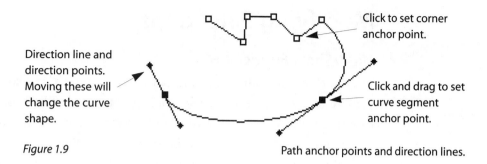

Direction line and direction points. Moving these will change the curve shape.

Click to set corner anchor point.

Click and drag to set curve segment anchor point.

*Figure 1.9*

Path anchor points and direction lines.

1. To use the Paths feature choose **Windows> Palettes> Show Paths**, or type T.

2. When the Paths Palette opens *(Figure 1.8)*, select the pen tool and click once in your window to create a control point and start a path. Curve control points are created by clicking and dragging.

3. By selecting the pointer tool in the Paths Palette, you can move control points and adjust the curve control arms.

4. Save your path by choosing the options triangle in the Paths Palette and pulling down to Save Path *(Figure 1.10)*.

5. The same Palette Options will allow you to turn your path into a selection by choosing Make Selection.

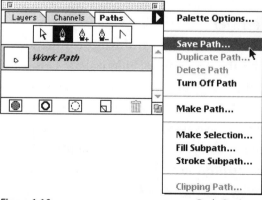

*Figure 1.10*

Path Options.

# Modifying Selections

### Hide/Show Edges ⌘ H

The marching ants can be hidden from view by typing ⌘ H, allowing you to more accurately access your selection. The selection is still in place—only its marquee is hidden. To show the edges type ⌘ H again. The hide and show edges command is located under the **Select** menu. This command is particularly useful when you are setting type in Photoshop because type first appears as a selection, making it difficult to see.

### Save/Load Selection

Selections can be saved along with the file by choosing **Select> Save Selection...** or clicking on the Selection icon in the Channels Palette *(Figure 1.11)*. Once saved, you can load your selection by choosing **Select> Load Selection...**, or drag your new channel into the Selection icon in the Channels Palette, or Option-click on the new channel.

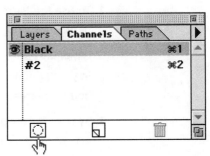

Figure 1.11        Save/Load selection icon.

Note that simply saving the file using the File menu item will not save the selection unless you have first saved the selection using the technique above. Also, saving the selection does *not* save the file to disk. You must first save the selection, and then save the file.

### Feather

Selections can be feathered as they are drawn with the Rectangular, Elliptical, or Lasso tools, or after they are created by choosing **Select> Feather**. If the feathering is applied *after* the selection is created, you will need to copy and paste, fill, move, or apply a filter, before you will see any effect of the feathering *(Figure 1.12)*.

Figure 1.12        Feathered marquee.

### Expand/Contract

Selections can be expanded or contracted by a specified number of pixels after they are created. Choose **Select> Modify> Expand... (or Contract...)**.

### Smooth

Selections with jagged edges can be smoothed by however many pixels you specify. Choose **Select> Modify> Smooth...**.

### Selection Marquees Can Be Moved

With one of the selection tools active, selection marquees can be moved *without moving the contents* by holding down the command and option keys before you click and drag to reposition the marquee. If you click and drag a selection without the Command and Option keys, you will cut a hole in the background where the selection was before the move *(Figure 1.13)*. You can use the arrow keys to nudge the marquee one pixel at a time in any direction.

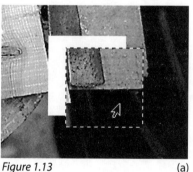 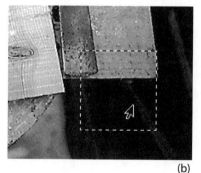

*Figure 1.13*            (a)                      (b)
Click and drag marquee to cut it out of the background (a); Hold down the Command and Option keys to move marquee without moving the contents (b).

### Adding to a Selection

Once a selection is made, you can add to it using any of the selection tools by first holding down the Shift key. With the Magic Wand, for example, if you click once after you have made a selection with it, a new selection will be made, discarding the original selected area. If you hold down the Shift key while clicking a second time (in a new area of the image) with the Magic Wand, the new selection will be *added* to the original selection.

## *Subtracting from a Selection*

Once a selection is made, you can subtract areas from it by first holding down the Command key and using any of the selection tools to define the area to be subtracted.

# The Basics

This is a subject that, like most things, is simple and complex at the same time. I'll stick to the simple, by example explaining only what you absolutely need to know, and leave it at that.

To begin with, you need to understand that anything you put into a computer is digitized. This means that it is broken down into a collection of numbers—the more numbers, the larger the file, because file size is a description of how many numbers are involved, and the size of a file is expressed in numbers.

## Bits & Bytes

One of the amazing aspects of computers is that for all of the elegant possibilities and awesome power packed into small spaces, they work on an incredibly simple principle: by turning on and off little switches. These switches have only two positions: on and off, or 0 and 1. Each two-digit switch is called a *bit*, which is an acronym for *Binary digIT*. It is because a computer does its work by manipulating these digits that its operations are called *digital*, and the information stored is referred to as being *digitized*. Your computer organizes bits into groups of eight called *bytes,* which are the basis for the numbering system used to describe file sizes.

## Deciphering the Numbers

An adaption of the metric system is used to describe the size of files:

| | |
|---|---|
| **8 bits = 1 byte** | **1024 bytes = 1 kilobyte** |
| **1024 kilobyte = 1 megabyte** | **1024 megabyes = 1 gigabyte** |

The reason for bothering about this is to clearly understand that your computer is working exclusively with these numbers behind the scenes. Behind the windows, menu bars, desktop, colors and sounds, in other words, the *graphic interface,* your computer is furiously manipulating trillions of bits, the simple on and off switches, in order to make it all happen.

## Analog vs. Digital

When you see a picture on your monitor, it is important to realize that it is not being displayed in the same way that a slide or film is projected, or the way that a print from a photographic negative is created. In the case of these photographic methods of imaging, there is always a negative or positive of some sort that is made up of *marks* on film or paper which collectively create the picture you see. This is an analog system.

In the case of the image on your computer screen, on the other hand, there is no negative or image of any sort embedded in your computer. There is only a collection of numbers or bits that are organized in a specific manner allowing your computer to assemble the original image. This is a digital system.

## Pixels & File Size

When you are working with a picture of any kind on your computer, the computer organizes the image by using a grid or map of *pixels.* A pixel (acronym for PICture ELement) is the basic building block of any image. In the simplest terms, the more pixels used to describe, or map, the image, the higher its resolution—and the larger the file size. Image files using pixels to describe the picture are called *bitmaps (Figure 2.1a).*

## Object-Oriented Files

Another method your computer uses to describe images is the *object-oriented* approach. Rather than using pixels to describe the image, object-oriented images use a system of shapes, such as circles, lines, rectangles, and curves described by *Bezier curves,* which are mathematical formulas defining *control points (Figure 2.1b).* The advantage of using object-oriented graphics for nonphotographic images is that they retain their quality at any size. Since there are no pixels used to create the image, the edges are always crisp and clean without the *jaggies* or staircasing that can occur with low resolution bitmapped files. In addition, since the image is created by using a system of control points to describe a shape, the file size can be smaller. The most commonly used object-oriented graphics are PostScript fonts. Programs

*Figure 2.1*                              (a)                              (b)
A bitmapped character created in Photoshop at low resolution (a), and an object-oriented character created in Illustrator showing control points (b).

such as Illustrator, Freehand, QuarkXPress, and Pagemaker all use an object-oriented approach. Usually, whenever both type and images are involved, an object-oriented program is used to set the type, and a bitmapping program like Photoshop is used for the pictures. The bitmapped file is then *placed* in the object-oriented application, where it can be scaled and moved around.

### ppi

Pixels are described by their frequency or ppi (pixels per inch), and their bit depth. The pixel resolution of a file is determined when you make the scan by adjusting the dpi (dots per inch) of the scanner driver. *Dpi* in this case is really referring to the ppi of the resulting scan. More about nomenclature in Chapter Four: *Pixels, Dots, & Spots.* As is evident in Figure 2.2, the higher the resolution or ppi of a file, the larger the file size, and the more information the file contains. Also evident is the fact that as the ppi increase, the pixels themselves get smaller to fit more and more into the same space.

### Bit Depth

Each pixel is defined by the number of bits used to describe it. For example a high-contrast black and white image, type, or line illustration is usually a one-bit file. Grayscale or continuous tone black-and-white images use 8 bits per pixel, and color files can use either 8, 24, or 32 bits per pixel *(Figure C.1)*. Don't give up on this yet, it's really not that complicated. An

*Figure 2.2*

10 ppi. File size: 3 Kb          20 ppi. File size: 5 Kb          72 ppi. File size: 39 Kb

Higher resolution yields larger file sizes.

8-bit grayscale file means that each and every pixel can be any one of 256 shades of gray. On any computer, the native or natural *color space* is RGB (red, green, blue), which means that there is one 8-bit channel for each of the three colors: one for the red, one for the green, and one for the blue. It follows then that each channel has the possibility of describing 256 shades of red, green, or blue.

An RGB color file will have the potential of displaying 16.7 million shades of color on your monitor providing you have a 24-bit video card installed. RGB is 24-bit because three 8-bit channels equal 24 bits total. How do you get 16.7 million? By multiplying 256 x 256 x 256, which is 16,777,216. If you don't have a 24-bit card installed in your computer, the chances are it will display 8-bit color. That means 256 colors only. Some monitors are 16-bit, which means they will display thousands of colors: 256 x 256 = 65,536. As I mentioned in the introduction, if you are planning to work with color for final output, you must have a 24-bit color monitor.

CMYK (cyan, magenta, yellow, and black) color has a bit depth of 32 bits per pixel: one 8-bit channel per color, 32 bits total.

## Putting It All Together

The size of a file in kilobytes is determined by:

1. **The pixel dimensions**
   a. **frequency (ppi)**

      b. height and width of the file in pixels

  2. **The bit depth:**

      **Grayscale, RGB, and CMYK, will all produce a different file size.**

Why do you need to be concerned about the size of your files? Because data storage is expensive, and you usually have a finite amount of space at any given time. A floppy disk will hold either 750 Kb or 1400 Kb depending on whether it is a double-sided regular density or double-sided high density disk. If you make and try to save a scan that is 1600 Kb on either of these disks, it simply will not fit. Likewise, no matter how large your hard drive is, you will eventually run out of space on it unless you carefully manage your files and file storage.

## *Optimum Resolution*

The first question you need to answer for yourself is: *How will this file be printed?* Resolution requirements vary depending on the method you intend to use to print the file. In general, the optimum resolution is determined by a combination of how much information you need, and the halftone frequency, or lines per inch (lpi), of the final print. Halftone dots will be discussed in Chapter Four: *Pixels, Dots, & Spots.* You should scan with the final resolution in mind because it is often not possible to successfully increase the resolution later. While it is technically *possible* to sample up, or interpolate and add pixels, your computer is essentially inventing data or information when it does this. The results of sampling up are never as good as if you had scanned at the higher resolution in the first place. Most often the results are fuzzy and lacking in detail *(Figure 2.4a and b)*. Often the best results are obtained by scanning at the optical resolution and sample *down* later in Photoshop (see Chapter Six: *Scanning*).

There are no *absolute* rules dictating the resolution of your file, but there are tried and true guidelines which, when adhered to, will usually produce the best result. In other words, if your resolution is too low for a particular printer or imagesetter, the file will still print—it just won't look very good. Conversely, if the resolution of your file is too high, the file will also still print, but you will have wasted a lot of time processing the file, and space on your drive storing it—with no improvement in the quality.

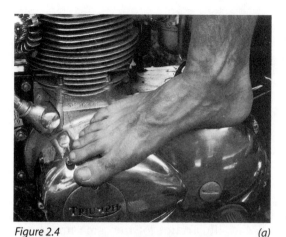 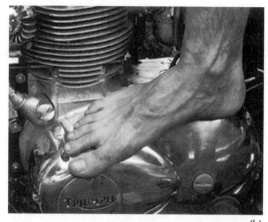

*Figure 2.4*                                    *(a)*                                                                                *(b)*

An image (a) scanned at 300 ppi; (b) scanned at 100 ppi and sampled up to 300 ppi in Photoshop. Even though it has the same resolution as the image on the left, the image on the right is distinctly lacking in sharpness and detail. Moral: You can't sample up very effectively—use the optical resolution of your scanner and sample down later in Photoshop.

# The Guidelines

As a general rule, you should try to keep the file resolution, the ppi, at 1.5 to 2 times the lpi of the printer or press you plan to output to. Again, I would like to stress that you are in complete control of the resolution of your file. There are no automatic safeguards, no bells and whistles that are going to go off if you create a file with either too low or too high a ppi. For a 5 x 7 inch image, here are examples of a 2:1 ratio between ppi and lpi for some printers, along with the resulting file sizes:

| | | | File Sizes | |
| --- | --- | --- | --- | --- |
| **Type of Printer** | **lpi** | **ppi** | **Grayscale** | **CMYK** |
| **300 dpi laser printer:** | 50 | 100 | 342 Kb | 1.34 Mb |
| **600 dpi laser printer:** | 75 | 150 | 770 Kb | 3.0 Mb |
| **Offset press:** | 150 | 300 | 3.0 Mb | 12 Mb |

In cases where there is no fine detail you will get perfectly good results using a 1:1 ratio between lpi and ppi:

| | | | | |
| --- | --- | --- | --- | --- |
| **Offset press:** | 175 | 175 | 1.02 Mb | 4.09 Mb |

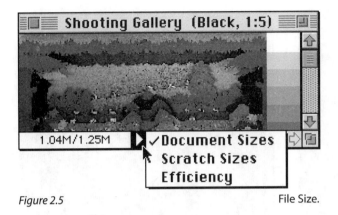

*Figure 2.5*                                    File Size.

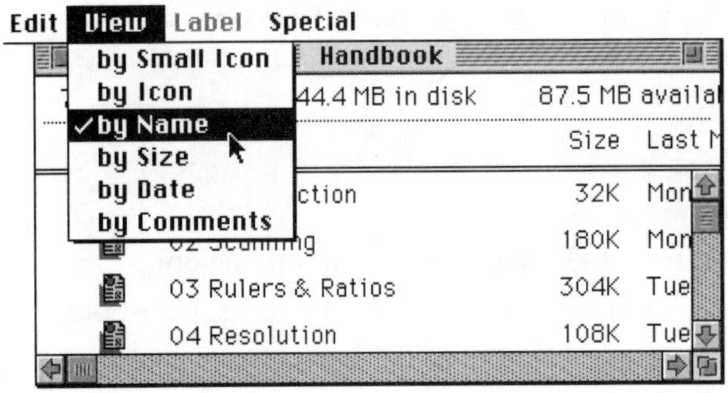

It is in your best interest to keep your files as small as possible while at the same time maintaining adequate resolution (ppi). Nothing is gained by having a ppi that is higher than necessary, and as you can see, when the ppi doubles, the file size—the amount of room required on disk—quadruples. See figure C.2 for an illustration of the same image reproduced with 150 and 300 ppi at 85, 110, and 150 lpi.

### Finding the File Size

How do you find out what the file size is? In Photoshop, the file size is displayed in the lower left-hand corner of the window unless you have used the option triangle to change the field to display the Scratch sizes or Efficiency percentage. The first value indicates the file size as it would be sent to a printer. The second value indicates the file size as it would be saved to disk with any additional channels or layers *(Figure 2.5)*.

*Figure 2.6*                                    View by Name.

Another way is to look at the file name as it is listed in the window of the volume where it is saved. To see this file size, you must View by Name *(Figure 2.6)*.

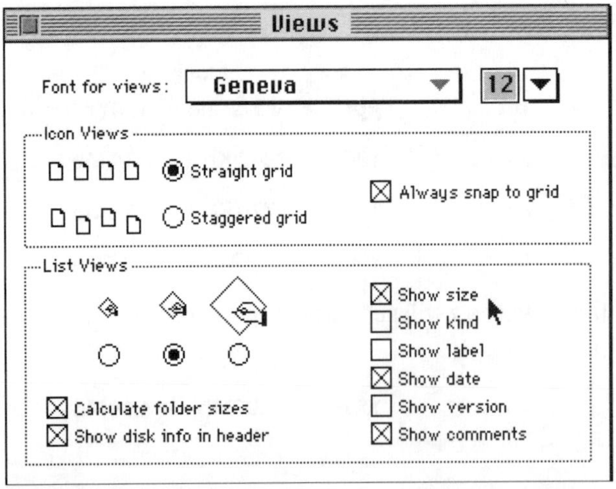

*Figure 2.7*                                    Views Control Panel.

Figure 2.8       Get Info.

In addition, you must have the Show File Sizes checked in the Views dialog box in the Control Panel *(Figure 2.7)*.

A third method of finding out about a file is to select it, either in a window or on the desktop, by clicking once on it and choosing **File> Get Info**, or simply type ⌘ I for Get Info *(Figure 2.8)*.

# Compression Schemes

My advice on compressing your files is—don't do it unless you have no other choice.

There are two types of compression categories: lossless and lossy. The names mean exactly what they imply. Lossless schemes will squash and re-expand your files with no loss of quality or data. Lossy schemes, on the other hand, will degrade the quality of the data.

The primary drawback to either type of compression is that it takes extra time to compress and extra time to decompress the files. If you are working with very large files, this extra time can amount to a considerable delay. So as for most things, there is no free lunch.

The most obvious and prevalent use of compression is for transmitting files via modem to a remote site—from your home or studio to a service bureau, for example—and it is important to keep the transmission time to a minimum. Consult with your service bureau on the best software to use for this purpose.

## *The Irony*

The irony of the situation is that the bigger the file, the more it is crying out for compression, but because of its large size, you might be able to play a round of golf before your computer finishes the compression. You can look forward to playing another nine holes while you are waiting for the decompression. Another consideration is that even in a compressed format *very* large files may still be too large for comfortable modem transmission.

## *Lossless*

To begin with, Photoshop automatically compresses files when you save them in its native format as Photoshop 3.0. This compression is most noticeable in files which have large areas of repetitious pixels.

Other lossless compression schemes are:

**RLE**       **(Run Length Encoding)**

**LZW**       **(Lempel-Ziv-Welch)**

Lossless archiving schemes are:

**Stuffit**

**Disk Doubler**

**Compact Pro**

**PKZIP**

## *Lossy*

The most prevalent lossy scheme is:

**JPEG**       **(Joint Photographic Experts Group)**

Santiago.110. (1:1)

## Seeing Is Not Believing

Your monitor is your visual link between your scanner, or input, and the world of printing, or output. No matter what size or brand monitor you are using, there is one important characteristic which is common to them all:

**The size your picture is displayed on the monitor is variable and may** *never* **be the actual size of the picture when it is printed.**

Sounds strange and even annoying, doesn't it? Perhaps so, but it's an aspect of electronic imaging you will just have to get used to. The reasons for this apparent incompatibility have to do with the relative pixel resolutions of the file and the monitor. If you are not already familiar with the difference between bitmapped and object-oriented types of files, now is a good time to read Chapter Two: *Resolution & File Size* for a brief explanation.

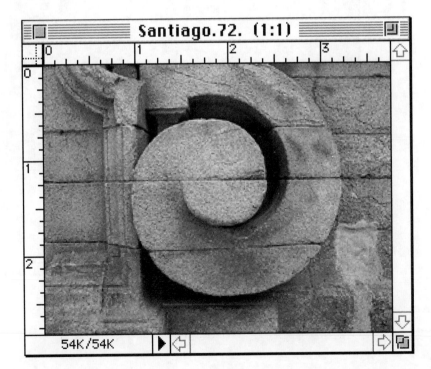

*Figure 3.1*
A 72 ppi file displayed at a 1:1 ratio.

# Ratios

Since your file is actually a collection of pixels which can vary in size and frequency (expressed as ppi), the size that it is displayed at a 1:1 ratio changes with its ppi. This is because your monitor has a *fixed* resolution. Even if you have a monitor/software configuration that allows for switchable resolutions, it is only using one resolution at a time and, for the sake of discussion, is fixed. This means that there is a predetermined grid, already established, into which the file's pixels must fit. It follows, therefore, that if your file resolution is different from your monitor resolution, the pixels of your file will be *forced* to fit the monitor grid. When you display your file

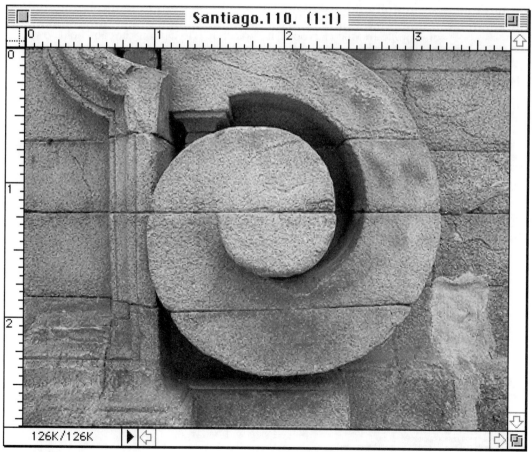

*Figure 3.2*                                    A 110 ppi file will be displayed too large at a 1:1 ratio.

at a 1:1 ratio, it will be the correct (printing) size *only* when the file resolution and the monitor resolution are the same.

> **You should think of the 1:1 ratio as** *display every pixel* **rather than** *display correct size.*

The file shown in Figure 3.1 will appear approximately the correct size at a 1:1 ratio on a monitor with a resolution coresponding to the ppi resolution of the file (72 ppi).

The file shown in Figure 3.2 will appear too large at a 1:1 ratio on the same monitor, since its 110 ppi is greater than the monitor's resolution. Notice how large the inches in the ruler are displayed.

## Finding the File's Resolution

The quickest and easiest way to find out what the actual physical dimensions of your file are when it is open in Photoshop is to Option-click and hold down the mouse button on the file size number in the lower left-hand corner of the window. This will give you a pop-up telling you not only the size, but the type of file, i.e., RGB, Grayscale, Bitmap, or CMYK, and its resolution *(Figure 3.3)*. When you put the pointer on the file size number and hold down the mouse button *without* the Option key, you get a preview diagram of how your image will print on the paper *(Figure 3.4)*. This print preview is responding to your page setup and whatever printer is selected in the Chooser.

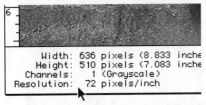

*Figure 3.3*      Option-click the file size.

In practical terms, if your monitor resolution is approximately 72 dpi (as many are), your image will be displayed at the correct size only when its resolution is 72 ppi *and* 1:1 is in the title bar. If your image resolution is lower, 60 ppi, for example, the displayed size will be smaller at 1:1. If your image resolution is higher, 150 ppi, for example, the displayed size will be larger at 1:1.

*Figure 3.4*      Click the file size.

### Image Size

Using the Image Size control in Photoshop (choose **Image> Image Size**), test this discussion by saving one of your picture files at two different resolutions, one matching your monitor's dpi, and another at a different resolution. Keep a transparent ruler handy to hold up to your screen with the screen rulers displayed. Compare the displayed inch to an actual inch and notice that the inches are the correct size only when the resolution of the file matches that of your monitor. Note also that if you are using a 72 dpi monitor and your image resolution is twice that, 144 ppi, you can display it at the correct size, but 2:1 will be in the title bar.

### What's Wrong with 72 ppi?

Why not always use a file resolution of 72 ppi and make life simple? Because 72 ppi is much too low for almost all output purposes. You will need a resolution of about 150 ppi for decent results when you are making final prints even from low resolution printers, and a resolution of 200 to 300 ppi or more for output to high resolution image setters for quality printing (see Chapter Two: *Resolution & File Size*).

### What's My Monitor's Resolution?

How do you find out what your monitor resolution is? Look at the documentation that came with it (there is usually a page called Specifications) and divide the horizontal pixel width by the horizontal viewing area. For example, in the case of an Apple 13-in. monitor, the resolution is described as 640 horizontal pixels with an active viewing area of 235mm horizontally. Converting 235mm to 9.4 in., and dividing by the 640 horizontal pixels, yields 68 as the fixed monitor resolution. If you bought a 24-bit video card, check the software that came with it (in the control panels) to see if it is modifying the displayed resolution.

# Rulers

For work that requires precision, using the rulers in Photoshop can be very helpful especially if you aren't used to the way your monitor can display your images at other than actual size.

### Show Rulers

An easy way to get a feel for the relationship between the physical dimensions of a file and its size as displayed on your monitor in Photoshop is to display the rulers (⌘R, or choose **View> Show Rulers**).

### Changing the Zero Point

You can reposition the ruler zero point both vertically and horizontally by dragging on the crosshairs in the upper left-hand corner where the rulers meet and dropping the new zero point wherever you want on the image. Changing the zero point can be very useful in cases where you are aligning elements within a picture with precision. For example, if you need to place two squares equidistant from the center, drag the ruler crosshairs to the center to reposition the zero point and the ruler will display equal measurements out from both sides of the zero point.

### Changing Units of Measurement

If it's more convenient, you can change the unit of measurement to pixels, centimeters, points, or picas instead of inches. To change the units of measurement, choose **Edit> Preferences> Units**.

## Precise Measuring

Another technique useful for precise measuring is to use the Rectangular Marquee tool in conjunction with the Info Palette:

1. In Photoshop, double-click on the Marquee tool (top left in the Tool Palette). When the Marquee Options Palette opens *(Figure 3.5)*, set the shape option to Rectangular and set the size to Normal unless you have an exact fixed size in mind, in which case you can enter it. Set the feather radius to zero pixels.

2. Choose **Window> Palettes> Show Info**, and the Info Palette will appear.

3. With the Marquee tool selected in the Tool Palette, draw a marquee by clicking and dragging the mouse. As you do this, notice that a new set of measurements appears at the bottom of the

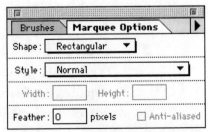

*Figure 3.5*          Marquee Options Palette.

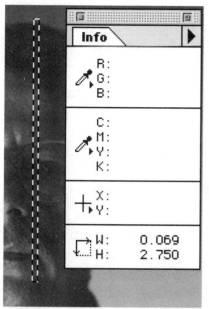

*Figure 3.6*    Width and Height readout.

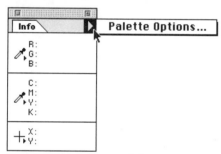

*Figure 3.7*    Palette Options.

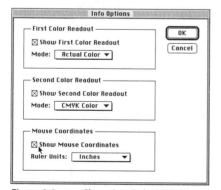

*Figure 3.8*    Changing Palette Options.

Info Palette which displays the exact width and height of the marquee you are drawing *(Figure 3.6)*.

After making a measurement simply click once anywhere in the window and the selection marquee will disappear.

## Show Mouse Coordinates

If the Info Palette does not display the marquee size, Go to the Options triangle at the top of the Info Palette, click and hold down the mouse button, and slide over to the Palette Options pop-up *(Figure 3.7)*. In the dialog box that appears, make sure that the Show Mouse Coordinates box is checked *(Figure 3.8)*.

*Hold down the Shift key to constrain the marquee shape to a perfect square. Hold down the Option and Shift keys to start drawing from the marquee center.*

## Make Selection a Path

To keep the marquee visible in the window without it being a selection, covert your selection into a path. As a path, it will be available as a reference without interfering with any other work.

To make a selection into a path:

1. Choose **Window> Palettes> Show Paths.**

2. When the Paths Palette appears, go to its option triangle and pull down to Make Path *(Figure 3.9)*. Set the Tolerance for 2 pixels and click OK.

3. To turn the path on and off, simply click on either the name (*Work Path* in this example) or the white space below it *(Figure 3.10)*.

4. You can save the path by going to the options triangle in the Paths Palette and pulling down to Save Path, where you will be given an opportunity to name it as you save.

## Paths as Guides

You can draw paths in straight lines (or any shape) by using the pen tool directly. To create a straight line path:

1. **With the Paths Palette open, select the Pen tool and click once to set the first point of your guide.**

2. **Hold the shift key down to constrain your guide to the X or Y axis while you click again to set the end point of your straight line guide.**

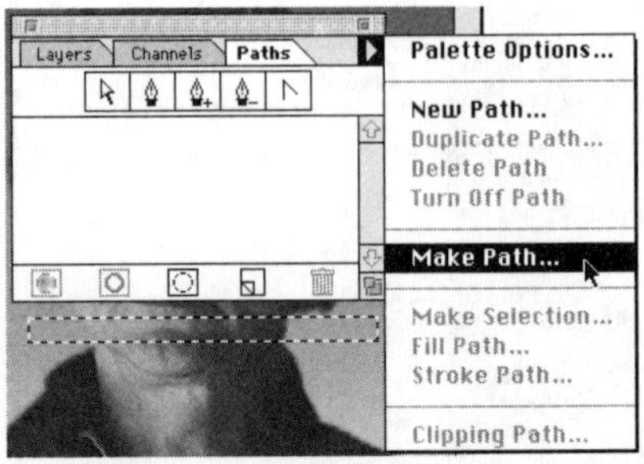

*Figure 3.9*     Paths Palette Options.

*Note that your path will not be saved with the file unless you save your path in the Paths Palette Options pop-up first (Figure 3.11).*

*Figure 3.10*
Click area below path name to turn path off.

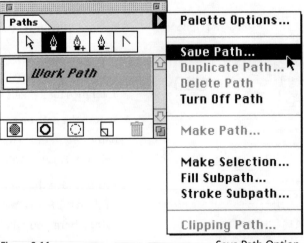

*Figure 3.11*     Save Path Option.

## The Big Three

Before going too far, you'll want a fundamental understanding of the way in which your computer organizes images and how various output devices go about using that information to output the files.

Basically, you need to get a grip on three kinds of marks your computer makes: *pixels, spots, and dots.* While these three kinds of marks are interrelated, they are not the same.

### Welcome to Babel

It is especially important to understand what each is and how it's working for you, because terminology varies widely, and in some cases the term DPI is used to describe all three. Dots are sometimes called spots, and spots are sometimes called dots. Confused yet? The only sure way to avoid terminal confusion is to have a rudimentary understanding of what's really happening. Once empowered with this new knowledge, you'll be able to decipher any discussion in which these terms are thrown about (even if they're used incorrectly or differently), based on the context in which a term is used.

### Industry Standard

Rather than invent new terms and make a confusing situation even more confusing, I'll use the industry standard for naming the three types of marks we will be discussing. Staying with the standard will give you at least a 50/50 chance of understanding and being understood by people who have been in the business for more than a year or two.

## Pixels

The pixel (derived from *picture element*) is the basic building block of your electronic image. You can think of it as roughly equivalent to the grain of conventional photographic processes. Pixels are the little squares you see on your monitor if you zoom way in on your image *(Figure 4.1)*, and are char-

acterized by their bit depth and frequency (see Chapter Two: *Resolution
& File Size*).

### ppi

The frequency of pixels in your file
determines the file's resolution and
is usually described in pixels per
inch—ppi. The higher the ppi, the
more detail or information a file will
have. That is not to say, however, that
you should aim for having the highest ppi possible. For most output

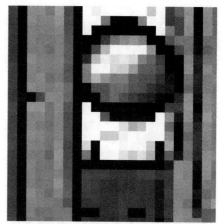

*Figure 4.1*                          Enlarged pixels.

devices, you reach a point of diminishing returns very quickly. Generally,
a 2:1 ratio between pixels and halftone frequency is maximum. For example, if the file is to print in 150 lpi (lines per inch), a ppi of 300 is all you need.
A higher ppi will only add useless information which will bog down all the
systems unnecessarily. Another downside of too high a ppi is the very large
files that result, and that will occupy valuable space on your drive.

# Dots

Most of the pictures we see today have been reproduced from the original
by a printing process of some sort, usually offset lithography. In spite of the
fact that we take the reproduction of color and black and white continuous
tone originals for granted, the whole affair is really a grand illusion, because
printing presses only print one color in one density at a time. If a press has
black ink on its rollers, it will print only solid (100%) black. In other
words—high contrast. So where do all those wonderful colors and grays come
from? You guessed it—the mighty halftone dot.

### Exactly What Is a Halftone Dot?

First used commercially in Philadelphia by Max and Louis Levy in 1883, the
halftone dot is the mechanism which transformed the world of reproduction.
Essentially, a halftone dot is one of a collection of small marks in a regular
grid pattern. When taken together, the grid of dots creates the illusion of a

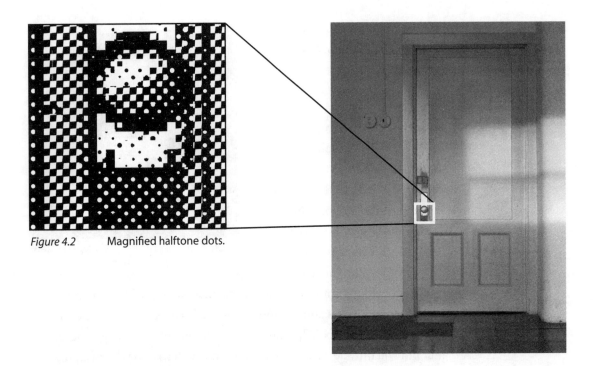

*Figure 4.2*      Magnified halftone dots.

continuous tone. When a photomechanical reproduction is enlarged sufficiently, you see the individual halftone dots that make up the image and create the illusion of tonality *(Figure 4.2).*

*Halftone dots are characterized by their frequency (lpi), shape, and angle.*

## lpi

Halftone dot frequency is described by lines per inch (lpi)—a little strange since we're really talking about rows of dots, not lines; but because they *line up,* someone thought "lpi" was a grand idea. Another wrinkle in the terminology fabric is that lpi is sometimes referred to as *screen frequency, screen ruling,* or, *line screen.* These terms are used more by older types who predate the desktop publishing revolution in the graphic arts. If you want to sound more graphically mature, use "screen ruling" when you visit your printer, instead of "lpi."

Figure 4.3 illustrates the same image reproduced with various lpi's.

*Figure 4.3*

10 lpi.

50 lpi.

100 lpi.

150 lpi.

*Figure 4.4*                                                        Three halftone dot shapes.

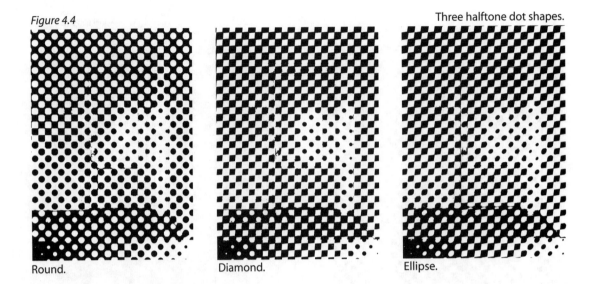

Round.                    Diamond.                    Ellipse.

## Dot Shape

In addition to their frequency, halftone dots are available in a variety of *shapes*. If you're saying to yourself: "uh-oh—here's another thing I have to worry about," put your fears aside because you really *don't* have to worry about it. I'll explain why in a bit, but for now you do need to be aware of the various dot shapes in the event that you need to alter the shape for purely stylistic reasons in an illustration where the dots are prominent, that is, you are working with a low frequency screen (lpi). Plus, you don't want to be empty handed at the next Desktop Publishing Society meeting when someone asks you what your favorite dot shape is.

## Holdover from the Conventional

Most of the halftone dot attributes and terminology for digital imaging have been adopted from conventional screening methods. This, of course, includes *dot shape*. If you browse around in the **Page Setup** of Photoshop, under **Screen...**, you'll notice you have a choice of seven different dot shape options: *custom, round, diamond, ellipse, line, square, cross*. The custom option is for when you have a lot of time on your hands to research and develop your own dot shape—useful for stylistic distortions rather than any serious reproduction. Figures 4.4 and 4.5 illustrate the digital dot shapes at 10 lpi. Most imaging software will offer you a similar selection.

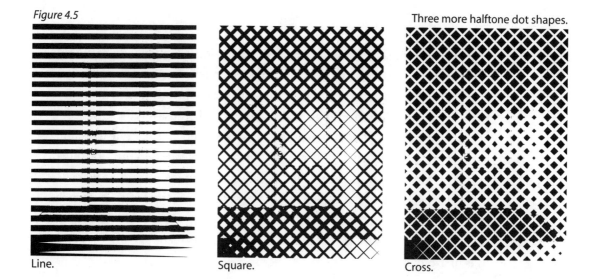

Figure 4.5

Three more halftone dot shapes.

Line.                    Square.                    Cross.

## *Faking It*

Some of these dot shapes are not quite the real thing. In conventional screening, there are a vast number of screens and shapes available, each designed to work best under specialized conditions. For example, there are special screens for every kind of press, from sheet-fed offset to gravure. In the conventional screening world, using a round dot screen would make it easier to prevent the shadows areas of an image from filling in or *plugging,* and using a square dot screen would produce an image with sharper detail. The digital dot shapes available through your image editing software, on the other hand, are poor cousins to the conventional dot shapes. In fact, if you try to send a file to the high resolution imagesetter with a square dot shape selected, you'll be very unpleasantly surprised, since the square dot shape you end up with is nothing like a conventional square dot and doesn't act the same. Not only is it not an actual square dot by conventional standards, but whatever you might have had in mind for dot % values will be disregarded by the imagesetter's inability to cope with the shape.

The point of all of this is that the alternative dot shapes aren't really alternatives, but merely stylistic options for use when dot shape might enhance the appearance of an image as an obvious element. Stick with diamond or ellipse for printing to your laser printer (or its default screens).

## Screen Angle

Every halftone screen has an angle. Since the dots are aligned in regularly spaced rows, the angle of these rows of dots is referred to relative to the 360 degrees of the circle *(Figure C.3)*. In single color printing (which would include black), the screen angle is always set at 45° because it is the least obvious for purely psychological reasons. Figures 4.6 and 4.7 illustrate the same dot shape and frequency at 0° and 45°. The real challenge is in printing multiple colors on top of each other, because any time you put two screens together you get what's called a *moiré* pattern. When the moiré pattern is of a low frequency, the pattern created is disturbing *(Figure 4.8)*. When the moiré is at a high frequency, however, it's called a *rosette (Figure C.3)* and is unavoidable.

## Conventional vs. Digital Screening

A conventional *halftone screen* is a dot matrix on a polyester base (exactly like a photographic negative) through which an exposure of a continuous tone original is made in a graphic arts or process camera. The halftone screen is placed in vacuum contact with the film being exposed and creates the halftone image of the original on the film. The film used for this process, by the way, is special high-contrast film (such as Kodalith) designed for this purpose.

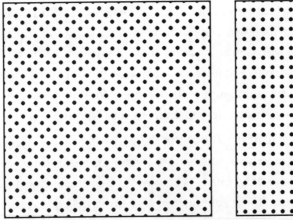

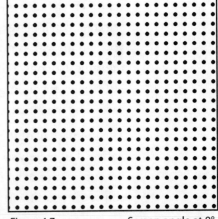

*Figure 4.6*          Screen angle at 45°.     *Figure 4.7*          Screen angle at 0°.

## *Soft Dot/Hard Dot*

Since a conventional halftone screen has a vignetted or soft-edged dot, the halftone dot it produces has a fringe area around its edges. Figure 4.9 illustrates an enlargement of the conventional halftone screen *itself*, not the halftone dots that result from its use. While this detail is certainly a level of minutia which is not essential to know to work with digital imagery, it is one of the main differences between a conventional and digital halftone. The result of this soft dot is that the negative can be manipulated by a process called *dot etching*, where the density of a dot can be altered. In addition, the conventional halftone negative made in a graphic arts camera will respond very differently to the plate-making stage of the printing process. Once the original camera negative is duplicated, the soft dot becomes a hard dot. What this all boils down to is that a conventionally made halftone negative might have somewhat more subtlety of tonal nuance in critical areas such as the bright highlights than a digital halftone. To achieve this and other similarly subtle advantages, some fine reproduction of black and white photographic originals is still made using conventional halftone screening methods.

## *Digital Screening*

The digital halftone is modeled after the conventional approach with respect to functionality, and most of the same terminology is in place. Like the con-

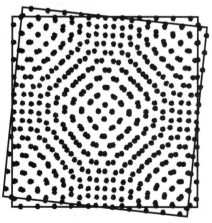

*Figure 4.8*   Low frequency moiré pattern.

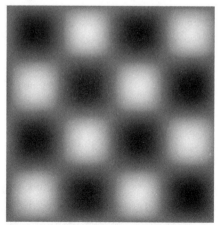

*Figure 4.9*   Conventional halftone screen.

ventional halftone, a digital halftone is characterized by frequency, dot shape, and angle, but it is produced in an entirely different way. To understand how digital halftones are made, you need to know a little about *spots*.

## Spots

Each individual halftone dot is made from even smaller marks used by the imagesetter or laser printer called *spots*. These spots are arranged in a regular pattern referred to as the *recorder grid*. The resolution of the recorder grid is expressed in spots per inch, and here's where terminology gets strange again—this resolution is referred to as *dpi* (dots per inch). Instead of the analog process of light passing through a vignetted screen and exposing a negative, the digital halftone dot is created through the use of a sub-grid of the recorder grid called the *halftone cell (Figure 4.10)*. The cell size is determined by the number of spots available, which in turn is determined by a combination of the resolution of the imagesetter and the lpi of the image at hand. Figure 4.10 shows a halftone cell that is 6 x 6 spots. The

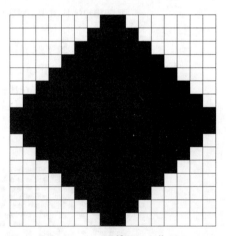

*Figure 4.10* Halftone cell: 37 possible grays.     *Figure 4.11*     Halftone cell: 257 grays.

halftone dot this cell produces can be any one of 36 levels of gray—actually 37 when white is included (all available spots turned off). Figure 4.11 illustrates one cell that is 16 x 16, spots which can produce a halftone dot with 256 possible grays plus white. The way in which high resolution imagesetters manage the creation of halftone dots is called *spot function*—that is,

*Figure 4.12*
Ragged edges
of digital
halftone dot.

the order in which the imagesetter decides to fill in the available spots and draw an individual halftone dot. Figure 4.12 illustrates how digital halftone dots might appear in an enlarged section of an image. Notice the ragged edges of each dot, which is characteristic of digital halftones.

## Gray Levels

256 is the magic (ideal) number of gray levels, and the maximum number available with current imaging technology. Why 256? Because it represents $2^8$—see Chapter Two: *Resolution & File Size* for more about how your Macintosh "thinks." In digital halftoning, the number of gray levels involved is critical, because too few will cause posterizing or banding in continuous tone graduations *(Figure 4.13)*.

## How Many Grays Do I Have?

The formula for figuring out the number of gray levels you will end up with when you print a file is:

$$\left(\frac{\text{dpi}}{\text{lpi}}\right)^2 + 1 = \text{shades of gray}$$

You flunked ninth grade math? Don't worry, it's really very simple. Let's say you're planning to print a grayscale file with a 150 lpi halftone screen and you are going to use a service bureau with a 2400 dpi imagesetter for making the film. Divide 2400 by 150, which results in 16. Multiply 16 by itself and you arrive at 256 + 1 (all spots off) = 257—the maximum number of gray levels (including white) you can have. You're golden. Figure 4.14 illustrates a file with the magic number of gray levels.

## How Many Gray Levels Do I Need?

Suddenly you (or your client) have become obsessed with printing with no less than a 200 lpi screen ruling. You run the numbers again: 2400 dpi divided by 200 lpi = 12. Then 12 times 12 results in 144 + 1 = 145 levels of gray. Not golden, *but* probably adequate for most images. In fact, I routinely run color and grayscale images with this configuration without problems. The same formula is used for calculating the number of gray levels in color

*Figure 4.13*          20 gray levels     *Figure 4.14*          257 gray levels

images. Anything fewer than 145 gray levels for full range photographs printed on coated stock would have me worried.

### Other Criteria

The number of gray levels you can get away with without compromising quality will depend on the type of image you are working with, the quality of paper (coated or uncoated), and even the kind and quality of press used for the printing. For most images, the 145 levels will work fine. Even as few as 100 gray levels might be enough for pictures with very limited tonal range and no graduations. For an Ansel Adams big sky photograph of Yosemite (again, printed with a 200 lpi screen), I would use an imagesetter with a resolution of 3600 dpi, or reduce the lpi to 150, either of which would bring me to the maximum number of available grays.

# Assigning Halftone Screen Attributes

In Photoshop, the screen attributes are accessed through the Page Setup dialog box under the **File** menu *(Figure 4.15)*. Click on the secondary button labeled **Screen...** and you're on your way. The screen settings will be saved with the file in Photoshop format and optionally in EPS (Encapsulated

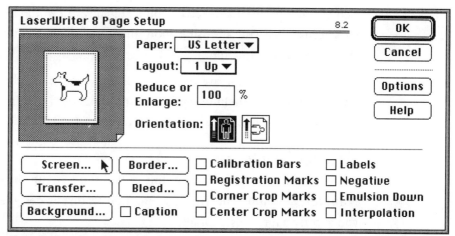

*Figure 4.15*                                                    Page Setup dialog box.

Postscript) format if you specify saving them, but not in other file formats *(Figures 4.16 and 4.17).*

## When Should You Specify Screens?

When you are printing from your own laser printer to optimize its capabilities. For example, if you have a 600 dpi printer you might prefer to use an 80 lpi screen ruling instead of Photoshop's default *Use Printers Screens*. Another example of when you might specify a screen ruling is when you are doing specialized work intended for a printmaking medium, such as silkscreen, photo-etching, or photo-woodcut. You might specify your own screen attributes if you are using the screen frequency as an obvious design

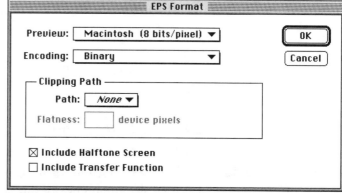

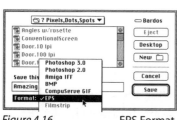

*Figure 4.16*          EPS Format.          *Figure 4.17*          Include Halftone Screen.

element, and need a 14 lpi screen ruling. Finally, you would need to specify screens when you are using more than one screen frequency on the same page or the same film.

In all of these instances, save your file in the EPS format and check **Include Halftone Screens** (**Include Transfer Function** should remain unchecked) in the secondary dialog box that appears *(Figure 4.17)*.

## Transfer Function

Directly under the **Screen...** button in the **Page Setup** dialog box is a **Transfer...** button. The Transfer Function feature is designed to allow you to correct for a miscalibrated imagesetter. For example, if you consistently get a 54% dot when you should be getting a 50% dot according to your Info Palette readout, you can correct for the error using Transfer Function *(Figure 4.18)*.

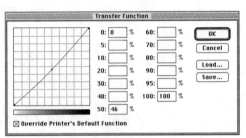

Figure 4.18        Transfer Function correction.

## When Should You Use Transfer Function?

Again, only when you are doing customized work to output to your own laser printer or alternative printmaking media where through trial and error you can arrive at the best settings with low risk to your wallet. Although the transfer function is intended to be used to correct for an imagesetter's miscalibration, if your service bureau's imagesetter is consistently out of calibration, don't try to fix it with Transfer Function—change service bureaus. If changing service bureaus isn't feasible, you should approach using the transfer function with great trepidation since it applies an *invisible* modification to your files which could easily get you into trouble if not applied very skillfully.

## Printing from a Laser Printer

I will regularly apply a transfer function to files printed from my Apple LaserWriter Select 360 (600 dpi) when I am specifying a screen ruling of 80 lpi or higher. Typical settings I use for this purpose are illustrated in Figure

4.19. Note that every laser printer will have its own ideal transfer function settings for getting the best-looking results. Some trial and error is the best way to arrive at what's best for your equipment.

To really get a feel for how your transfer function is working, set your screen frequency to about 85 lpi, and print a test proof with Calibration Bars checked in the Page Setup *(Figure 4.15)*. This will give you a small grayscale at the bottom of your image. Make a print with and without your Transfer curve and compare the results. Notice that using the transfer function opened up the separation in the shadow end of the calibration bar, compensating for the compression in the shadows which resulted from the higher lpi.

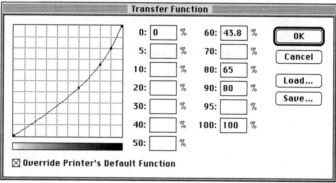

Figure 4.19                                          Transfer Function curve.

## Calibrating with Dot Gain

If your printed image is overall too light or too dark, adjust the dot gain % in the Printing Inks Setup. Make sure you have the *Use Dot Gain for Grayscale* checkbox checked in the Printing Inks Setup dialog box (choose **File> Preferences> Printing Inks Setup...** ). This will change your monitor to match your laser printer results.

For example, if your print came out too dark, adjust the dot gain % upwards to darken your monitor's display and match the dark laser print. What good did that do, you're asking yourself—now the print *and* the monitor are too dark.

*The key is in the next step:* adjust the image using Levels or Curves, back to the correct overall brightness on the monitor. Make a new print and it will match your monitor as will all subsequent prints from that monitor and printer setup. You have now calibrated your monitor to your printer. Keep in mind that the dot gain % that works *is for your particular laser printer only.* When you send a file to a different printer, you will have to calibrate again by following the same steps:

1. Make a test print.

2. Compare it to your monitor and adjust the dot gain % in the Printing Inks Setup dialog box so your monitor matches the print.

3. Use Levels or Curves to adjust the file so that it looks the way you want it to on your monitor and save it.

4. Make a final print.

### Smart People at Work

For serious production work it is generally a mistake to specify your own screens when using a high resolution imagesetter. Determining exactly what the best halftone dot shape and angle is for any particular imageset-ter is a science in itself. Legions of scientists and technicians spend entire careers optimizing *spot function* (the way in which an imagesetter creates a halftone dot). The major players in this environment name and market their systems' screening technology very aggressively. Scitex Screening, Agfa Balanced Screening, and Linotype-Hell's HQS are just a few such systems. Because of the intense competitive atmosphere of marketing graphic arts systems, and the special challenges associated with digital screening, you can be fairly certain of getting the best results from any given equipment by using the manufacturers screening technology. Unless you have a compelling reason to do otherwise, limit yourself to specifying only the screen frequency (lpi), and leave the dot shape and angle to the experts.

# Stochastic Screening

Recently, a technique for screening that does not involve halftone dots has been introduced. The technique is called stochastic or frequency modulated (FM) screening *(Figure 4.19)*. Frequency modulated screening works by creating an image with millions of marks which are all the same size, but vary in the number of marks for any given area of the image. The frequency of FM screening is much higher than that of halftoning and requires more care on the part of the printer in film making, and platemaking, as well as on press.

The advantages of FM screening are the absence of moiré patterns, since the marks are not arranged in a regular grid, and extraordinary sharpness and color saturation. Since there are no screen angles to deal with, more than four colors can be used on any given image without interference. Other advantages of FM screening are lower imagesetter and scanning resolutions than that of the standard halftone or AM (amplitude modulated) screening technology. All in all, the results look much more like those of continuous tone printing techniques. As yet, due to the increased difficulty of managing FM or stochastic screening, it hasn't become commonplace, though it is used occasionally to obtain especially high quality results.

The major players in the imaging field call their FM screening technology by compelling names such as CristalRaster (Agfa), Diamond Screening (Linotype-Hell), and FullTone (Scitex).

*Figure 4.19*                (a)                                                                (b)
Conventional halftone screen at 50 lpi (a), and Stochastic screen (b).

# SETTING UP YOUR MONITOR 5

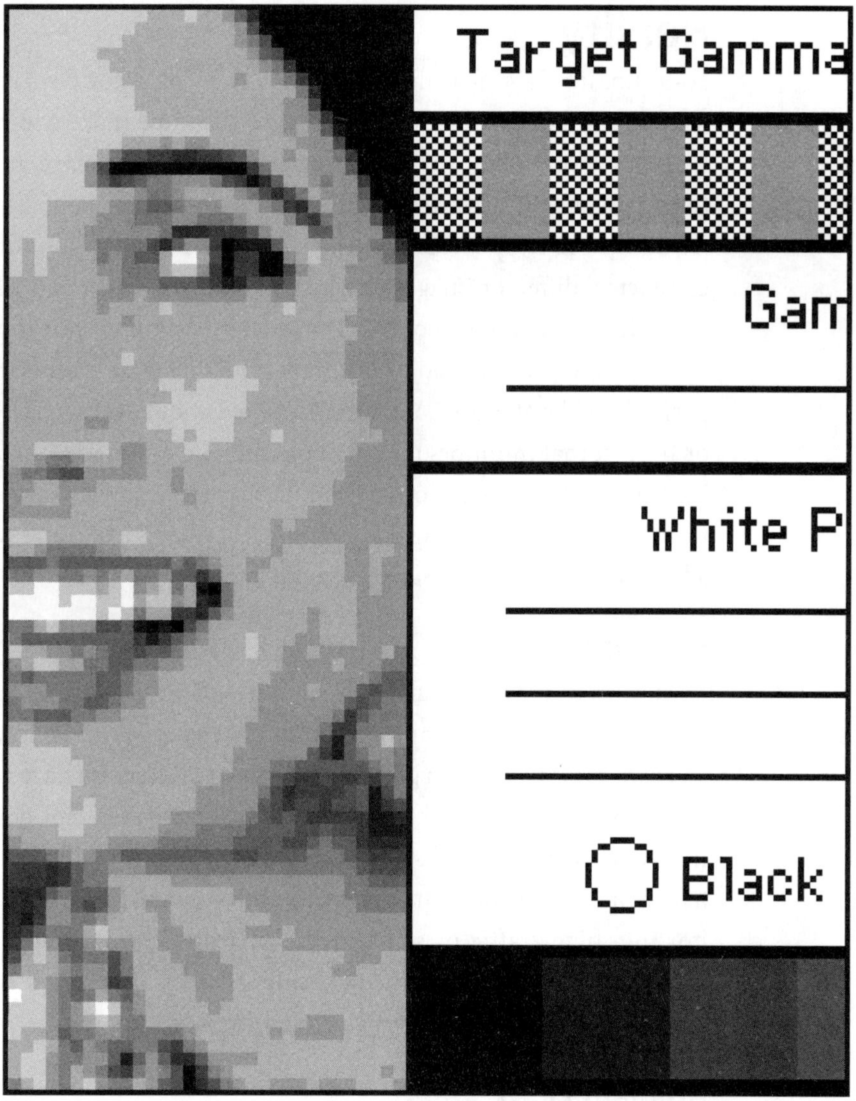

## Reality

Your monitor is your reality. Just about every monitor displays color differently from every other monitor—even the same make and model often look different. When you work long and hard on an image, making carefully considered and heartfelt decisions about the subtle relationships of color, it's dismaying to open the same file on someone else's monitor and find a completely different image. So which one do you trust, and which monitor is displaying the real color? The answer is simple: your monitor. Your mission is to get any kind of output to look like your monitor, which is a perfectly achievable goal. You aren't worried about everyone else's monitor or the fact that monitors may all look different—you are (theoretically, at least) happy with your monitor and the way it displays color—so you start from there. Understanding this concept is very important and will save you a lot of confusion and disappointment later.

### Stabilize!

Regardless of the age, quality, or condition of your display, *it is important to stabilize it*. If your monitor is constantly changing in the way it displays color, you will never get a grip on your output. After you have achieved the optimum settings for your monitor, leave it alone—even tape down the contrast and brightness knobs if your monitor has them. I will assume that you have a monitor in an environment you can control. If you work on a monitor in a high traffic or semi-public environment such as a classroom, stabilizing it can be very difficult to impossible, since everyone who uses it will have a different idea about what looks good.

### Ambient Light

In addition to stabilizing your monitor, you will want to stabilize the ambient light in the room where you work. The room light, daylight or artificial, has a major impact on the appearance of images on your monitor. Factors such as the time of day, the color of the walls, and the proximity of any other light source, all play a part in how your monitor looks. If you work in a room with windows, and you work at various hours throughout the day, it would be a good idea to hang curtains or get blinds to control the intensity of daylight entering the room. Not only will the intensity of the daylight affect the appearance of the color on your monitor, but the color of the daylight as it changes throughout the day will also have an effect.

## White Point

You should adjust the brightness, contrast, and color temperature of your monitor so that it closely approximates white paper. Of course there is no getting around the fact that your monitor is an RGB device—essentially a video display just like your television set—and will never display images exactly like those printed on paper and viewed by reflected light. The idea, however, is to adjust your monitor so that it comes as close as possible to the look of images viewed by reflected light; and despite the fact that a perfect match may never be achieved, you can come very close—certainly closer than most monitors look with no attempt to adjust them whatsoever. For the most part, monitors which are uncalibrated, "out of the box," are far too blue and bright to function well for careful and controlled color work.

There are two (at least) schools of thought on this subject. Many long-time (pre-desktop publishing) professionals in the graphic arts field insist that getting your monitor to look close to a printed result is impossible, so don't bother trying. Proponents of this approach like to go by the numbers (i.e., the percent of each color as measured by an on-screen densitometer such as Photoshop's Info Palette), and through experience, judge what a color will print like based on the densitometric readout, ignoring the color the monitor actually displays. While this approach has a place in the world of reproduction specialists, it is one that leaves out anyone who doesn't have many years experience in visualizing final color from a set of numbers. The second approach is the one we are taking, that is, to bring your monitor into a reasonable *gamut* (range of colors displayed), stabilize it, and learn to calibrate to any output medium.

### Viewing Box

You should make or buy a viewing box *(Figure 5.1)* with a built-in 5000° light source so that you can compare originals and printed results to your monitor in a stable lighting situation. A viewer is important also because the color of any image, whether the original is a print or a transparency, can change dramatically with the color of light it is viewed by. This may seem extreme if you're not used to working in a professional environment, but it is an essen-

Figure 5.1                                    GTI D5000 transparency/print viewer (left).

tial part of the calibration process. Professionals in the graphic arts and printing industries have adopted a standard of 5000° Kelvin as the light source for critical color evaluation. 5000° Kelvin is a cool but not blue color of light approximating north sky daylight at mid-day. Using a viewer can make a big difference in how you perceive prints, transparencies, or press proofs, since it will allow you to work with a lower ambient light level, reducing the glare on your monitor, and maintain adequate and stable lighting on the artwork.

# Before Beginning

The Photoshop control panel device Knoll Gamma is used in the steps below to control the color and *gamma* (brightness range) of your monitor.

If you have third-party calibration software installed, such as Radius IntelliColor or Precision Color, use that instead of the Gamma utility if you prefer, but don't use both. In following these steps, don't be too concerned with exactness. Remember, it's your monitor, and you want to set it up in a way that pleases you. Also keep in mind that your goal is to calm down the video feel of your monitor and get it to appear more like an image viewed by reflected light. This usually means calming down the brightness considerably (use a white piece of paper as a reference), and getting rid of the typical blue cast. You might want to go through the following steps more than once in order to get a sense of what these controls can do for you. If you are accustomed to working with an unadjusted monitor, i.e., too bright and too blue, following these steps will make your monitor seem somewhat dimmed and warmer in color. Give yourself a chance to get used to a "calmed down" or calibrated monitor before you make any judgments about the effectiveness of the new adjustments. Once you get used to it, you will wonder how anyone can stand the typical uncalibrated settings.

## Reference Proof

Since you are going to use your monitor as your basis for digital reality— what things really look like—you need to calibrate your monitor carefully.

In order to adjust your monitor using Knoll Gamma or a similar control panel utility, it is essential to produce a color target print to refer to. Your target print must include a sample of all the CMYK color combinations in addition to an image with a wide variety of colors. It just so happens that Photoshop ships with a ready-made calibration file, called Olé No Moiré. This file is buried in the Photoshop folder under **Goodies> Calibration> Separation Sources** *(Figure C.4)*. You can add ramps (graduated color bars) of the individual primary and secondary colors to the file if you feel confident about using the Gradient tool, as well as a CMY ramp which can be useful for accessing color *(Figure C.5)*. The Olé No Moiré file as supplied, however, will do the trick nicely.

*It is very important that you do not alter the* Olé No Moiré *file in any way, other than adding ramps if you choose to do so. The file that you use to com-*

*pare to your target proof must be exactly the same file used to produce the proof. If you do add ramps to the file, make certain that you do it in the CMYK mode.*

For the sake of simplicity, I will assume that you are going to use the Olé No Moiré calibration file that is supplied with Photoshop, which is the safest bet for the time being. An advantage of using the Olé No Moiré file is that many service bureaus and printers are familiar with it, and may be able to provide you with a proof if you ask for it. Also, everybody who uses Photoshop has exactly the same file in their Separation Sources folder, making it a universal reference point.

## Making a Proof

Since the proof you are going to make will be used to check and make the final adjustments to your monitor, this is a good place to discuss the proof in a little more detail. For the purposes of calibrating your monitor, the most useful type of proof to have made from the Olé No Moiré file is a contact proof from film. Aside from a press proof, a contact proof from film is the most accurate representation of the file you can acquire, since digital proofs will vary widely in color and rendition of the highlight values. Prepress proofing systems, on the other hand, conform closely to rigid standards for pigment color and dot gain and are, therefore, remarkably consistent provided you stay with the *same* system. Even if offset is not your primary medium, have a contact proof from film made for reference purposes in order to establish a norm for your monitor. Then have press proofs made of the Olé No Moiré file in whatever mediums you plan to use the most and use the proofs for building the printer profiles discussed in Chapter Eighteen: *Managing Color.*

## Not the Same Difference

Consistency of proofing materials is vitally important. Most service bureaus offer a variety of digital and film (analog) proofing systems. There are subtle differences between a 3M MatchPrint and an AgfaProof made from the same films.

*When you have proofs made from film, be certain to specify the proofing system you and your printer prefer using to avoid getting a 3M MatchPrint one day and an AgfaProof the next.*

In the same vein, don't mix up digital proofs and treat them as the same animal, because the color will vary between devices. For example, if you work from a Tektronics dye sublimation proof as an interim step toward final output, don't arbitrarily switch to a dye sublimation print made by a Kodak or an Epson device.

### Digital vs. Analog Proofing

Digital proofs such as those from Iris Ink Jet, Canon Color Laser Printer, dye sublimation, color laser, and thermal wax printers can be useful for a rough check of your file before going to film and contact proofs. In some cases, if your images are not destined to be offset printed, these prints can be the final output and used for exhibition purposes with great success. If you are heading for a printing press, however, be aware that most proofs from digital proofing systems will not be the same as a contact proof from film. Most significantly, the highlight values, 5% and less, tend to disappear on many digital proofs, the exceptions being those from the Iris Ink Jet printer and Kodak's Approval system, both of which can, if calibrated carefully, hold the highlights and very closely match a film proof. How much the highlight deficiency of some digital proofs affects your work will vary with the importance and amount of bright highlight areas in individual images.

# Setting Up Your Monitor

To calibrate for real, you need a *colorimeter* and its software. A colorimeter or color calibrator is a device with a sensor that attaches to your monitor with a suction cup and measures the intensity, chroma, and luminance of each gun. The accompanying software records your monitor's response and adjusts it to your preference in terms of color temperature and gamma. The value of using a colorimeter is not so much to allow you to set your monitor's response—you can do a very reasonable job using Knoll Gamma or similar software—but to ensure that your monitor remains stable over time. When you use a calibrator, your monitor's response is noted and

*Figure 5.2*                      Colorimeter.

recorded. In a month or two, when you repeat the process, the calibrator and its software will set your monitor back to where it was if it has drifted. It takes about three minutes to calibrate a monitor with a colorimeter such as the one sold by Radius *(Figure 5.2)*. Calibrating your monitor with a colorimeter or Knoll Gamma doesn't necessarily mean that your output will match your monitor's display—there's a little more to it as you'll see in Chapter Eighteen: *Managing Color*. The steps below assume you are using the Knoll Gamma control panel utility.

1. **Turn on your monitor and let it warm up for at least half an hour.**

2. **Adjust the room lighting to the standard you will be working in.**

3. **Set your desktop pattern to a neutral medium gray. This is important since one's perception of color is affected by adjacent colors. To set the desktop pattern, choose Apple Menu> Control Panels> General Controls *(Figure 5.3)*.**
   **In the General Controls window, click on the small direction triangles at the top of the desktop image until the light gray neutral pattern comes up. Then click once on the gray area directly below the triangles and the selected pattern will be initiated. System 7.5 has a separate Desktop Patterns utility in the Control Panels *(Figure 5.4)*. It offers the same neutral gray so just scroll to it and select.**

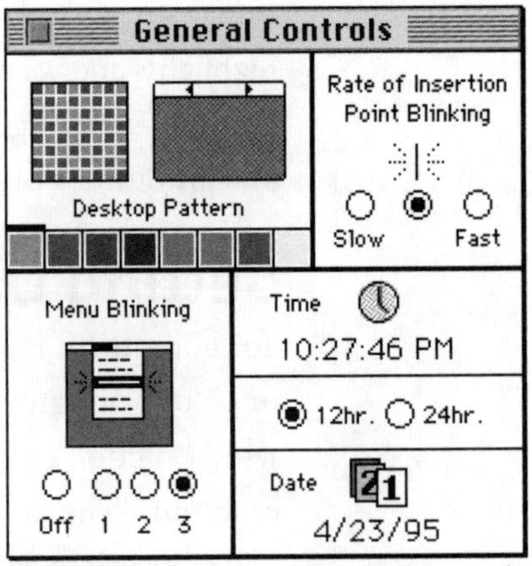

4. **Adjust the brightness and contrast knobs on your monitor to more or less their central position. (Never have the brightness turned up too far, since it will prematurely burn out your monitor's phosphors.) You might have to come back to these controls later, so don't tape them down yet. If your mon-**

*Figure 5.3*                      General Controls.

itor has a contrast control knob, you will probably find that you need to turn it down a little further than its midpoint.

5. Launch Photoshop and open the Olé No Moiré image.

6. Choose **Apple Menu> Control Panels> Gamma** *(Figure 5.5)*. Make sure it is turned on (On/Off buttons in lower left of Gamma window.) and start by selecting the 1.8 Target Gamma. If you don't have the Gamma utility installed, you will find it two levels down in the Photoshop folder: **Goodies> Calibration**. Drag it into your System folder and click OK when you are asked if you want it in the Control Panels where it belongs.

7. Click on the White Pt button and adjust the color of a white area of the monitor to match the color of a neutral piece of white paper in your viewing box. Usually you will need to move the blue slider a little to the left to "warm up" the color a bit, counteracting the excessive blue cast. You may also have to move the green slider slightly to the left to get rid of a reddish cast if there is one.

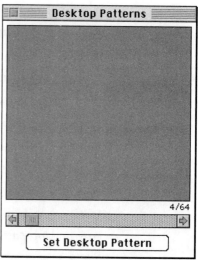

*Figure 5.4*                    Desktop Patterns.

*Figure 5.5*                    Gamma.

8. Drag the Gamma Adjustment slider until the gray area above it is a continuous gray tone.

9. Click on the Balance button and move the three color sliders until the grayscale at the bottom of the Knoll dialog box is free of any color tints.

10. Click on the Black Pt button and move the color sliders until the shadow portion of the same grayscale is free of any color tints.

11. Compare your monitor to the Olé No Moiré proof in your viewing box and make any subtle adjustments necessary.

12. Tweak the brightness and contrast controls on your monitor if necessary to come as close as possible to the Olé No Moiré proof.

13. Click on the Save button, and save the settings to Photoshop's Calibration folder, or anywhere else convenient for you.

*Note that as you are making these adjustments you will be referring not only to the grayscale at the bottom of the Gamma window, but also to the neutral gray desktop pattern, as well as the Olé No Moiré image you opened in Photoshop.*

Don't despair if you find it difficult to get a perfect match between your monitor and the Olé No Moiré proof in your viewing box. Achieving the best possible match requires very subtle balancing between the monitor's brightness and contrast controls, and the Knoll Gamma control panel utility. You'll have to go back and forth a few times before you get a handle on where the controls need to be set.

## Setting Up Photoshop

Once your Knoll Gamma utility and brightness and contrast controls are adjusted, you need to tell Photoshop what you've done to avoid conflicts. There are two areas in Photoshop that affect the monitor display and that you will need to set up. If you are using another image processing program, check its documentation for any preferences that might affect how the monitor displays color and proceed accordingly.

## Monitor Setup

1. Launch Photoshop if it isn't already running.

2. Choose **File> Preferences> Monitor Setup** *(Figure 5.6)*.

3. Select your monitor from the Monitor pop-up menu. If your monitor isn't listed, use 13-in. Apple if it has Trinitron phosphors, or contact the manufacturer and ask if they have a profile you can acquire.

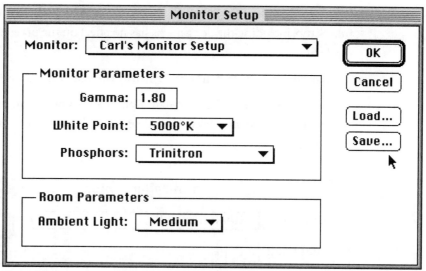

Figure 5.6                                                    Monitor Setup.

4. Enter 1.80 in the Gamma box.

5. Select 5000°K from the White Point pop-up menu.

6. Select Trinitron from the Phosphors pop-up menu, or another type for your monitor if available.

7. Select High, Low, or Medium from the Ambient Light pop-up menu.

8. Click on the Save button, name the file appropriately, and save it.

9. Click OK.

Note that the settings in the Monitor Setup dialog box only affect the preview of files that are in the CMYK or LAB mode (more about color spaces in Chapter Seventeen: *Color Models*).

## *Printing Inks Setup*

This dialog box defines the exact ink colors you expect to be used when your file is printed. SWOP (Standard Web Offset Proofing) is one of the most typical used in the United States and is a good place to start. When you change the Ink Colors in Photoshop, the way an RGB file is separated and a CMYK file is displayed is affected accordingly. The Dot Gain % tells Photoshop how light or dark any printing method is relative to your monitor and will affect the brightness of a grayscale or duotone file when the box in the lower left of the Printing Inks Setup dialog box is checked. Note that the Printing Inks Setup, including the dot gain %, has no effect on the preview of an RGB mode file.

1. Choose **File**> **Preferences**> **Printing Inks Setup** *(Figure 5.7)*.

2. For starters, select SWOP (Coated) from the Ink Colors pop-up menu. The Gray Balance and other Ink Color options will be discussed in Chapter Eighteen: *Managing Color*.

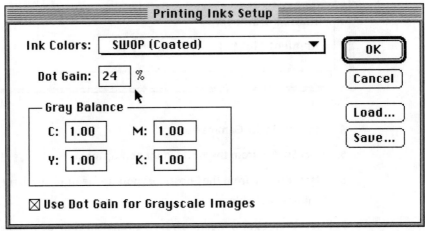

Figure 5.7                                                                 Printing Inks Setup.

3. Change the value in the Dot Gain % field to 24.

4. Click on the Use Dot Gain for Grayscale Images checkbox.

5. Click OK.

At this point your monitor should be in a reasonable range of calibration to begin working.

# SCANNING

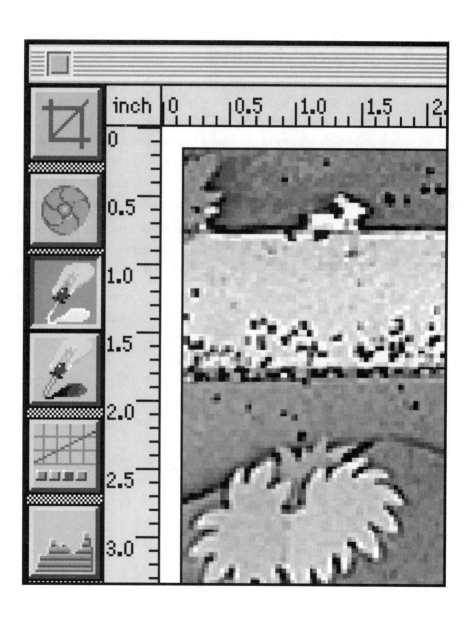

# Before Starting

If you are working with images of any kind, the scan is where you will usually begin. The quality of the scan, whether high or low, is not *entirely* up to the scanner itself: how you operate the scanner has more than a little to do with the quality of the results. In other words, you can produce a low quality scan on an expensive scanner if you don't know what you're doing, and a decent (not great, but usable) scan on a low-end inexpensive scanner if you are careful and proceed with an informed strategy.

The dynamics of the particular scanner itself will, of course, limit what is possible. Another way to put this is that you will probably not get as good a scan from a device costing $1,000 as you will from one costing $20,000 or more.

This chapter is devoted to getting the best possible scan from inexpensive equipment, which is what most of us are up against most of the time.

# Types of Scanners

For the sake of perspective, I'll start with a brief rundown of the types of scanners available.

### Hand-held

The least expensive and least capable kind of scanner. This type of device works by being rolled over the original to be scanned. It might provide some quick-and-dirty FPO (For Position Only) scans, but would be utterly useless for most serious work.

### Sheetfed

There don't seem to be very many of these around anymore. A sheetfed scanner works by feeding the original much like a fax machine. The original must be flexible enough to feed, a limitation serious enough to make you think twice before buying one except for special functions such as OCR (Optical Character Recognition).

### Flatbed

The most prevalent type of scanner for desktop use. Comes in low-end (cheap) as well as high-end (very expensive) varieties. Often can be purchased with an attachment for scanning transparencies.

### Slide

Very common in desktop environments. Also available in a vast range of price and quality. Scanners of this type, even the expensive models, are a desktop invention. Usually dedicated to 35mm format.

### Drum

The real thing, what the big girls and boys play with in serious production environments. This type of scanner is what professional color separators and large color printers have used for decades for the best possible results. Can be very expensive (hundreds of thousands of dollars), and capable of scanning both reflection and transparent originals.

More affordable ($20,000 and up) desktop drum scanners have been introduced in the last few years. These more modest devices, while more capable than low-end flatbed scanners, are usually not up to producing the size and quality of scan that you get from "the real thing"—you get what you pay for.

Figure C.6 illustrates the same print scanned on three different flatbed scanners and a drum scanner.

## Scanner Characteristics

All of the scanners just described can be characterized by resolution, dynamic range, and bit depth.

### Resolution

Resolution is the pixels per inch (ppi) or number of samples per inch the scanner is capable of capturing. This is usually referred to as dpi (see Chapter Two: *Resolution & File Size*). Note that the advertised maximum resolution of a scanner is often not its optical or actual resolution, but rather, the interpolated resolution—that is, the optical resolution sampled up or manipulated by the software to change a 300 ppi scan into a 600 ppi scan. The results, therefore, are synthetic and not as good as a true 600 ppi scan.

When a scanner's specifications are given as two numbers, 600 x 1200, for example, the first number refers to the resolution across the short dimension of the bed (glass area), and is the optical resolution, while the second refers to the resolution down the long dimension of the bed. The second number, then, tells you that the scanner will take samples in increments of 1200 per inch in the long dimension. Resolution may be the *least important* characteristic in evaluating a scanner's performance.

## Dynamic Range

Dynamic range is the maximum difference in brightness between the lightest and darkest values of an original that a scanner is capable of detecting. It is determined by the quality and configuration of CCDs (Charge Coupled Devices) the scanner is equipped with (PMTs or Photo-Multiplier Tubes in the case of drum scanners). Dynamic range is measured in a logarithmic scale from 0 to 4.0. The dynamic range of an original transparency is about 3.5, and a print is about 1.5 to 2.0.

Most low-end flatbed scanners have a dynamic range of about 1.8 to 2.0. Mid-range flatbeds are at about 3.0, with drum scanners ranging from 3.2 to 4.0. You usually won't see a specification for the dynamic range of an inexpensive scanner, since it's too embarrassing, but mid-range and high-end scanner specifications always publish the figure.

## CCD Sensors

The CCDs are the receptors that respond to the brightness levels of light projected on to them by a set of mirrors and lenses which vary from scanner to scanner. Flatbed scanners use an array of thousands of CCD elements arranged in a row. When light falls on the CCD array, it is converted into a proportional electrical charge or analog voltage. The voltages are then chopped into steps or levels by an A/D (analog-to-digital) converter.

### Noise

The purity of this tiny signal can easily be corrupted by interference from a number of sources resulting in *noise*. "Noise" in this sense means a signal containing data that didn't come from light reflected from the original image. Too much noise, and your ability to enhance or even reproduce the visual data in threshold areas such as the deep shadows is seriously, compromised.

There may be considerable differences in quality (absence of noise) between scanners that seem to have the same overall specifications. The differences are usually in how much noise-free detail or subtle changes in value one scanner can detect in the highlights and deep shadow areas of an original compared with another scanner. The device that does better has a superior dynamic range.

### Bit Depth

Bit depth is the number of bits per pixel a scanner is capable of capturing. The least expensive scanners on the market these days, whether color or black and white, are 8-bit-per-channel scanners. In the case of color, that usually means 8 bits per red, green, and blue channels, totaling 24 bits (see Chapter Two: *Resolution & File Size* for more detail on bit depth). 10-bit is becoming the norm for low-end flatbed scanners, with 12-bit scanners available for only slightly more money.

Usually a greater bit depth results in a higher quality scan. Even though most applications work with only 8 bits per channel (Photoshop supports 48-bit files), if a scanner can capture 12 bits, it retains only the best of the 8 bits to deliver to your application. This means that the scanner can toss out 4 bits of data on the extreme ends of the range, which, by the way, are usually the noisiest bits.

These three characteristics—resolution, dynamic range, and bit depth—taken together are what determine the quality of scan the device is capable of.

# Strategy

Before getting down to business I'd like to point out three very important basic strategies for obtaining the best results from your scanner. The first two should be adhered to until you have taken the time to perform the simple test of your scanner driver outlined later in this chapter. The third, avoiding clipping, should always be your goal.

Scanner software varies in quality. It may well be that your scanner came with very capable software which you can actually use without trashing your data. Agfa's FotoLook, which is bundled with its Arcus II flatbed scanner, falls into the capable category. On the other hand, some scanners, especially very inexpensive models, come with software that will definitely ruin your scanned data and should be avoided at all costs.

The bottom line is, stick to the strategy outlined here, and assume the worst, at least until you test your scanner software to make sure it's not degrading the quality of the hardware's performance.

### Scan at the Optical Resolution

Whenever possible, scan at the optical (actual) resolution of the scanner. In the case of a slide scanner, this may not be possible, but it usually is possible if you are using a flatbed scanner. The reason for doing this is to avoid interpolation or resampling (changing) the scan resolution with the scanner driver. Even though you may need a resolution lower (or higher) than the optical resolution of your scanner, use the optical resolution anyway and resample later as outlined in the step-by-step instructions. Your scans will almost invariably be sharper and cleaner. Check the documentation you received with your scanner to find out what the optical resolution is.

### Avoid Scanner Software

Never use software that came with the scanner to adjust the results of the scan until you test the software. These adjustments are usually brightness, gamma, and curves. The reason for this is the same reason you scan at the optical resolution: while the manufacturer may have your best interests at heart, remember that if you are using a low-end device, it has distinct limitations in the software as well as the hardware departments. In other words, the software is usually not as capable as your primary image manipulation program such as Photoshop. To put it bluntly, your strategy is to avoid messing up the scan with low-end software and making all adjustments later with a more carefully written and capable program. In general, this strategy also applies to third-party programs—use your primary image processing program instead, unless you have carefully tested the software in question and proven it to be free from distortions.

## *Avoid Clipping*

Clipping is the failure to capture the full range of values from the deepest shadows to the brightest highlights. To a large extent, any scanner's ability to capture the full range of an original depends on its dynamic range, or gamma. If a scanner ain't got it in it, it ain't gonna do it. Nevertheless, even if you have a very capable drum scanner, you need to be aware of the clipping issue to avoid it. You can clip a scan in either the shadows or highlights by setting up the software carelessly despite the fact that your scanner may be capable of scanning without clipping the information.

For example, if a highlight in the original has a slight tone of, say, 3%, and you scan that area of the original to be 0%, you have failed to capture some of the information that was in the original. Instead, you should make sure that the brightest value in your completed scan is no less than about 5%— even for areas in the original that may be paper white with no tone whatsoever. This way, you are making sure that you have captured all the available tones, and you give yourself the option of very carefully adjusting the highlight value in Photoshop (see Chapter Ten: *Adjust Gray Values*). If you blow off (clip) some subtle but valuable data going in, you diminish your ability to produce a high quality finished file with as much information as possible.

Likewise, in the shadow areas, you want to avoid turning a dark gray into a 100% black, and thereby failing to capture valuable shadow separation. Make sure your highest value is no more than about 95% in the unadjusted or raw scan. You will carefully adjust the file later in Photoshop, but you have to have the raw material (information) to start with.

Your goal should be to scan grayscale for a range of 5% to 95%, and color for a range of about 250% to 10% for all three channels—red, green, and blue.

## Save the Original Scan

Since you'll probably do a considerable amount of work on most of your scans, it's a good idea always to save your original scan so that in the event that you make a mistake, you can always start over without having to re-scan.

## The Histogram

This device is used to display the tonal distribution of pixels in a scan over the 0–255 range. It tells you how many pixels are at each brightness level. For a visual artist, this device is somewhat overrated. It may not be particularly useful, for example, to know that the standard deviation of pixels (how widely the pixels vary) is 60.46, or that there are 2,716 pixels at gray level

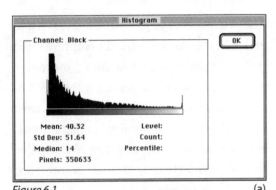 

*Figure 6.1*                                                  (a)                                                  (b)
You don't need a histogram (a) to know that the image (b) is too dark.

*Figure 6.2*                                                  (a)                                                  (b)
You don't need a histogram (a) to know that the image (b) is normal.

25. Nor do you need to display the histogram of an image that is too dark and see the mountain on the shadow end of the graph to know that the image is too dark—you already know that by looking at your monitor display *(Figures 6.1 and 6.2)*.

The most useful information a histogram might provide you with is the quality of your scan. When you see gaps or white spaces in the histogram, it means that there is no information at that level; the scan will thus appear posterized where it jumps from one level to another *(Figure 6.3)*. Since the histogram is also displayed in the Levels dialog box (without the numerical data), you may find that you rarely need to refer to the Histogram display found under the Image menu.

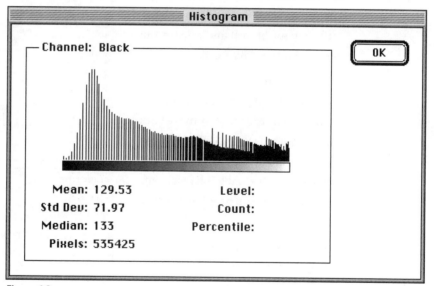

Figure 6.3                                                           Histogram showing gaps.

## Don't Rush

Take your time. I know you thought your computer was going to make your life easier and your work go faster, and it may—but not until you have lots of experience. Performing all the steps involved in preparing any file you plan to go to press with may take many hours to execute, so don't be impatient.

# Flatbed Scanning I

The following steps are for scans made with a Microtek scanner but the procedure is the same for any one of a variety of low-end scanners, though the design of the software interface will vary. These steps assume that a Photoshop plug-in came with your scanner software.

1. Launch Photoshop by double-clicking on the application icon in the Photoshop folder.

2. In the main menu, choose **File>Acquire> ScanMaker Plug-in** (substitute your brand) and release the mouse button *(Figure 6.4)*.

3. After the scanner dialog box opens, begin by clicking on the Reset button if there is one to set the software back to its defaults *(Figure 6.5)*. This will override adjustments that have been made by someone else to the Enhancements options, which you definitely want to avoid using.

4. Select either **Gray-scale** or **Color>Gray-scale Prescan** from the Scan Mode options *(Figure 6.6)*.

   Never use Line Art or Halftone modes. Remember, you are going to avoid any manipulation of the scan by the driver, and these two modes employ modifications after the scan which are better done in Photoshop.

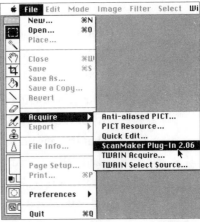

*Figure 6.4*                    Acquire.

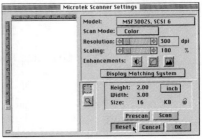

*Figure 6.5*                    Reset.

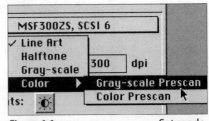

*Figure 6.6*                    Set mode.

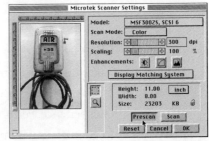

*Figure 6.7*                    Click Prescan.

5. Open the cover and place your original artwork face down on the scanner bed glass toward the top (check the rulers for the zero point). Place your artwork square to the edges and close the cover. (If you are scanning from a book, just leave the scanner cover open.)

   It is important to get a close fit between your original and the glass. If your original is wrinkled or warped, or if the cover of your scanner doesn't close tightly, put a light weight on top after closing. Usually a few books will do.

6. Click Prescan *(Figure 6. 7)* in order to locate your original on the dialog box representation of the glass scanner bed.

7. Use the crop marquee tools *(Figure 6. 8)* to draw a marquee around the area you want to scan. Cropping is important because you don't want to scan an area any larger than necessary. Notice that the size in KB (kilobytes) is only 235 when the area to be scanned is small *(Figure 6.9)*. The size has increased more than 100 times to 30,107 KB when the area to be scanned is opened to include the entire scanner bed *(Figure 6.10)*. It is important to be aware of the file size you are creating to avoid unnecessarily large files, which will take up disk space and slow down your computer.

8. After the marquee is drawn and you have checked to make sure you have the correct mode, resolution, and scale, click on Scan *(Figure 6.11)*.

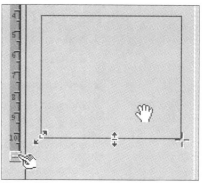

*Figure 6.8*                    Marquee Controls.

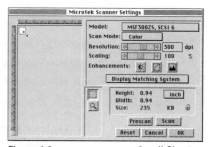

*Figure 6.9*                    Small file size.

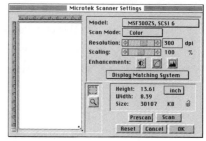

*Figure 6.10*                    Large file size.

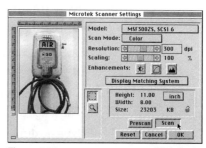

*Figure 6.11*                    Click Scan.

# Test Drive Your Driver

1. Make sure the enhancements of your scanner driver are turned off (or click on Reset if available).

2. Select a small test image or use a small area (about 6 inches square) of an original with sharp detail and continuous blends. You will be scanning exactly the same area twice. You can do this test in either RGB or Grayscale mode, but if you have a color scanner you might learn more from the RGB mode.

3. Set the resolution to the optical resolution of your scanner and the scaling at 100%. Prescan to select the area you want to include in the scan, and Scan. Save the resulting file and name it "Optical Res."

4. Set the resolution to a number different from the optical resolution—pick any arbitrary resolution, lower than the optical resolution. Leave the scaling at 100% and everything else the same and Scan. Save the result using the resolution you scanned at as the file name, e.g., "255 Res" *(Figure 6.12a)*. Leave both files open in Photoshop.

5. Next you are going to sample down the optical resolution scan to the same resolution as your second scan. In other words, you are going to throw away some of the pixels just as the scanner driver automatically did for you when you set the resolution at 255 dpi instead of the optical resolution—except that in this test, you are going to let Photoshop do it instead of the scanner driver. Before resampling (or interpolating), you need to check to make sure that Photoshop is set for its best method of interpolating.

   Choose **File**> **Preferences**> **General**, and make sure your interpolation method is set for Bicubic, which is the most accurate way to resample. Click on OK *(Figure 6.13)*.

6. Click once on the optical resolution scan (to make it the active file) and choose **Image**> **Image Size**. Make sure that the Constrain File Size box is unchecked, and change the resolution to 255. Click OK.

7. Now line up the two files *(Figure 6.12a and b)* side by side and set the display ratio (in the title bar) at 1:1 for both files. This step is very important! Careful evaluation of any file should be carried out with the display ratio at 1:1 (or greater, e.g., 2:1). Never try to evaluate a file for any critical considerations when it is being displayed smaller than 1:1 on your monitor. The reason for this rule

Figure 6.12                                                    (a)                                                    (b)
(a) 255 Res and (b) scanned at optical resolution and sampled down in Photoshop to 255 ppi.

is that at smaller ratios, your computer is eliminating some of the pixels in order to create a smaller image on the monitor, and, in effect, is scrambling the true pixel display to some extent.

8. Look carefully at the edges of the detail in your image for any difference between the two files. Also look for any artifacts in the smoothly graduated tones. Typically, the optical resolution file that you sampled down in Photoshop will have cleaner and sharper edges, and it will be free from artifacts that might be evident in the other file.

## The Proof Is in the Scan

So what does this prove? If you can't see any difference between the two scans, it proves your scanner software is doing a good job and you don't have to be afraid to use it.

If you do see a difference, it proves that Photoshop's algorithms are more sophisticated and capable than those of your scanner driver—perhaps dramatically so. If you want the best results from your equipment, you will scan only at the optical resolution, 100% scaling, with no enhancements, then sample down later in Photoshop.

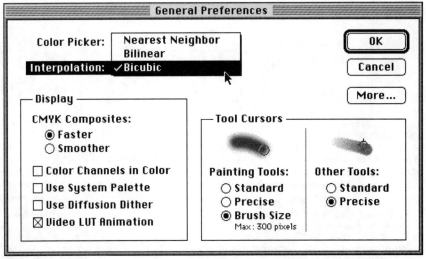

*Figure 6.13*                                    General Preferences.

# Flatbed Scanning II

If you're lucky enough to have one of the slightly more expensive and capable flatbed scanners such as Agfa's Arcus II, the driver is quite trustworthy but the scanning sequence can be more involved. The Arcus II has an optical resolution of 600 x 1200 ppi, a dynamic range of 3.0, and a 12-bit-per-channel sample depth. Using this scanner involves the following steps:

1. In Photoshop, choose **File> Acquire> FotoLook PS.**

2. When the FotoLook dialog box opens *(Figure 6.14)*, select either Color or Gray-scale from the Mode options, and type of original from the Original options (Gray-Scale was selected for this example).

3. The Input resolution is a pop-up menu with various options, all of which are sub-resolutions of the optical resolution. Using one of these will give you better results than a completely random resolution setting which you type in.

4. Click on Preview and adjust the size of the marquee to include only the area you want in the scan.

5. From the Range option, select Set White/Black Point *(Figure 6.15)*.

6. Click on the Tone Curve Editor icon (fifth from top) and the Tone Curve Editor dialog box opens, allowing you to construct a custom curve in grayscale or RGB, or select one of the curves already available *(Figure 6.17)*. Choose the Gamma 1.8 curve and click OK.

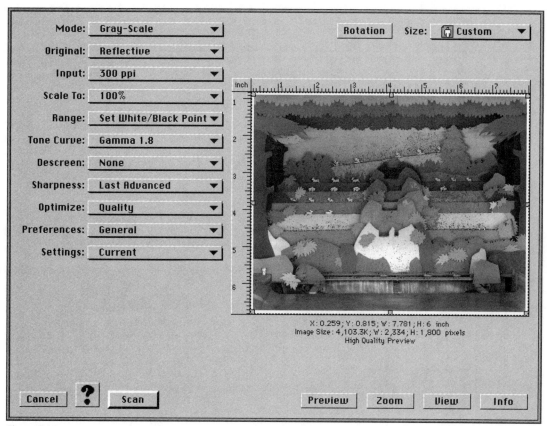

*Figure 6.14*                                          Acquire FotoLook.

7. **Double-click on the Set White Point icon (third from the top in Figure 6.17),** and set the white point to 5%. Locate the brightest highlight in your image and click once to set its value to 5% and avoid clipping the highlights.

*Figure 6.15*                    Range Options.

8. **Next double-click on the Set Black Point icon (fourth from the top (Figure 6.17),** and set the black point to 95%. Locate the darkest shadow in your image and click once to set the value of this area to 95% and avoid clipping the shadows.

9. Click on the Close box (upper left of the window) which returns you to the main window and click Scan.

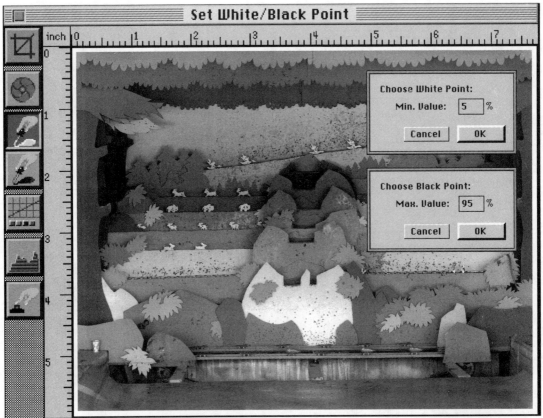

*Figure 6.16*                                                    Set White/Black Point.

This driver offers options such as descreening (for scanning originals printed with a halftone screen), sharpening, and batch processing. By carefully setting the white and black points you can avoid clipping any of the original information, and the curves can by optimized to enhance shadow or highlight detail.

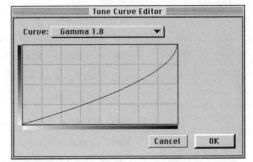

*Figure 6.17*                    Tone Curve Editor.

# Flatbed Scanning III

The UMax PowerLook scanner has a resolution of 600 x 1200 ppi with a 10 bit-per-channel sample depth. Experiment with the controls offered with this driver, but start by following these steps:

1. Choose **File> Acquire> UMAX MagicScan**.

2. When the MagicScan dialog box opens *(Figure 6.18)*, choose the appropriate Scan Mode, Source, Destination, Resolution, and set the Gamma to 1.8.

Settings ⟶

Set Gamma ⟶

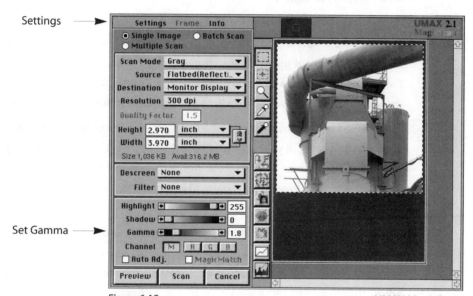

*Figure 6.18*                                                                    UMAX MagicScan.

3. Choose **Settings> Output...** and make sure you use about 250 for the Max (highlights), and not less than about 10 for Min (shadows) in order to avoid clipping *(Figure 6.19)*.

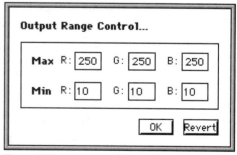

4. Click on Preview and adjust the marquee to include only the area you want in the scan.

*Figure 6.19*                Output Range Control....

5. Click Scan.

# Summary

1.  As this book goes to press there is an explosion of new flatbed and slide scan-
    ners on the market for under $2000. Even at the $1000. level, there are a
    number of flatbed scanners  with 600 ppi optical resolution and 10 bit-per-
    channel sample depth. If you're planning to buy a scanner, do your homework
    and read the reviews carefully—there is a vast difference in the quality of scans
    from the various scanners on the market—even between scanners that sell
    for about the same price.

2.  A scanners resolution is the *least* important factor in evaluating a scanner. The
    quality of the results and absence of *noise* from any scanner is determined by
    the overall quality of the electronic engineering, the quality of the CCDs (or
    PMTs), the bit depth, and the dynamic range. These factors are far more
    important determiners of quality than raw optical resolution.

3.  Make careful tests of your scanner driver to determine if you can trust it to not
    degrade the quality of your scans. If Photoshop will do it better, avoid using
    the software that came with your scanner to manipulate the scan (see page
    76: *Test Drive Your Driver*). This is particularly important if you have an 8 bit-
    per-channel scanner.

4.  If your scanner has a 10 or 12 bit-per-channel depth and the driver is trust-
    worthy, use it to adjust color balance and gamma to come as close as possible
    to a corrected scan and then fine tune in Photoshop. This means that you should
    adjust the gamma to 1.8 or even 2.0 when scanning to ensure capturing all
    the information contained in the original. This is especially important if your
    monitor is properly set up and you are scanning for reproduction. Otherwise,
    you will find yourself making major Curves or Levels adjustments in Photoshop
    to brighten the scan and consequently degrading your scan unnecessarily.

5.  Avoid clipping. If you don't capture the information contained in the original,
    there is no way to recover it later.

6.  Always save the original *raw* scan. This will save you the trouble of rescanning
    if your correction strategy goes awry.

Photo CD is very cool. Conceived of by Kodak as a consumer product, it has blossomed into a serious EDP (Electronic Document Preparation) tool. Originally, Kodak thought it would be nifty if when you brought your snapshots to K-Mart for processing you could get the pictures written to a CD ROM disc to show to your friends on your TV. For whatever reasons, this concept never really took off, but the systems that Kodak developed to scan, compress, and write the images to disc turned out to be remarkable.

## What Is Photo CD?

In its basic form, Photo CD Master is a system that gives you about one hundred 35mm images on a single CD ROM disc. Each image is stored and available in five resolutions, the largest file size of which decompresses to an 18 Mb file.

Kodak also offers Pro Photo CD for 35mm, medium format, and 4 x 5 in. size films, which holds fewer images depending on the size of the original.

Pro Photo CD offers a sixth resolution resulting in a file size of 72 Mb.

The Kodak Photo CD Catalog is for storing and distributing up to 6,000 images on a single disc. This is for retailers, stock agencies, galleries, real estate agencies, and other businesses. The images are low resolution and only for viewing on a TV or computer monitor.

The Kodak Photo CD Portfolio integrates still images, sound, and video for multimedia presentations.

### Sources

You have the option of using Photo CD for positives or negatives in either black and white or color in 35mm, $2^{1}/_{4}$ in., and 4 x 5 in. formats. Roll film and 35mm can either be mounted or in strips. If you have an entire roll of film processed *and* scanned for Photo CD at the same time, the price is considerably lower per image.

# How Photo CDs Are Made

Your images are scanned on a Kodak Professional Imaging Workstation (PIW), which automatically captures the five hierarchical resolutions called the Photo CD IMAGE PAC file format and writes the data in a compressed format to the CD disc. Kodak's PIW system consists of the scanner, a Sun workstation, the CD writer, and a dye sublimation printer which produces the thumbnails for the inside of the jewel case the disc comes in. The 18 Mb scans are made in about 10 seconds.

## Compression

The 18 Mb file is compressed to 4.5 Mb using Kodak's YCC color model, which separates the image into three channels: one for the grayscale (luminance) information, and two for the color (hue) information. Kodak describes its compression scheme as *visually lossless*. Only the Base x 4, 16, and 64 files are compressed.

## Resolution

The five sizes you get from 35mm in the Master CD format are:

| | | |
|---|---|---|
| Base x 16 | 2048 x 3072 | 18 Mb file |
| Base x 4 | 1024 x 1536 | 4.5 Mb file |
| Base | 512 x 768 | 1.12 Mb file |
| Base/4 | 256 x384 | 280 Kb file |
| Base/16 | 128 x 192 | 70 Kb file |

These figures translate into printing about a 9 x 13.5 in. image at 150 lpi (using a 1:1.5 ppi-to-lpi ratio).

The Pro Photo CD format offers you the Base x 64 resolution resulting in a 72 Mb file, which would get you on press with an 18 x 27 in. image using the same 1:1.5 ratio.

## Quality

The quality of the scans is quite high. Actually it's great, when you factor in the cost—about $3.00 or less per image plus about $10.00 for the disc, it's awesome, which is why the Photo CD format is the rage it is. Most desktop slide scanners can't touch the quality of these scans, and flatbed scanners with transparency adapters—forget it. You can't see a difference on press between a $3.00 Photo CD scan and a scan from a high-end drum scanner at about $30.00 an image *(Figure C.7)*.

### Multisession

An added attraction is that even though each disc will hold about 100 images, you don't have to go for filling the disc all at once. You can have as few or many images (up to the maximum capacity) scanned and written to your disc on one of several sessions—hence the name *multisession*. Labs have a small minimum charge to discourage you from bringing them one or two slides to scan, but beyond that there usually aren't any restrictions. The more sessions you take to fill any particular CD, however, the fewer images you will get on it, since some space is taken up by directory information between sessions.

## How to Use Photo CD

To begin with, you need a multisession CD drive hooked up to your computer. Double or Quad speed will do the trick. Any recent CD drive will be multisession unless you bought it more than three years ago or from a guy on the street in Times Square, in which case, check to see if it actually has a drive mechanism inside. If you happen to have a single-session drive, you will be able to read the first session but not additions written to the disc in subsequent sessions.

### Opening the Photo CD Images

Once you have the CD in your drive and its icon showing up on your desktop, opening your images is really very simple. There are a few pitfalls along the way, however, so follow these instructions carefully. I'll leave it to a discussion between you and your CD ROM drive manufacturer to get to first base: the CD mounted and available on your desktop. Once you're there, and with Photoshop running, proceed as follows:

1. Choose **File> Open...**.

2. In the open dialog box locate your CD on the desktop and double-click on it or select it by clicking on it once and click Open *(Figure 7.1)*.

*Figure 7.1*                Open CD.

*Figure 7.2*          Open Photo CD.

*Figure 7.3*            Open Images.

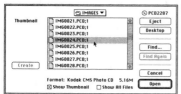

*Figure 7.4*            Select image.

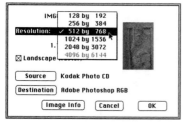

*Figure 7.5*        Choose resolution.

**3. Open the folder named Photo_CD** *(Figure 7.2)*.

*It is important not to use the Photos folder, which will open the images without using Kodak's CMS system.*

*If you choose to circumvent Kodak's CMS system and open your images as straight PICT files, you may end up clipping your images (see Chapter Six: Scanning) in addition to not getting the best color balance and contrast possible.*

**4. Open the Images folder** *(Figure 7.3)*.

**5. Refer to the Thumbnail images in the jewel case to select the number of the image you want to open, scroll to it and double-click on it** *(Figure 7.4)*.

**6. Select the resolution you want from the pop-up Resolution window** *(Figure 7.5)*.

**7. Click once on the Source button** *(Figure 7.6)*.

**8. In the next dialog box, select the original emulsion type you gave the lab to make the scan and click OK** *(Figure 7.7)*.

*This is a critical step in opening your image with the best color quality. Kodak recommends using the Universal Ektachrome V2.0 option for all color reversal film even if the original film type is unknown.*

*Use the Universal Kodachrome option only for film using Kodachrome K-14 processing.*

*Use Color Negative V2.0 for color negative films.*

**9. Click once on the Destination button** *(Figure 7.8)*.

**10. Select Adobe Photoshop RGB and click OK** *(Figure 7.9)*.

*If you have a good reason (you heard somewhere that it's more professional is not a good reason) to use the Adobe Photoshop CIELAB option, make sure you read the technotes that came with your Photoshop application carefully. The Monitor Preferences affect the way this transformation looks when it opens, and Kodak recommends having the Ambient Light set to High for "optimal image fidelity."*

*Figure 7.6*          Click on Source.

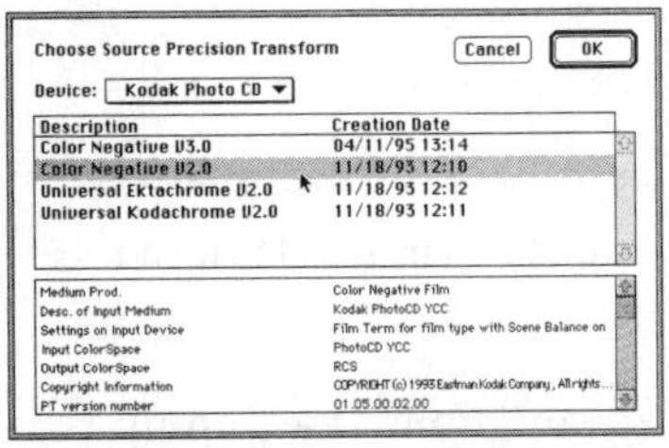

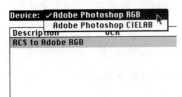

*Figure 7.7*     Choose emulsion type.

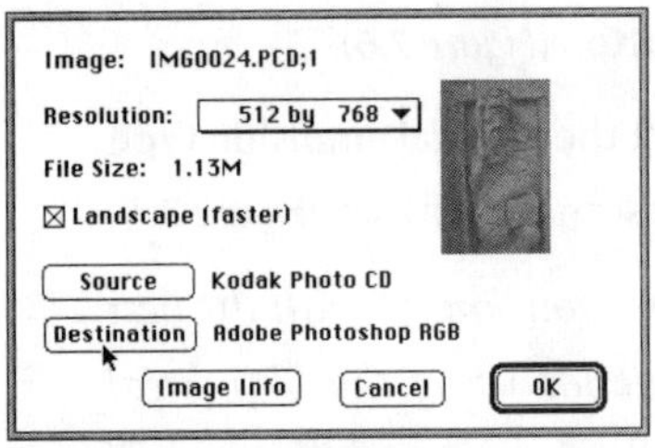

*Figure 7.8*     Click on destination.

**Choose Destination Precision Transform**

*Figure 7.9*     Select the destination.

*Figure 7.10*          Click OK to open.

*Note that if you use the CIELAB option and subsequently change the mode to RGB, the results may not be the same as if you used RGB in the first place. Again, don't open in CIELAB unless you understand all the ramifications of using it.*

**11. Click OK to open your image using Kodak's Precision Color Management System** *(Figure 7.10)*.

The Source and Destination settings you used to open your image will remain in place until you change them. Make sure to check your original film type when opening any image, since the Source designation you select has a dramatic impact on the color and contrast your image opens with. Try using the various options to see for yourself how critical this step really is.

*Figure 7.11*          **Image> Rotate....**

Once your image opens, if it is a vertical image it will be lying on its side. Choose **Image> Rotate> 90° CW** to straighten it up *(Figure 7.11)*.

# Sharpening

Like any scan, your freshly opened Photo CD image will need to have Unsharp Masking applied. Refer to Chapter Thirteen: *Unsharp Masking* for details on how to use this filter.

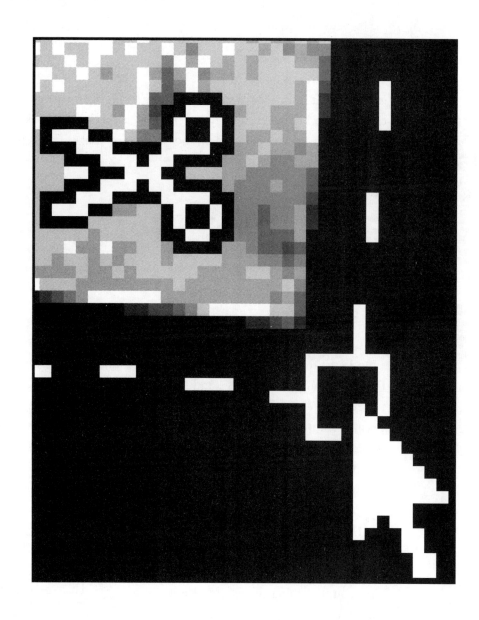

## The Raw Data

Once your freshly scanned image opens in Photoshop, the chances are excellent that it won't be perfect—in many respects. You are going to proceed with an informed strategy, a step-by-step check list of tasks that you will probably need to perform on most scans you make. The steps are:

1. Rotate and crop precisely.

2. Adjust size and resolution.

3. Adjust grayscale values or color correct.

4. Perform any stylistic modifications.

5. Apply Unsharp Masking.

6. Clean up dust or other defects.

7. Perform any local color or contrast adjustments.

*Figure 8.1*
Cropping Tool.

Follow these steps one by one making as few adjustments to the file as possible. Resist the temptation to color correct or adjust the brightness of the file before you perform steps 1 and 2. Think of your file as a piece of exquisite jewelry you are crafting from raw precious metal. The more you bend, twist, or hammer the raw metal, the further you move away from being able to recover its original form. Each alteration you make commits you more and more irrevocably to the direction you are moving in. This chapter covers step 1, and steps 2 through 7 are covered in the chapters following.

## The Cropping Tool

The first step on the road to perfection is to rotate and crop your new scan precisely, and in doing so, get rid of any unnecessary space around the image which is causing the file to be larger in kilobytes than it needs to be.

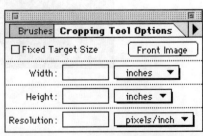

*Figure 8.2*    Cropping Tool Options.

1. **Choose the Cropping tool from the toolbox by clicking on it once *(Figure 8.1)*. (If you click twice, the Cropping Tool Options Palette will appear, which allows you to specify an exact width, height, and resolution by clicking on the Fixed Target Size checkbox.)**

*Caution: If you enter a number in the Resolution box, Photoshop will resample your file. This could have a potentially negative effect on quality if you cause Photoshop to sample up. It's best to avoid this option unless you have a clear understanding of what's happening. If you enter a width and height and leave the resolution box blank, Photoshop will not resample.*

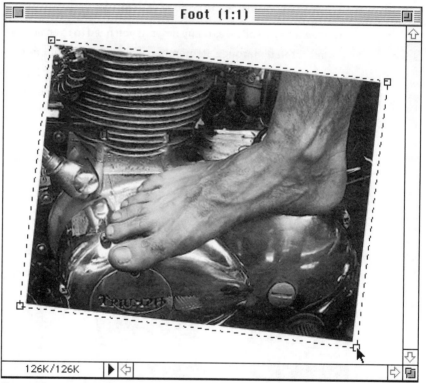

Figure 8.3

Option drag any corner to rotate.

Leave the Cropping Tool Options Palette blank for now since you are going to use the Cropping tool to straighten up the scan if you didn't place it exactly square on the scanner bed (which is usually the case), and crop to the image with greater precision *(Figure 8.2)*.

2. Click and drag a marquee roughly around your image. You don't have to make this perfect because you can adjust it later with the control boxes in each corner.

3. Put the pointer on one of the corners, hold down the Option key, and click and drag to rotate the crop marquee to align with your image *(Figure 8.3)*.

*Caution: Be careful to click and drag only when you see the pointer in one of the control boxes. Otherwise you will either cancel or activate the cropping (Figure 8.4).*

4. Put the pointer on one of the corners and adjust the size of the marquee to just a fraction inside the edge of your image.

5. Repeat steps 3 and 4 as many times as you need to to achieve a perfectly sized and rotated marquee. Remember that you can zoom in on the image for more critical adjustments (see Chapter One: *Photoshop Essentials*). Move the cursor inside the marquee and click once when you see the scissors to activate the crop.

6. Choose **Save As...** and make sure you use Photoshop's proprietary format for now. See Chapter Sixteen: *Saving Your File* for more about file formats.

*Figure 8.4*                                                          Cropping Tool Controls.

Pointer to adjust.          Click to Cancel.          Click to activate crop.

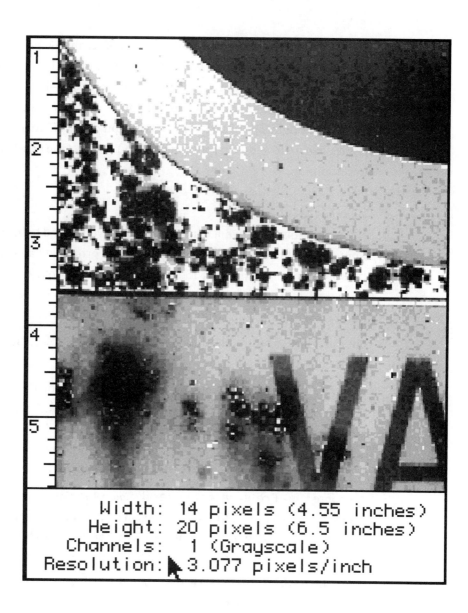

Width:  14 pixels (4.55 inches)
Height:  20 pixels (6.5 inches)
Channels:   1 (Grayscale)
Resolution: 3.077 pixels/inch

# ADJUST SIZE & RESOLUTION 9

At this point you should be working with a cleanly cropped and aligned version of your file at the optical resolution of your scanner. Theoretically, you have a very good idea of how you plan to use this image—that is, what size you will print it and in what medium. If you don't know, it's best to leave the file at its original optical resolution until you decide. Remember, if you sample down or lower the resolution now, you can't get the data back without rescanning.

## Example One

Let's say it is a black and white photograph which you intend to use in a page layout at a final size of 4 x 5 in. This page will be printed on a high quality offset press on coated paper at 150 lpi (lines per inch). Your original photographic print was 8 x 10 in. and you scanned it at 300 ppi, which is the optical resolution of your scanner with scaling set at 100%.

Your mission is to reduce the dimensions of the image to 4 x 5 in. and keep the resolution at 300 ppi.

First you will check to make sure that Photoshop's interpolation method is set to Bicubic. You won't need to do this every time you work with the program because it will stay the way you set it (that is, provided no one else uses the machine and changes it; if you work in an environment where other people use your machine, you will want to check this every time).

1. Choose **File> Preferences> General** *(Figure 9.1)*. Make sure that Bicubic interpolation is selected from the pop-up menu. Bicubic is the most accurate method, and Nearest Neighbor the least. (There are instances, however, when you may want to use the Nearest Neighbor method for special effects.)

2. Choose **Image> Image Size**. The Image Size dialog box opens, displaying the current size of your file in the top portion, and the new size in the bottom portion *(Figure 9.2)*. When it first opens, the information in both portions will be the same.

One of the most important features of this dialog box is the innocent looking little checkbox in the lower right-hand corner called File Size. When checked, the file size is constrained (kept the same in spite of any changes you make in the Width, Height, or Resolution). When unchecked, the file size will be adjusted accordingly, based on any changes you make to the Width, Height, or Resolution.

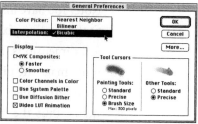

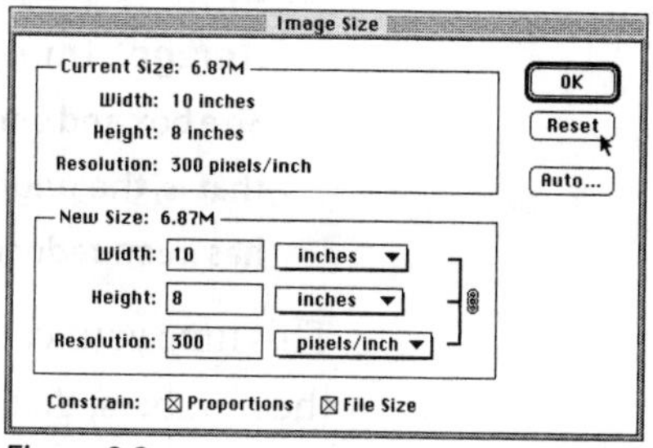

*Figure 9.1*      Bicubic Interpolation.

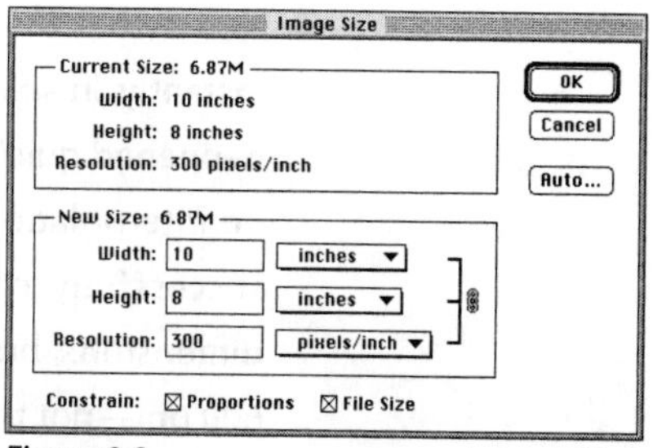

*When the File Size box is checked, Photoshop will not resample. When the File Size box is unchecked, Photoshop will resample your file.*

Option-clicking on the Cancel button will reset the dialog box back to how it originally opened *(Figure 9.3)*.

*Figure 9.2*      Image Size.

As you know from the discussion in the Scanning and Resolution chapters, resampling, or interpolating either up or down, is tricky business and should be approached cautiously. In other words,

*Figure 9.3*      Reset.

you should know when you are resampling and when you are not. Furthermore, you should know that whenever you resample you are messing with the pixels in your file—either adding or deleting pixels.

As an exercise, we are going to do this wrong first, Undo the change, and then do it right.

3. **With the File Size box checked, click once on the word "Width" to highlight the box and enter 5. Notice that the entry in the Height box automatically changed to 4 because the Proportions are constrained, i.e., the file will not change shape, only size. Notice also that the Resolution has changed to 600 ppi and that the New Size is the same as the Current Size *(Figure 9.4)*. Click OK.**

Note: You have instructed Photoshop to fit the existing pixels into smaller physical dimensions. To do this Photoshop must make the pixels smaller and consequently there will be more per inch—thus the higher ppi. No pixels were created or discarded.

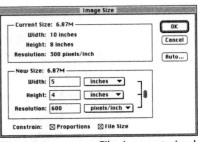

*Figure 9.4*        File size constrained.

4. Notice that the file was restructured instantly, in spite of how large it is. It happened quickly because there was no interpolation necessary. We have successfully changed the physical dimensions, but the resolution is at 600 ppi—not the 300 ppi we require. Choose **Edit**> **Undo** (or type ⌘ **Z**).

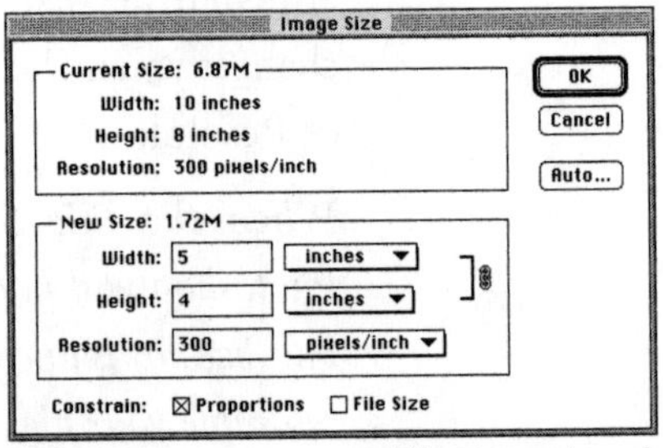

*Figure 9.5*        File size reduced.

5. Open the Image Size dialog box again (**Image**> **Image Size**). This time we'll do it right. Uncheck the Constrain File Size box and enter 5 in the Width box. Now we will end up with what we want, that is, the original file sized to 4 x 5 in. and 300 ppi. Notice that the file size has been reduced to 1.72 Mb *(Figure 9.5)*. Click OK or press Return.

This time your computer might have hesitated a bit while it was crunching the numbers, that is, working on how to discard three quarters of the total pixels involved.

Why are we reducing the file size? Because disk space is valuable, and at 300 ppi we are at a perfect 2:1 ratio (see Chapter Two: *Resolution & File Size*) to the lpi (lines per inch or halftone screen frequency). Any more than a 2:1 ratio is at the point of diminishing returns—it is excess resolution that is not improving the image quality and is taking up space as well as slowing down the process unnecessarily.

# Example Two

In this example you have scanned a color picture in the RGB mode at 600 ppi (this is the optical resolution of your other scanner) with the Scaling set at 100%. Let's say that the original is 3 x 5 in. and you plan to use it in a page layout at a final size of 6 x 10 in. Again this file will be printed on a high quality offset press at 150 lpi.

Your mission in this case will be to increase the physical dimensions of the file and reduce the resolution to 200 ppi. Why 200 ppi instead of 300 ppi, which would result in the "*ideal*" 2:1 ratio between ppi and lpi? Because at 300 ppi the file size is 15.5 Mb (which will increase to a whopping 20.6 Mb when you change the file to CMYK mode making your color separations). You are going to have several images in this page layout; you simply can't afford the disk space to save and store images at 300 ppi. While the result represents a ratio of about 1.33:1, less than the theoretically ideal of 2:1, the 200 ppi will work just fine. In fact, any resolution of 1:1 (150 ppi in this case) or better will suffice for most images. (See Figure C.13 for an illustration of various ppi to lpi ratios.)

1. Choose **Image**> **Image Size**. The Image Size dialog box opens, displaying the current size of your file in the top portion, and the new size in the bottom portion *(Figure 9.6)*. When it first opens, the information in both portions will be the same. Notice that the file size is 15.5 Mb.

2. With the File Size box unchecked (you don't want to constrain the file size, you want to reduce it), click once on the word "Width" to highlight the box and enter 10. Notice that the entry in the Height box automatically changes to 6 because the Proportions are constrained.

3. Click once on the word "Resolution" and enter 200. Notice that the "New Size" changes to 6.87M, which is exactly what you want *(Figure 9.7)*.

4. Click OK or press Return.

*Figure 9.6*     File size too large.

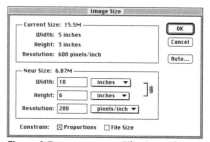

*Figure 9.7*     File size reduced.

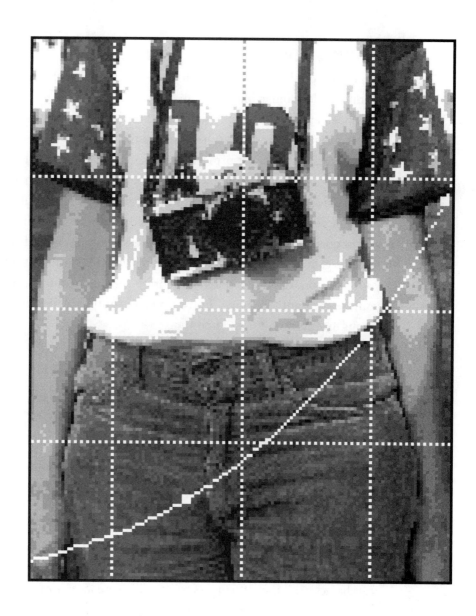

## Overview

Depending on the equipment you used to scan the original image—flatbed scanner, slide scanner, photo CD, and so on—the grayscale or RGB file you have open in Photoshop will usually need some adjustment. Keep in mind that it is best to make critical alterations to the file as few times as possible, because each time you perform an adjustment you are discarding data. Here is where your monitor and how you have set it up becomes an important part of the calibration link. It won't be until you have gone through the entire process several times, right through to printed results, and including the final and important step of comparing the results to your monitor, that you will begin to gain some confidence in how much you can trust what you see on your monitor. You should think of calibration as an ongoing process which you are constantly refining. Every time you output a file, compare the results to your monitor and fine-tune.

### Objective

Your objective is to make corrections to the scan which are designed to produce the print quality you want—in whatever medium you choose to use to output the file. For the purposes of this discussion I will assume the final output will be sheetfed offset lithography on coated paper. You will be using the same techniques to tailor files for any other output medium with different target values. In order for any file to print correctly, it must have the appropriate dot percent values (as indicated by the Info Palette) in the shadows, midtones, and highlights. While this may sound like the *go by the numbers* approach instead of the *trust your monitor* approach, the fact is that for most control you will be relying on both approaches. Due to various physical characteristics, an offset press tends to increase the size of a halftone dot in decreasing amounts from the shadows to the highlights. This characteristic is known as *dot gain*. Depending on the type of press and the paper being printed on, some amount of compensation needs to be built into the file.

For a sheetfed press using coated stock, you will want a final grayscale image with about a 95% dot in the shadow area that represents the blackest black (no detail), and about a 5% dot in the highlight areas representing the lightest detail. Spectral highlights—small areas such as light glinting off chrome—can be allowed to go to 0% dot. Your midtone or middle gray values will have about a 40% dot.

## Reality Check

I am approximating these dot percent values, because there are actually quite a number of variables which will affect the result beyond the characteristics of the press itself. These variables include the efficiency of the platemaking procedure in the particular printing plant, the type of printing plates used, the type of ink used, the density of ink printed, and the screen frequency (lpi). In fact, every detail of the process will have an effect on the quality and consistency of the result. Your best chance for consistent and predictable results is to close the calibration loop as much as possible. In other words, the more you use the same service bureau, the same printer, the same paper and ink, the more closely you will be able to control the quality and predictability of the result. All of the same considerations apply to output to any medium—Canon color laser, Iris ink jet, dye sublimation, and so on. As yet, there is no magic formula to absolutely guarantee predictably great results.

## The Mystical Dot Gain

The dot gain % you use in the Printing Inks Setup dialog box *(Figure 10.1)* is an important yet much misunderstood factor in the equation of controlling quality. Exactly how this number relates to the dot gain your printer is talking about if she tells you that a certain press has a dot gain of, say, 12% is the mystical part. That dot gain figure is a description of actual physical dot gain between film and press sheet due to a myriad of factors, some of which I have just mentioned.

Photoshop uses 20% (in a scale of – 10% to 40%) as an average dot gain for offset presses. In practice, setting your dot gain at 20% will usually result in your images printing too dark, which accounts for the suggested setting of 24% in Chapter Five: *Setting Up Your Monitor*. For more about dot gain and color images, see Chapter Eighteen: *Managing Color*. Because of the way Photoshop's color management system works, however, there really isn't any reason to be concerned about how the dot gain % is calculated—only that it's the right number for the relationship between your monitor and the press or other output device in question—and whether it is or not is determined visually by comparison of a press proof with the image on your monitor.

In the final analysis, whatever dot gain % you use is the result of all of the factors that regulate your monitor's display, such as the Knoll Gamma or other utility, the gamma you use in Photoshop's Monitor Preferences, how you have your contrast and brightness adjusted, the make and model of monitor you use, your monitor's age, and the ambient light you typically work in. With all of these variables in play, it's unlikely that the same file will look the same on ten different monitors despite using the same dot gain setting. The only reasonable way to proceed, as suggested in Chapter Five: *Setting Up Your Monitor*, is to accept *your* monitor as your reality.

## *Seriously Numinous*

You use the dot gain setting in the grayscale mode to adjust the lightness or darkness of the image on the monitor in order to approximate the printed result, whether it will be offset or another output medium. Two things (at least) are important to understand:

1. **In the grayscale mode, changing the dot gain value will change the appearance of the image on your monitor (if you have *Use Dot Gain for Grayscale Images* checked in the Printing Inks Setup, *Figure 10.1*), but it will have no effect on the file itself. In other words, the file will always print exactly the same way despite the dot gain % you enter and despite the way the image looks on the monitor.**

Changing the dot gain value alters the appearance of the file on the monitor in order to give you the opportunity to correct its appearance using the Contrast/Brightness, Levels, or Curves controls. When you use these controls to correct the file's appearance, you are

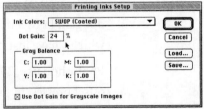

*Figure 10.1*     Printing Inks Setup.

in fact altering the file data itself, and the file will respond in print. The dot gain value you enter in the Printing Inks Setup is simply a device for visualizing what happens when you print. Dot gain works differently in the color modes, which are discussed in Chapter Eighteen: *Managing Color*.

2. **In order to use the dot gain control you must have a printed result from the device or press you are attempting to calibrate to.**

After all is said and done, the calibration process is very simple and painless. First: you make a proof. It doesn't matter if the proof looks right or not. Second: you compare the proof to your monitor and adjust the dot gain % until your monitor matches the proof.

Having adjusted the file on your monitor so that it looks good with your newly discovered dot gain % entered, the next print you make from the same device will be very close to what you expect. Each printing device may have its own dot gain %.

## Getting Ready

Before beginning your adjustments, remember to set up the Printing Inks Setup box as illustrated in Figure 10.1. The Dot Gain % will affect how your grayscale image is displayed with the checkbox checked, which it should be. Next choose **Window> Palettes> Show Info** *(Figure 10.2)*. This on-screen densitometer will become your constant companion while adjusting either grayscale or color images. The values displayed in the Info Palette reflect the halftone dot % that will result when your file is imaged by a calibrated imagesetter. Notice that the Info box displays a second set of numbers separated by a slash when any of

| Info | | |
|---|---|---|
| K: | 17%/ | 11% |
| C: | 17%/ | 11% |
| M: | 9%/ | 5% |
| Y: | 8%/ | 5% |
| K: | 0%/ | 0% |
| X: | 2.444 | |
| Y: | 0.083 | |

Figure 10.2
Info Palette.

the dialog boxes under the **Image> Adjust** menu are open. The number on the left represents the dot % before the change. The number on the right represents the dot % after the change.

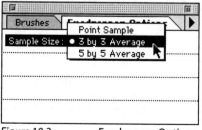

Figure 10.3        Eyedropper Options.

The last step in getting ready is to double-click on the eyedropper tool in the toolbox and set the Sample Size to 3 by 3 Average *(Figure 10.3)*. Point Sample is too fine a sample, since it is reading one pixel at a time and could be misleading, and 5 by 5 Average could be misleading because it is too coarse. I suggest setting your General Preferences to display Precise in the Other Tools section of the Tool Cursors *(Figure 10.4)*.

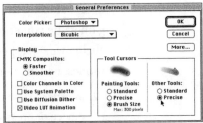

Figure 10.4          General Preferences.

### *Monitor Limitations*

However wonderful your monitor might be, you must get comfortable with using the Info Palette for accessing the highlight values. Even the finest monitors simply will not be able to show you variations of a few percent in the lightest highlights, that is, with values of 10% or less. Here is where using the eyedropper tool in conjunction with the Info Palette is essential.

# The Controls

Let's assume your scan is a bit too dark and lacking in contrast. You have three options available in Photoshop with which to make corrections, with increasing levels of control:

1. **Contrast and Brightness**

2. **Levels**

3. **Curves**

All three are located in the **Image> Adjust** menu. Before making adjustments we'll look at the controls and describe how they work.

# Brightness/Contrast

This control offers the least precision of the three, and for that reason I rarely use it and don't recommend it for critical work. How it works is fairly self-evident *(Figure 10.5)*.

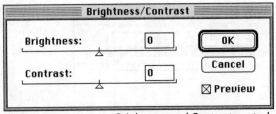

Figure 10.5          Brightness and Contrast control.

# Levels

The Levels dialog box *(Figure 10.6)* offers far more control and precision than Brightness/Contrast, and there are many instances in which it proves invaluable.

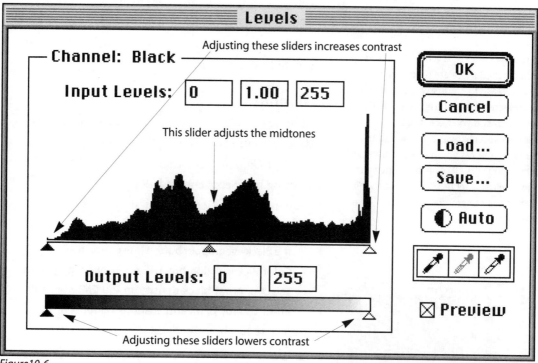

*Figure10-6*                                                                                          Levels dialog box.

## *Finding the Outer Limits*

One of the most valuable functions of the Levels dialog box is to assist you in locating the darkest and lightest places in your picture. To use this feature you need to have the Video LUT Animation checked in the General Preferences dialog box, and the Preview box unchecked in the Levels dialog box *(Figure 10.7)*. Open the image file you are going to adjust and choose **Image> Adjust> Levels**. Hold down the Option key and drag either the shadow or highlight slider to the opposite side of the histogram to locate the darkest and brightest areas. The image will be displayed with

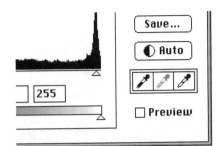

*Figure 10.7*

**Preview checkbox:** When the box is checked, changes are made only after you release the mouse button, and only to selected areas (if there were active selections). If you leave the box unchecked, changes are made to the entire screen as you move the sliders. Once you click OK, only the active window will be affected. This is true for all other adjustment dialog boxes with a Preview checkbox.

*Figure 10.8*        Brightest highlights.

high contrast, allowing you to easily determine the lightest *(Figure 10.8)* and darkest *(Figure 10.9)* areas.

## Eyedropper Buttons

The eyedropper buttons within both the Levels and Curves dialog boxes are there to allow you to automatically or manually adjust the image to preset values—that is, to set the maximum shadow and highlight dot percent.

## Manual

In order to make either the manual or automatic eyedropper options work properly you must have the *Use Dot Gain for Grayscale Images* checkbox in the Printing Inks Setup checked. Begin by setting the target densities for each as follows:

1. With the Levels dialog box open, double-click on the Black eyedropper button (the one on the left). The Color Picker dialog box will open, allowing you to select a target black density. In the CMYK% fields, enter 0% for C, M, and Y and 95% for K or black *(Figure 10.10)*, and click OK.

2. Double-click on the White eyedropper button (the one on the right). When the Color Picker dialog box opens, enter 0% for C, M, and Y, and 5% for K *(Figure 10.11)*, and click OK.

3. With the Black eyedropper button selected, click once on the area of your image which represents the maximum shadow density. Photoshop will set that point to 95%.

4. Click once on the White eyedropper button and click on the lightest area of the image with detail. Photoshop will set that point to 5%.

*Figure 10.9*          Darkest shadows.

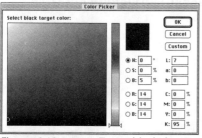

*Figure 10.10*          Target black density.

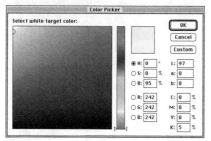

*Figure 10.11*          Target white density.

The manual eyedropper function allows you to select densities anywhere in the image and set them to the preset values instantly.

## Automatic

The easiest of all: simply click once on the Auto button in the Levels dialog box and Photoshop will select the lowest and highest values and set them to the percents you preset in the Color Picker.

These controls work the same way in both the Levels and the Curves dialog boxes. Now that you know how these automatic and manual eyedropper controls work, use them cautiously. They can get you into trouble and may not produce optimum results.

## Using Levels

The Levels tool shows a histogram *(Figure 10.6)*, which is a visual representation of how the pixels are distributed in the image in terms of grayscale levels from 0 to 255. There are two sliding bars which allow you to adjust the Input and Output levels, both of which operate either by using the sliders or by inputting values directly into the box. The Levels dialog box also allows you to save and reload adjustments if you want to apply the same settings to several different files. Using Levels can be a quick and easy way to lighten or darken an image by adjusting the midtone slider in the Input section. Moving the midtone slider to the left will lighten the midtones, and moving it to the right will darken them. The Output sliders offer an easy method of limiting the maximum black values and brightest highlights. Adjusting the black Output slider to the right will lighten the shadows, and moving the white Output slider to the left will darken the highlights. The overall effect of using the Output sliders is to lower the contrast of the image.

## Correcting a Dark Image Using Levels

Starting with a dark image *(Figure 10.12a)*, open the Levels dialog box by typing ⌘L *(Figure 10.13)*. Notice in Figure 10.13 that the midtone slider has been moved to the left to shift the midtone toward the shadows, thereby lightening the image *(Figure 10.12b)*. By referring to the Info Palette I noticed that this move caused the darkest shadow (in the chair where the eyedropper tool is positioned) to get too light. To correct this, I moved the black Input slider very slightly to the right to get the 95% shadow dot I wanted. Finally, I moved the white highlight Input slider slightly to the left to brighten the highlight dot. Not surprisingly, the histogram (choose **Image> Histogram**) before-and-after illustrations show that the pixels have been remapped to be distributed more evenly throughout the grayscale after the corrections *(Figure 10.14a and b)*.

*Note: If you want to apply the same Levels adjustments to multiple files, hold the Option key while choosing Levels in the* **Image> Adjust** *menu. The dialog box will open with the last settings entered.*

*Figure 10.12*          (a)                                                                          (b)

Dark image before Levels adjustment (a), and after Levels adjustment (b).

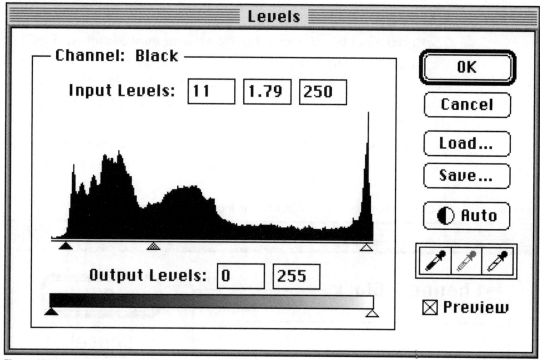

*Figure 10.13*

Levels dialog box.

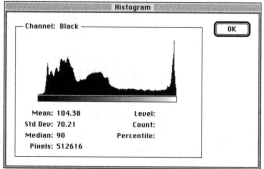

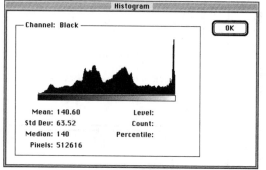

*Figure 10.14*          (a) Histogram before.          (b) Histogram after.

# Curves

The Curves dialog box *(Figure 10.15)* offers you the most control over how the values of your image are distributed. It offers precise control over the shadow, $^3/_4$ tone, midtone, $^1/_4$ tone, and highlight areas. You have the option of working with dot % or RGB values. To make life a little easier, you can click on the Zoom box in the upper right-hand corner of the title bar to toggle between two sizes for the dialog box *(Figure 10.15)*. Curves also allows you to click on an area of your image and identify the location of that value

*Figure 10.15*          Curves dialog box.          Click here to toggle between large and small window

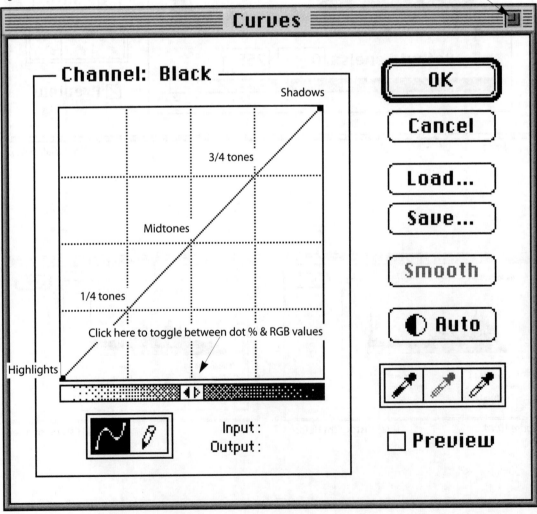

on the curve itself. If you prefer a tighter grid pattern in the Curves dialog box, you can Option-click anywhere on the grid to toggle between a tight and loose grid *(Figure 10.16)*.

## Correcting a Dark Image Using Curves

Figure 10.17 illustrates a Curves dialog box with the curve adjusted to correct for a dark image *(Figure 18a)*. With the Curves dialog box open, click and drag anywhere on the curve to modify its shape. Anywhere you click on the curve will create a new control point, and in this example *(Figure 10.17)*, I have created three new control points to keep the curve from bending too abruptly. The results of the curve adjustment are illustrated in Figure 10.18b.

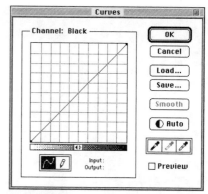

Figure 10.16
By Option-clicking anywhere on the grid area you will toggle between a loose or tight grid pattern.

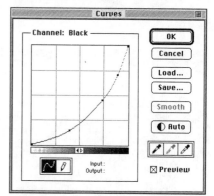

*Figure 10.17*          Curve adjustment.

*Figure 10.18*                    (a)                                            (b)
Dark image before Curves adjustment (a), and after Curves adjustment (b).

(a)

(b)

*Figure 10.19*
Low contrast scan (a), and the same image after adjustment (b).

## Correcting for Low Contrast

A typical correction for a low contrast or flat scan might be made for an image like the one in Figure 10.19a. Notice that I am working with the shadows on the left side of the curve this time *(Figure 10.20)*. By creating a control point in the $^3/_4$ tone area of the curve and dragging down to darken the shadows, and creating another in the $^1/_4$ tone area and dragging up to lighten the highlights, a gentle "S" curve can be made which will effectively increase the contrast. The result of the adjustment is illustrated in Figure 10.19b.

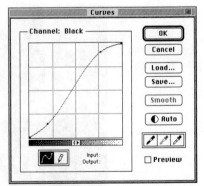

*Figure 10.20*
Curve adjustment to increase contrast.

*Figure 10.21*
Results of a
Distorted curve.

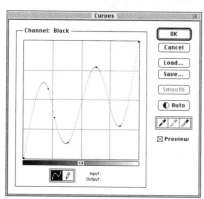

## *Distorted Curves*

Be careful not to bend the curve in a radical way
unless you are trying to achieve a distorted effect
(*Figures 10.21 and 10.22*).

*Figure 10.22*
Distorted curve.

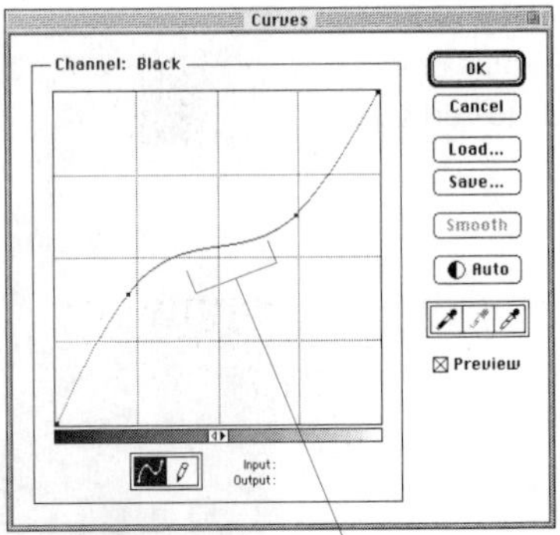

Figure 10.23
Flattened curve.

Figure 10.24
Results of flattened curve.

Notice how the flat-tened area of the curve results in lack of separa-ration in the image.

## *Flattened Values*

Avoid horizontal areas in the curve as well. In other words, if the curve is too *flattened* the area of the image represented by that section of the curve will lose separation and become flat *(Figures 10.23 and 10.24).*

### Identifying Specific Values

With your image open in Photoshop, click and hold the mouse button down on an area you wish to adjust. When you look at the curve you will notice a circle which identifies the exact location on the curve of the value you clicked on. This allows you to adjust the curve in that specific area for maximum effect on the gray value you want to alter *(Figure 10.25)*.

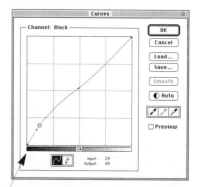

*Figure 10.25*                Identifying specific values.

## The Controls

In addition to Brightness/Contrast, Levels, and Curves, there are four tools
with which you can adjust the overall color balance or specific colors in your
image: Color Balance, Hue/Saturation, Selective Color, and Variations.

In any of the color modes (RGB, CMYK, or LAB), Levels and Curves work
in very much the same way as discussed in Chapter Ten: *Adjust Gray Values*

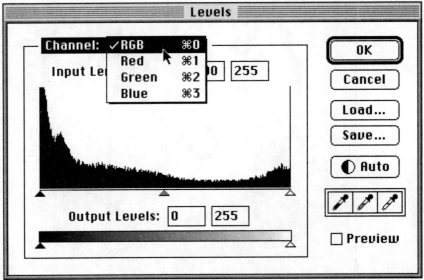

Figure 11.1                                                    Channel pop-up.

except that you will have the option of a pop-up in the dialog boxes to adjust
the color channels individually *(Figure 11.1)*.

You will find that you may want to use more than one of these tools to completely correct some images. For example, if a scan is far too dark or light
to begin with, you might use Levels to correct that problem. If the scan's color
also needs adjusting, you might find it easier to make that correction using

Color Balance rather than using Levels. Since color perception varies so unpredictably between individuals, you'll need to discover which approach works best for you.

# Color Balance

With the possible exception of the Variations command (**Image> Adjust> Variations**), perhaps the easiest way to adjust an RGB scan that has an objectionable overall color cast is with the Color Balance tool (**Image> Adjust> Color Balance...** or type ⌘ Y) *(Figure 11.2)*. It has clearly labeled sliders which allow for intuitive color correction, as well as Shadows, Midtones, and Highlights buttons. In addition, it has an invaluable checkbox allowing you to Preserve Luminosity—in other words, make color changes without altering the overall lightness and darkness of the image. If you wish, you can make adjustments by entering numeric values in the appropriate fields.

If the color designations seem confusing at first, a little trial and error will quickly clear up how the sliders work. One way to think about it is that if an image is too red, for example, moving the slider *away* from Red will reduce its redness. This approach will work for all the colors in this dialog box even if you don't understand exactly why at first. Experimenting with this control is a good way to get a handle on the integral relationship between the RGB and CMYK color modes, and the symmetrical system of thirds governing them.

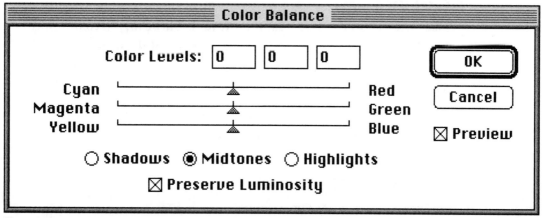

*Figure 11.2*                                                                 Color Balance dialog box.

One drawback of using Color Balance is that it will not allow you to save and load settings; but like the other Image Adjust tools, if you hold the Option key down while accessing this tool, it will open with the last settings in place. Color Balance would be my first choice of color correction tools to make broad overall color shifts in an image.

# Levels

Figure C.8 in the color section illustrates using Levels to correct a scan that is too dark and has a green cast *(Figure C.8a)*:

1. **Open Levels (type ⌘L).**

2. **Move the center slider to the left to brighten the image *(Figure C.8b)*.**

3. **Change the Channel to Green using the pop-up menu (see *Figure 11.1*) or by typing ⌘2.**

3. **Move the center slider slightly to the right to reduce the amount of green *(Figure C.8c)*.**

4. **Click OK or press Return.**

Figure C.8c shows the results of the corrections. While Levels is a great tool for correcting overall color casts, it is difficult to change midtones and highlights independently of one another with precision. And, of course, there is no reason to fight it—you would use Curves for the most sophisticated and independent control over the different areas of the image.

# Curves

Like the Levels tool, Curves (**Image> Adjust> Curves...**) in color works exactly like it does in grayscale, with the addition of the pop-up channel option. With Curves you can make very subtle corrections to the highlights, for example, without disturbing other areas of the image.

*As when adjusting grayscale files, make sure you have the Info Palette open to access the effect of the changes you are making.*

In this example *(Figure C.9a)*, you want to correct a slight green cast in the highlights only and proceed as follows:

1. **Type ⌘M to open the Curves control.**

2. Place the cursor (eyedropper icon) on the area you want to adjust and press the mouse button. A circle appears on the curve indicating the location on the curve of the color you want to adjust *(Figure 11.3)*.

3. Next, you need to bolt down the other parts of the curve to keep it from moving around. Simply place the cursor on the ³/₄ tone intersection and click once to place an anchor point; repeat for the midtone intersection. Place the anchor points carefully to avoid repositioning the curve.

*Note that in the Curves control in Figure 11.3 the shadows are on the left, which is my personal preference. Click on the buttons in the center of the grayscale to toggle between shadows on left or right. This also toggles the numerical readout between RGB values and dot %.*

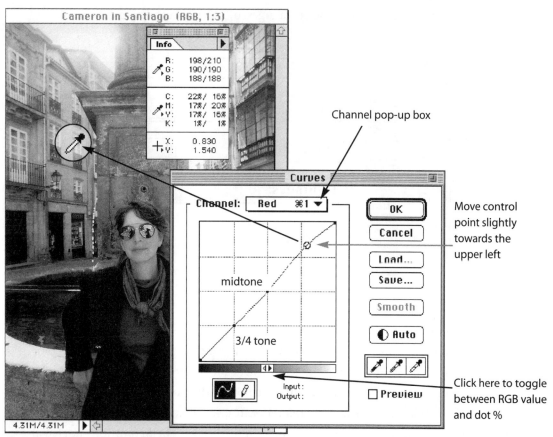

Channel pop-up box

Move control point slightly towards the upper left

Click here to toggle between RGB value and dot %

*Figure 11.3*

Color correcting with Curves.

4. **Put the pointer on the pop-up Channel box and select Red. You are going to lessen the amount of red in the critical area (the Red value in the RGB readout of your Info Palette will increase), which in effect will lessen the amount of cyan and yellow and increase the magenta slightly. Click and drag on the part of the curve you want to adjust (near the $^1/_4$ tone in this example), and move it slightly toward the upper left corner.**

5. **Click OK or press Return.**

Figure C.9b shows the corrected image.

# Hue/Saturation

The Hue/Saturation control (**Image> Adjust> Hue/Saturation...**) is one you might not use a lot, but when you need it, you *really* need it. It certainly wouldn't be your first choice for making general color corrections, but it is invaluable for making local changes, or changes to a single color.

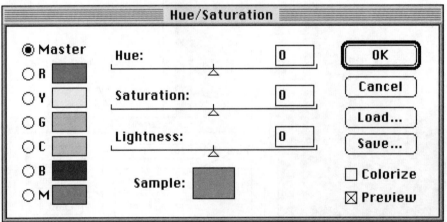

Figure 11.4                                                                                    Hue/Saturation control.

On the left side of the dialog box *(Figure 11.4)* are a Master and six color radio buttons. When you move the Hue slider, it moves around the color wheel *(Figure C.10)*. When the Master radio button is clicked, which it is by default, the sliders change all the colors at the same time. The color in the Sample patch is there as a reference. You can change it to a specific color in your image by clicking anywhere in the image. The Saturation slider will increase the saturation as you drag the triangle to the right, and decrease it as you drag the triangle to the left. The Lightness slider works in the same way.

As an example of color correcting using Hue/Saturation, in Figure C.12a, I wanted to increase the saturation of the blue sky. With this control it's as simple as clicking on the blue (B) radio button and moving the saturation slider a little to the right *(Figure C.12b)*. I also wanted to take out some of the red in the building and neutralize its color a little. To do this:

1. **Click on the Red (R) radio button.**

2. **Move the Hue slider a little to the right.**

3. **Move the Saturation slider a little to the left** *(Figure C.12c)*.

4. **Click OK or press Return.**

Figure C.12c shows the corrected image.

## *Colorize Option*

One of the coolest uses of the Hue/Saturation control is the Colorize check-box, which gives you almost instant tinted images *(Figure 11.5.* For a sepia-toned print, start with either a grayscale or color original. If you start with grayscale, change the mode to RGB color before beginning.

1. **Click on the Colorize checkbox.**

2. **Move the Hue slider to the right to 40.**

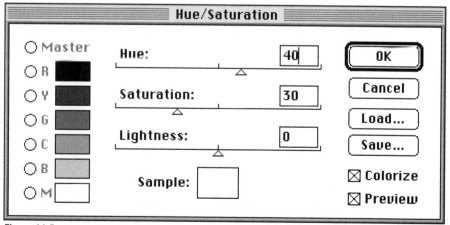

*Figure 11.5*                                                     Colorize option.

3. **Move the Saturation slider to the left to 30.**

4. **Adjust to taste.**

5. **Click OK or press Return.**

# Selective Color

Selective Color (**Image> Adjust> Selective Color**) adjusts the amount of subtractive color inks used to create a color *(Figure 11.6)*. Rather than allowing you to change a specific color, Selective Color will allow you, for example, to add a little yellow to *all* the reds in the image to warm them up. This command is most effective once you have converted your file from RGB

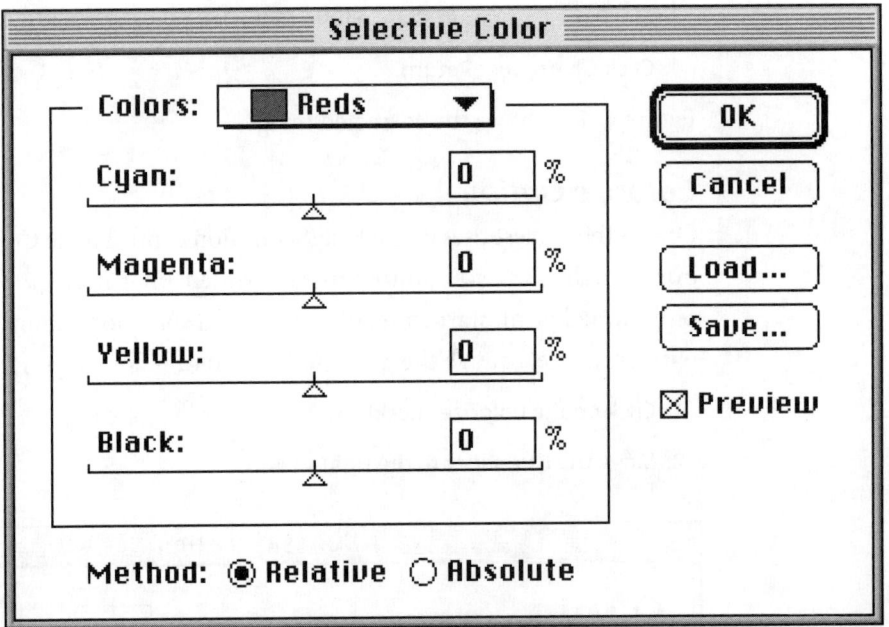

*Figure 11.6*                                                                                    Selective Color.

to CMYK, but will work in any color mode. You can use it as a final control to remove tints or color casts to subtle areas such as neutrals and highlights.

The Method radio buttons allow you to switch between Relative and Absolute. When you are using the Relative method, the changes you make are calculated based on the existing CMYK color percentages. For example, a 10% addition to 50% of any color results in 55% [50% + (10% of 50%)

= 55%]. If you use the Absolute method, the same 10% addition results in 60% (50% + 10% = 60%). The Relative method results in more subtle changes than the Absolute method.

Note that if you are working in the RGB mode, the CMYK values are calculated based on how you have your Monitor, Printing Inks, and Separation Setup Preferences set. See Chapter Eighteen: *Managing Color* for more about color separation controls.

# Variations

This command (**Image> Adjust> Variations...** )is a fairly painless way to make overall corrections to the color balance, brightness, and saturation of your image. I rarely use it, however, since the thumbnails provided are really too small for my taste, even on a 20 in. monitor. Variations can offer an alternative to the controls already discussed if you're stuck—that is, if Color Balance, Levels, or Curves won't quite do it for you *(Figure 11.7)*.

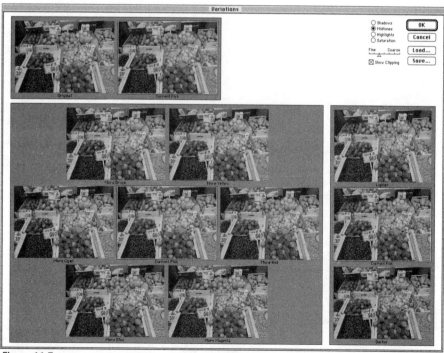

*Figure 11.7*

Variations dialog box.

# COMBINING IMAGES 12

At this point your image is well along the trail of being ready for printing. It's cropped precisely, and you've adjusted the size and resolution and fine-tuned the gray values or color balance. If you are working on a file that is designed to reproduce an original, you won't be using any of the techniques in this chapter, but if you are in the process of creating a new original, now is a good time to have fun and play with your image, trying various filters, combining images, and exploring one of Photoshop's greatest strengths—image manipulation and enhancement. This is a time for you to go exploring on your own, using whatever resources you have available to come up with an image that satisfies you as a creative being.

Since it's really beyond the scope of this book to lay out or explain the wealth of options you have at your fingertips while using Photoshop, I'll confine this chapter to a mini-tutorial of the more precarious waters you'll be navigating—pointing out a few aspects of combining two or more images that will drive you absolutely crazy, but for which there are very simple guidelines to keep you from being certified.

## Common Hazards

First, I want to point out some potentially hazardous areas, maneuvers that would unnecessarily degrade the image quality, and then briefly point out a few aspects of Photoshop's layering function which might save you a little trouble if you haven't worked with it a lot.

### Nervous Clicking

How many cups of coffee did you say you need to begin the day? This is one of the most frustrating pitfalls to people new to Photoshop: inadvertent or random clicking of the mouse button results in unintentional deselection or a trip to the Finder.

## Deselection

*One single click* of the mouse button will place a floating selection. For example, let's say you have worked for 20 minutes creating an elaborate selection around the outline of a head in order to separate it from the background. One minute you see the dancing ants demarcating your precious selection and the next minute they're gone. Reason: the one random click anywhere in the active window. Even more exasperating, once you have lost your selection, if you don't realize what has happened, you will usually click a few more times here and there in a desperate attempt to recover it. This only makes matters worse since you can't then use the Undo command, which would have "undone" the damage.

## Unscheduled Trip to Finder

Another very common and frustrating result of the random click is that you find yourself suddenly in the Finder and are left wondering where Photoshop went. Again, don't panic. Instead, get into the habit of checking the icon in the upper right corner of your monitor. If you see the small computer icon, it means you are in the Finder and not in Photoshop. You went to the Finder because you clicked once on your desktop. When you see the Photoshop icon in the upper right corner, you're in Photoshop.

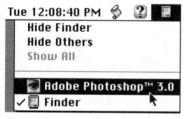

Figure 12.1     Back to Photoshop.

The cure is simple: click once on any Photoshop element or go to the Finder icon in the upper right corner and drag down to Photoshop and release the mouse button *(Figure 12.1)* and you're back in Photoshop.

**To summarize:** do not click randomly. If you have an active selection, one single click will deselect it. If you happen to have a mouse with a hair trigger and accidentally click—don't panic and click again. Instead, choose **Edit> Undo**, and the damage will be repaired: your selection will reappear.

Be careful about clicking on the desktop area, which will instantly send you to the Finder. Get into the habit of checking the icon in the upper right of your monitor to find out where you are.

# Combining Two or More Images

Frequently you will be slicing and dicing images from a number of different files and recombining them into one new original. The simplest strategy for going about this is to select the image you visualize as being the *base* image, onto which other images will be added in some way. Begin by opening the base image as well as one or two files which you will be using as sources for imagery to add to the base image.

## Scaling

When combining images by pasting one into another, you will frequently adjust the size of the pasted image using the **Image> Effects> Scale** control. Once you have implemented the scale change by clicking with the gavel icon 🔨, *never* reselect the pasted image and scale up (make it larger). Instead, if you feel you have made the pasted image too small, delete it, repaste from the original file, and adjust the scale again. The bottom line is: *Avoid sampling up. Sampling up will unnecessarily degrade the quality of the pasted image.*

*Figure 12.2*          File size.

*Figure 12.3*          File resolution.

## Size Surprise

When combining images, check the relative resolutions of each file. Unless they are the same, the image you are adding will be either larger or smaller than you expect. For example, if the base or destination file has a resolution of 200 ppi and the file (or portion of the file) you are pasting has a resolution of 300 ppi, the pasted image will end up larger than you expect it to be once it is pasted in. In the same way, if the file you are pasting has a lower resolution than the base or destination file, it will end up smaller than you expect once it is pasted in. The easiest way to check the resolution of a file is to press the Option key and hold down the mouse button with the pointer on the file size number in the lower left corner of the window *(Figures 12.2 and 12.3)*. While you don't have to manually change the resolutions of the two files

(Photoshop will do it for you automatically), you need to pay attention to their relative resolutions to avoid annoying surprises.

There are three ways to add one image (whole or in part) to another:

1. **Copy & Paste (old method).**
2. **Drag & Drop selection (new method).**
3. **Drag & Drop layer (coolest method).**

In addition to being easier and quicker than method 1, methods 2 and 3 above have the advantage of transferring the selection or layer without using the Clipboard. In Photoshop, the Clipboard is an invisible buffer area used to store *copied* data. When you select and copy all or part of an image, the data stored in the Clipboard uses some of your computer's memory. If you have selected and copied a large file, the space used by the Clipboard could have a significant negative impact on your computer's performance.

*If you have used method 1 (Copy & Paste) for a large file, it's a good idea to clear the Clipboard immediately so that your computer isn't unnecessarily encumbered with the data. To clear the Clipboard simply select and copy a very small area at random. This new smaller chunk of data will replace the large file since the Clipboard can contain only one copied element at a time.*

When working in Photoshop 3.x, it's best to take full advantage of its layering and Drag & Drop capabilities. This means that every element you add to a base image will have its own layer, giving you maximum flexibility to move, resize, filter, or delete that element, and you'll avoid the Copy & Paste method whenever possible.

## *Copy & Paste*

1. Open your base image and one other image file (from which you want to copy) in Photoshop.

2. Open the Layers Palette by choosing **Window> Palettes> Show Layers.**

3. Make the file from which you want to copy the *active* file (click once anywhere in its window) and *select* the area you want to copy. There are several ways to make a selection (check your *Adobe Photoshop User Guide* under "Working with Selections"), but for now simply click on the rectangular marquee tool (top left in the toolbox) and click and drag a selection marquee around the area

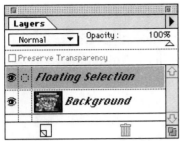

*Figure 12.4*          Floating Selection.

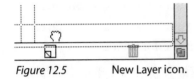

*Figure 12.5*          New Layer icon.

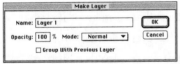

*Figure 12.6*          Make Layer.

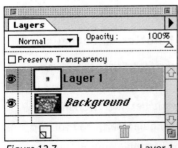

*Figure 12.7*          Layer 1.

you want to copy. If you want the entire image, choose **Select> Select All** or simply type ⌘ A.

4. Choose **Edit: Copy** from the menu.

5. Make the base image the active file (click once anywhere in its window).

6. Choose **Edit> Paste** from the menu.

7. The area you selected and copied will appear in the center of the base file's window.

The pasted image lands as a *floating* selection. This means that if you click and drag inside the *dancing ants*, you can move the selection around. In the Layers Palette it appears as a temporary layer called *Floating Selection (Figure 12.4)*. Next, make the floating selection into an actual layer.

## Make the Floating Selection a Layer

1. Double-click on the Floating Selection layer in the Layers Palette *(Figure 12.4)*, or drag the Floating Selection layer into the New Layer icon at the bottom left in the Layers Palette *(Figure 12.5)*.

2. A *Make Layer* dialog box appears, allowing you to type in a name for the new layer. Type in an appropriate name or just click OK, going with the generic Layer 1 name provided *(Figure 12.6)*.

3. The Layers Palette shows the newly created Layer 1 *(Figure 12.7)*.

   Easier still, simply Option-click on the New Layer icon at the bottom left of the Layers Palette and Layer 1 is created from the Floating Selection layer.

## Drag & Drop Selection

Starting after step 3 in the Copy & Paste instructions:

1. Arrange the base image and the image you are copying from next to each other *(Figure 12.8)*.

2. Drag the selection from the source window and drop it (release the mouse button) on the base image. The selected image you dragged into the base image will land as a Floating Selection *(Figure 12.9)*.

3. Follow instructions for making a floating selection a layer (above).

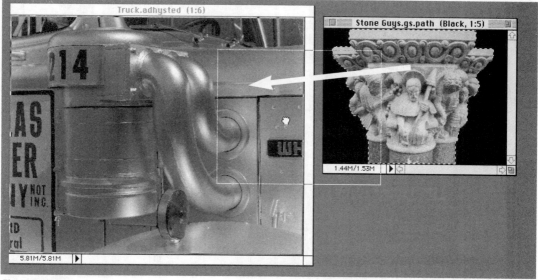

Figure 12.8

Drag selections between windows and drop.

Figure 12.9
Combined images.

## Drag & Drop Layer

Now for the coolest method of moving one image or a layer of an image to another. The advantage of this method (and the reason it's so cool) is that

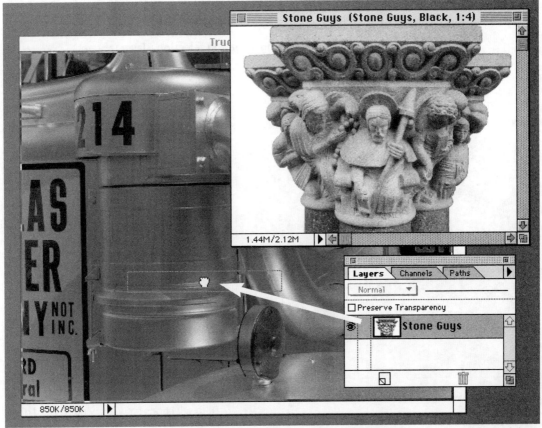

*Figure 12.10*     Drag layer from Layers Palette of *Stone Guys* file to window of *Truck* file and drop.

when you drag a layer from one image to another, it lands ready to go as a new layer in the destination file, complete with its name from the source file.

Starting after step 2 in the Copy & Paste instructions:

1. **With the source file the active file (Stone Guys in this example), and from the source Layers Palette,** *not it's window,* **drag the layer you want to add to the base image into the base image's window and drop it** *(Figure 12.10).*

2. **Voilà! Done** *(Figure 12.11).*

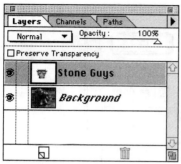

*Figure 12.11*
Layer from the *Stone Guys* file is added to the base image file with the layer name intact.

# Working with Layers

As I mentioned a little earlier in this chapter, making a new layer for the various parts of a picture you are creating is a sound approach, and one which takes the fullest advantage of Photoshop 3.0's greatest strengths—the flexibility of swapping position, transparency, modes, color, and other aspects of the elements you use.

## *Target Layer*

Once you have created two or more layers in a document you are given the choice of which layer is the active or *target layer*. The target layer is indicated by a gray background in the layer name area *(Figure 12.11)*. Being aware of which layer is the target layer is (yet another) very important habit to get into.

### *What's a Target Layer Good For?*

Very simply, whatever commands you execute will *only* affect the target layer. Any drawing, painting, erasing, or filtering will only hit the target layer. This is a necessary and very straightforward approach which works beautifully as long as you're *aware* of how it works. Otherwise, like many things in life, strange things may happen that you didn't intend.

If you have an active selection in a Photoshop file with multiple layers, you need to know (at least) two things:

1. **The selection will show up on all layers with its dancing ants marquee.**
2. **The selection will act on the target layer.**

In other words, all I've said about target layers also applies to selections. Painfully obvious, I know, but I felt it needed to be pointed out.

### *What's the Eye Icon Good For?*

The eye icon on the left of the Layers Palette is used to hide and make visible the layer. Clicking once on the eye icon causes the layer to become invisible. Clicking again where the eye icon used to be causes the layer to reappear. Very handy in sorting elements out when you are working with a file with many layers.

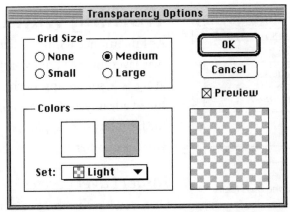

*Figure 12.12*        Transparency Options.

## Transparent or White?

This is definitely an aspect of Photoshop 3.x that will drive you nuts at first—guaranteed. What looks like a white area can be either white or transparent in some cases. The difference is just as you'd expect: a white area acts just like opaque white paper, while a transparent area acts invisible. To tell the difference, make sure you have a transparency pattern turned on in your Photoshop Preferences file. Choose **File> Preferences> Transparency...** *(Figure 12.12)*. With None selected for Grid Size in this dialog box, white and transparent areas will look the same. With Small, Medium, or Large Grid Size selected, transparent areas will have a checkerboard pattern identifying them.

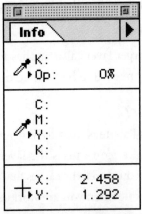

*Figure 12.13*      Info Palette.

Another way to tell which is which, even without a transparency grid turned on, is to check the Info Palette. If an area is transparent, the Info Palette will show an 0% opacity reading under the K reading *(Figure 12.13)*.

## How Do White and Transparent Work Differently?

When you import one image into another using any of the methods described, the white area will be opaque white, while the transparent area will disappear *(Figure 12.14)*.

## *How Do I Change a White Area to Transparent?*

1. **With the target layer other than Background Layer, select the area you want to change.**

*Figure 12.14*                    White and transparent areas of an image after it has been imported.

2. **Make sure the background color in the toolbox is white. The easiest way to accomplish this is to type D (for Default Colors), or click on the Default Colors icon in the toolbox.**

3. **Type ⌦ Delete to fill with the background color, or choose `Edit> Fill...`, select Background Color in the Fill dialog box, and click OK.**

*Note: An important condition for these instructions to work is that the area you want to change to transparent cannot be on the layer called Background Layer. To change the background layer to transparent, simply rename it Layer 0. Accomplish this by double-clicking on the background layer and, when the New Layer dialog box appears, giving it a new name or clicking OK to accept the Layer 0 name provided.*

If you have a layer beneath the one in which you created a transparent area, you will see whatever is on that layer instead of a grid pattern. This can be confusing if the area on the layer below is white. To confirm that your newly created transparent area is, in fact, transparent, hide all the layers below your target layer by clicking on their eye icons and you will see the grid pattern.

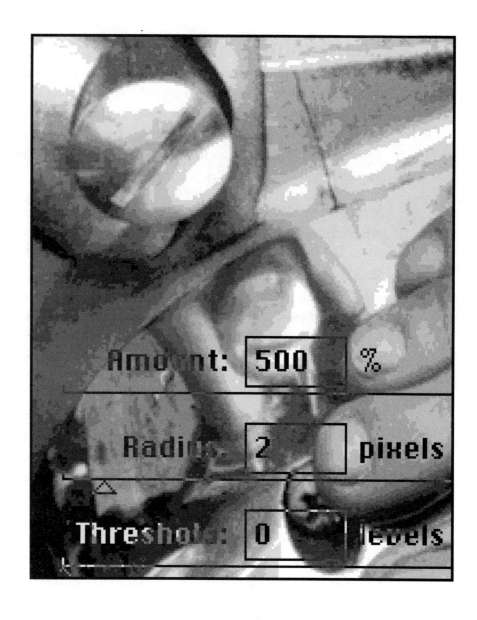

# Sharpening

Just about every image you work with will require some degree of sharpening, and exactly how you go about applying the sharpening is very critical. The fact that your scans require some sharpening does not indicate a flaw in the equipment. *All* scans are sharpened—even those from high-end equipment which usually have the sharpening routines built into the software and applied automatically.

## Sharpen vs. Unsharp Mask

When it comes to sharpening your images, photographic originals or otherwise, *the Unsharp Mask filter is the only way to go.* While the Sharpen and Sharpen More filters may have their uses, they don't offer the control available with the Unsharp Mask filter. The reason they are less effective is that they will sharpen the entire image, including smooth tonal graduations, which is usually not desirable. The Unsharp Mask filter, on the other hand, looks at the *edges* of the detail in your image, and allows you to control just how much you want to enhance those edges.

## Why Is It Called Unsharp Masking?

A really good question, and there are, believe it or not, a couple of good answers. First, the term is a carryover from the ancient history of the graphic arts when in order to enhance sharpness, particularly in color correction masking, a real, live, unsharp mask was made. The unsharp mask was made by sandwiching a sheet of frosted acetate between the camera negative and a new piece of film. After exposure in a contact frame, the new film was placed back in contact with a separation negative and another generation was created on high contrast film. The end result turned out sharper than the original due to the use of the unsharp mask. There you have reason number one—there actually was a physical *unsharp* film mask.

The second reason is that digital systems, in emulating the effectiveness of analog systems for sharpening, use a similar strategy. That is, first the edges are blurred, and then the contrast is amplified using a sequence of equations.

# Hazards

While the Unsharp Mask filter can be one of the final touches that will transform your carefully adjusted image into a masterpiece, it can also be the image wrecker when applied overzealously.

### *Halos and Key Lines*

Since unsharp masking works by creating a lighter halo and darker key line around your edges, too much of a good thing is a disaster *(Figure 13.1)*. The pixel resolution and the nature of the image itself both have a big impact on the amount of unsharp masking you can successfully apply. In general,

(a)

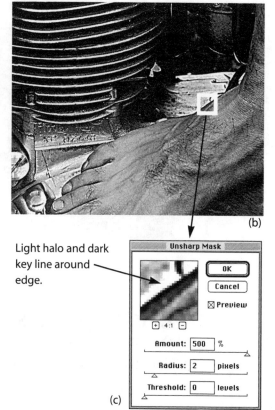

(b)

*Figure 13.1*
(a) Image before any unsharp masking, and (b) the effect of excessive unsharp masking as applied in dialog box (c) at right.

Light halo and dark key line around edge.

(c)

you will have to do a little trial and error on an image-by-image basis to determine what works best.

### Noise

One of the most aggravating factors in effectively applying unsharp masking is a poor quality or noisy scan. Noise is an artifact generated by the scanner itself—the addition of out of place or randomly placed pixels that do not have an equivalent in the original image. When noise is excessive, it limits the amount of unsharp masking you can apply, because the unsharp masking also amplifies the noise and creates an undesirable effect, especially in the shadow areas. Figure 13.2 illustrates a noisy scan unsharpened, and oversharpened to show the excessive noise level. What can you do if a scan is too noisy? If scanning with a higher quality scanner is not an option, careful use of the Threshold option in Photoshop's Unsharp Mask filter dialog box can help enormously.

*Figure 13.2*                (a)                                                 (b)
A noisy scan (a) unsharpened and (b) over-sharpened, with noisy shadow exaggerated.

# Unsharp Masking in Photoshop

Now that you know a few of the hazards to watch out for, let's get down to using the filter correctly to its best advantage. First a rundown of the controls available.

### *The Controls*

To access Photoshop's Unsharp Mask filter dialog box choose **Filter> Sharpen> Unsharp Mask...**. The dialog box opens *(Figure 13.3)* and you are given options for adjusting Amount, Radius, and Threshold, along with a Preview which allows you to zoom in and out. Keep in mind that you need to use all three controls together to achieve the best results. The Amount that is correct for a 1 pixel Radius may not work with a smaller or greater Radius, and the Threshold level will affect both the Amount and Radius settings.

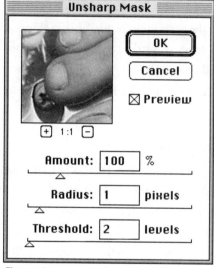

*Figure 13.3*     Unsharp Mask dialog box.

### *Amount*

The amount is adjustable from 1% to 500%. This control adjusts the intensity of the effect—not the width of the halos, just the amplitude.

### *Radius*

The Radius is adjustable between 0.1 to 250 pixels. This setting controls the depth of pixels from an edge that are being affected. The width of the halos or key lines is controlled by Radius.

### Threshold

Adjustable between 0 and 255 levels, the Threshold controls the amount of difference between pixels before unsharp masking will be applied. This control allows you to specify a higher contrast between the edges you want to affect. The higher the Threshold level, the greater difference between pixels before they will be sharpened. Put another way, the higher the level, the less impact the first two controls will have. You will use Threshold to prevent *mottling* of smooth areas such as skin, and control the amount of noise amplification in the shadows.

# Down to Business

Despite the wide control available in this dialog box, you will be using a very narrow range of settings to achieve optimum results, since any radical settings will simply *fry* your image. This makes applying unsharp masking easier than it looks at first, and happily you will be able to see the results on your monitor.

### The Tricky Part

Evaluating the results of your unsharp masking can be deceptive, but only at first. As I pointed out in Chapter Six: *Scanning,* "Test Drive Your Driver," and Chapter Three, *Ratios & Rulers,* **you can only judge the quality of your image at a 1:1 ratio**—that is, when you are seeing every pixel of your file. You should consider making a sign for the top of your monitor with the inscription: **Evaluate at 1:1 only!** Because of the monitor compression of your image data at smaller views (1:2, 1:3, etc.), you cannot evaluate the effects of any operation, the quality of the scan, or unsharp masking unless you view the file at 1:1 or greater. But that alone is not the tricky part—the tricky part is that when you display a 300 ppi file at 1:1, the image is about four times its actual size. What's tricky about that? When you view your skillfully sharpened image at four times its actual size, you will accurately see the effects on detail and edges, *but you have to visualize them at one quarter the size you see on your monitor.*

### *Realistic Settings*

You've seen the effects of too much of a good thing; now let's look at a few examples of settings for the Unsharp Mask dialog box that are more in the range of what you'll be using. Forget about the rules and formulas; what counts is what works. In my experience, the settings that work best are illustrated below.

Figure 13.4 uses an Amount of 250%. The Amount can vary considerably (from 100% up to 500%) depending on the nature of the image, the resolution, and the quality of the scan. I find that a Radius of .5 pixel works well for most photographic originals with a resolution of 300 ppi or lower, and varying the Amount and Threshold can tailor the effect to suit almost any image. A setting of Amount: 200; Radius: 1; Threshold: 4, will produce results almost identical to those in Figure 13.4 and might be preferable for very grainy originals. Figure 13.5 illustrates the almost imperceptible difference between a Radius of .5 pixel (Amount 300%) and a Radius of 1 pixel (Amount 200%). Experimentation and careful evaluation at a 1:1 ratio on your monitor are the keys to success.

*Figure 13.4*        (a)        (b)
(a) An unsharpened image and (b) the same image sharpened, using Amount: 250, Radius: .5, and Threshold: 4. Both images are 300 ppi printed at 150 lpi.

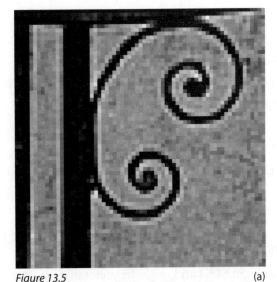

*Figure 13.5*                                     (a)                                                      (b)
Results are almost identical using settings of (a) Amount: 300, Radius: .5, and (b) Amount: 200, Radius: 1.

For images where the quality of the result is critical, try various settings and output paper proofs from the imagesetter or press to find the ideal settings.

### Small Radius

The reason I prefer a very small Radius setting is because a larger halo seems to offer no advantage. In fact, larger halos only tend to create a coarser effect. Figure 13.6 shows an enlarged detail of Figure 13.4, revealing a halo and key line that are ideal.

## Other Considerations

Almost invariably you will run into a few unusual situations, some which I'll touch on here.

### Unsharp Masking and Resolution

The settings used in Figure 13.4 work well for most images *provided* the file resolution is within a range between 200 to 300 ppi. This is the range you are most likely to be working with for images going to press, and probably covers most other output devices. If you are working with significantly lower or higher resolutions, a little experimentation would be advisable in order to determine the ideal settings. A radius of between 1.5 and 2.5 will

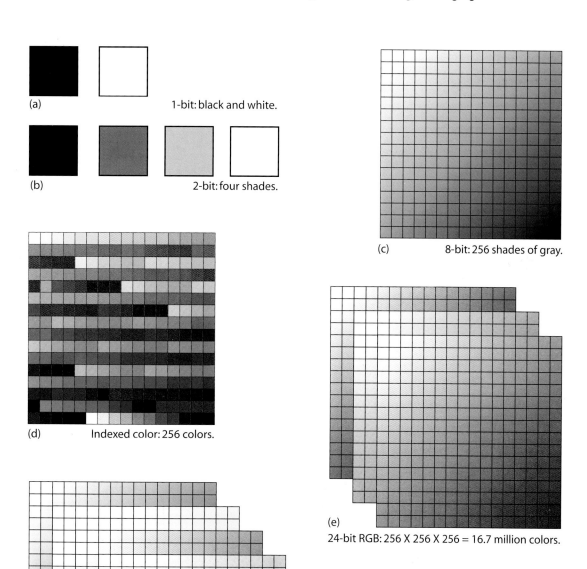

(a)  1-bit: black and white.

(b)  2-bit: four shades.

(c)  8-bit: 256 shades of gray.

(d)  Indexed color: 256 colors.

(e)  24-bit RGB: 256 X 256 X 256 = 16.7 million colors.

(f)  32-bit CMYK.

*Figure C.1*

# Bit Depth

(a) One-bit files are black and white (called Bitmap mode in Photoshop), two-bit files (b) have four shades of gray, and grayscale files (c) have 256 shades of gray. In the RGB mode, each and every pixel is one of 16.7 million colors (c), and each pixel is one of 256 colors in the Indexed color mode (d). The CMYK mode (f) has four eight-bit channels.

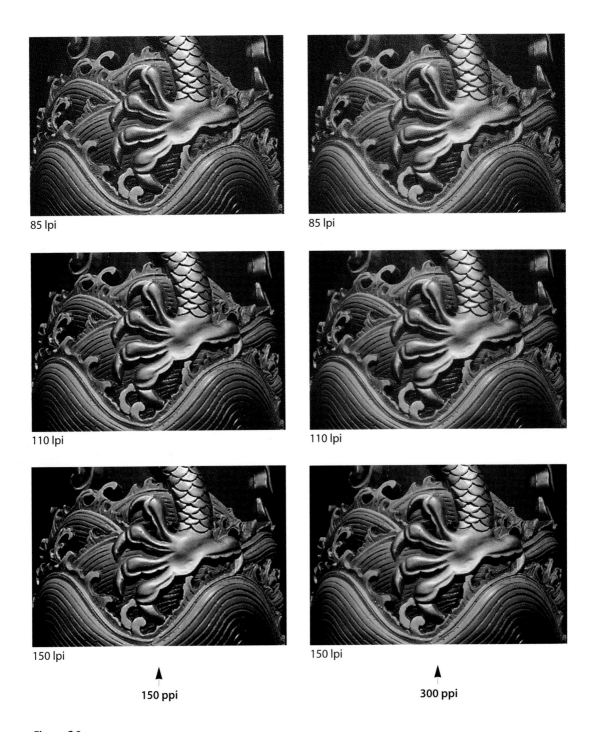

85 lpi

85 lpi

110 lpi

110 lpi

150 lpi

150 lpi

150 ppi

300 ppi

**Figure C.2**
Scans made with a Polaroid SprintScan 35. Bottom left illustrates a 1:1 ppi (pixels per inch) to lpi (lines per inch) ratio. Bottom right shows a 2:1 ppi to lpi ratio. See Chapter Two: *Resolution & File Size*.

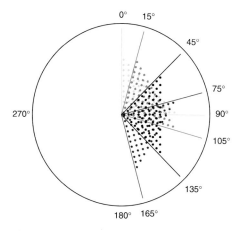

**Figure C.3**
Standard screen angles:
Cyan:      105°
Magenta:   75°
Yellow:    90°
Black:     45°

The center where all four colors superimpose shows a typical four color process rosette pattern.

Notice that screens have an x and y axis so that yellow can be said to be at 0° or 90° which mean the same thing. Likewise, the cyan screen angle can be described as either 15° or 105°.

**Figure C.4**      Olé No Moiré

**Figure C.5**
Custom calibration image with ramps and dot % scales to make identifying the minimum dot % easier.

*Figure C.6*
The same 8" x 10" contact print scanned with three low-end flatbed scanners and a high-end drum scanner. All scans have had unsharp masking applied and have been color corrected for optimum repro-duction of the original print.

*(a)*
Microtek
ScanMaker 600ZS
24-bit flatbed.

*(b)*
UMax PowerLook
30-bit flatbed.

*(c)*
Agfa Arcus II
36-bit flatbed.

*(d)*
Linotype-Hell 3800
drum scanner.

*(a)* Color slide from Photo CD.

*(b)* Color slide from Drum Scanner.

*Figure C.7*
The same 35mm color transparency scanned with (a) Kodak Photo CD and (b) a drum scanner.

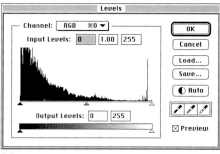

*(a)*

Starting with an image that is booth too dark and too green, open the Levels dialog box (type ⌘ L).

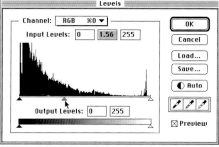

*(b)*

Move the center slider to the left to brighten the image.

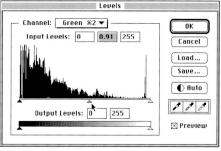

*(c)*

Change the Channel to green using the pop-up menu, and move the center slider slightly to the right to reduce the amount of green.

*Figure C.8*
Correcting brightness and color using Levels (see page 120).

(a)

(b)

**Figure C.9**
Example of using curves to alter a specific area of an image *(see page 120)*.

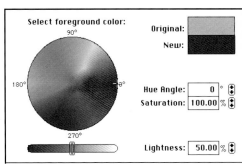

**Figure C.10**     Apple Color Picker Color Wheel.

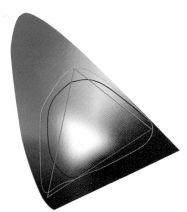

**Figure C.11**
Relative gamuts: CIE l*a*b*, monitor, CMYK, & PANTONE®.

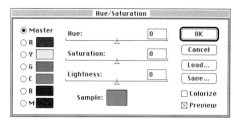

*(a)*
Starting with an image that needs increased saturation in the sky and less red in the building, open the Hue/Saturation dialog box by typing ⌘ U.

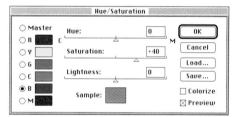

*(b)*
Click on the blue (B) radio button and move the saturation slider a little to the right.

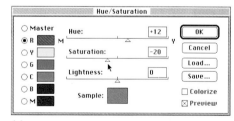

*(c)*
Click on the red (R) radio button, move the Hue slider a little to the right, and move the saturation slider a little to the left.

*Figure C.12*
Color correcting using Hue/Saturation (see page 123).

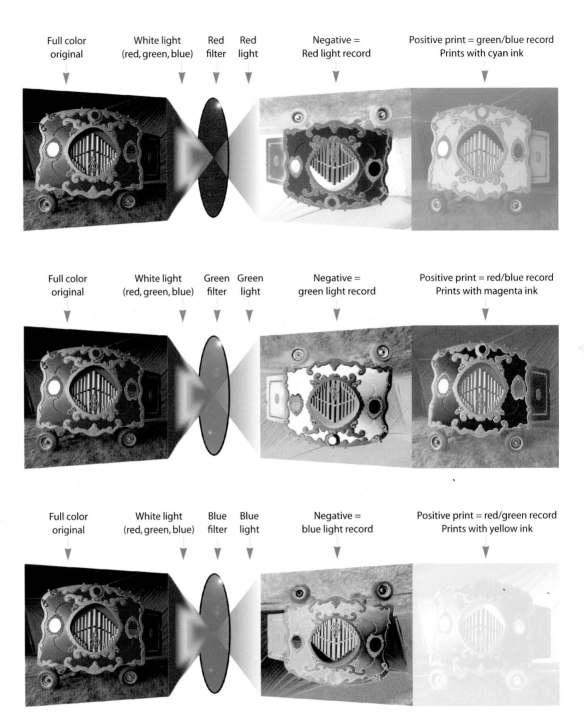

*Figure C.13*
Conventional color separations.

*Figure C.14*
Additive Color Mixing.
Any color including white
can be created by mixing
red, green, and blue light:
the additive primaries.

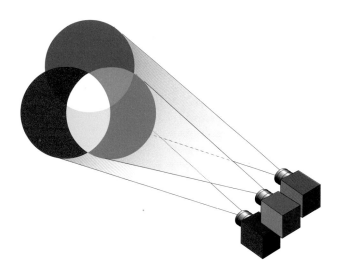

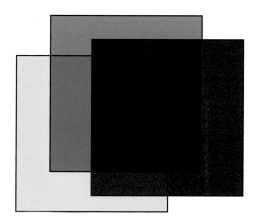

*Figure C.15*
Subtractive Color Mixing
Cyan, magenta, & yellow inks are the subtractive primaries and act like filters to subtract portions of the white light reflected from paper.

Theoretically, CMY solids superimposed should produce black (absence of light), but inefficiencies in the inks combined with the very thin ink film produce a murky brown instead. The addition of black ink (center square) produces a more convincing black.

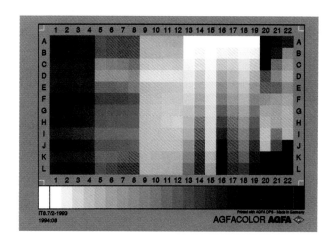

*Figure C.16*
Standard IT8 Reflection
Calibration reference chart.

Cyan

Magenta

Yellow

Black

Cyan/magenta

Cyan/magenta/yellow

# Four Color Process

*Figure C.17*
Four color process and
the individual colors.
Left: cyan/magenta, and
cyan/magenta/yellow
progressive colors.

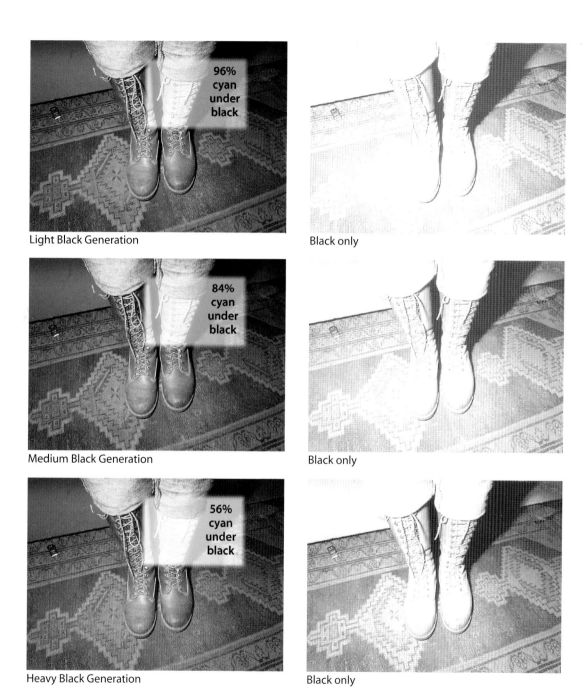

**Light Black Generation** — 96% cyan under black

**Black only**

**Medium Black Generation** — 84% cyan under black

**Black only**

**Heavy Black Generation** — 56% cyan under black

**Black only**

*Figure C.18*
GCR Separations from the same RGB image. Notice that as the amount of Black Generation increases from top to bottom, the other colors decrease to compensate (only cyan is illustrated). The end result can be a loss of richness in the dark values due to too much GCR.

**A.** Knockout (no trap): Blue knocks out of red background with no overlap making registration on press too critical.

**B.** .144 point trap: Blue spreads .144 point larger than knockout in red background.

**C.** .2 point trap: Blue spreads .2 point larger than knockout in red background.

**D.** 1 point trap: Blue spreads 1 point larger than knockout in red background.

**E.** Overprint: Blue prints solid over red background.

**F.** Quark will spread colors over a picture but won't choke (shrink) the picture under type.

**G.** Quark will not trap to blends.

*Figure C.19*

# Quark's Trapping Limitations

For more capable trapping use Adobe Illustrator (for occasional instances) and import into Quark, or have your document trapped by your service bureau with a program like Aldus TrapWise. Notice that in B., C., & D., the blue type spreads even when it's not over the red causing a bloated look—not what you want.

*Figure C.20*
Photo collagraph. This image was created by scanning an original and outputting separations which were used to screen print adhesive. The adhesive was sprinkled with carborundum and sealed with polyurethane to form the relief printing surface. The print reproduced here was scanned at 200 ppi using an Arcus II flatbed.

*Figure C.21*
Photo silkscreen. This image was created by scanning an original and manipulating it in Photoshop. Laser print separations on paper were used to expose the screens coated with photo screen emulsion.

*Figure 13.6*                                    (a)                                                     (b)

(a) Enlarged detail of Figure 13.4 unsharpened, and (b) sharpened showing halo and key line.

be more appropriate for files with resolutions of 400 ppi and higher. In any case, it is unlikely that you will ever need a Radius of less than .5 pixel or more than 2.5 pixels.

## *Unsharp Masking and Resampling*

If your file is going to require sampling up or down, here are a few guidelines to follow. While it's always best to avoid sampling up, if for some reason it's unavoidable (you've lost the original and can't rescan), apply the unsharp masking *after* you sample up. This way the Unsharp Mask filter will have more information (more pixels) to work with and you will also have the opportunity to correct for any fuzziness resulting from sampling up.

If you are planning to sample down (you scanned at 300 ppi for offset and it turns out you will be printing from your laser printer instead), apply the unsharp masking *after* you sample down. This way the the halos and keylines created by the Unsharp Mask filter can be optimized at the final resolution. If the file you are sampling down has already had the Unsharp Mask filter applied, you may find that applying it again at the lower resolution will improve the results.

### Sharpening Channels

When working with color images in either RGB or CMYK, there may be times you will get better results with unsharp masking by applying it to one or more channels individually. If you are into exploring what usually turn out to be minute differences or improvements, you might try sharpening the black channel of a CMYK file more than the other channels—or only sharpen the black channel. With certain images, very grainy or fuzzy ones, for example, the grain is more pronounced in some channels, suggesting less sharpening for those channels.

Keep in mind as you explore these options that the techniques that work with one image might not be appropriate for another, and that the color range of a particular original will have a dramatic impact on how you approach sharpening it.

### Sharpening Scans from Life

Flatbed scanners are great tools for scanning objects directly. In fact, the low-end scanners do a much better job scanning an object, such as a wrench, fabric, or wood, than they do scanning from reflection originals, such as photographs, drawings, paintings. When you are applying an unsharp mask filter to objects you've scanned, you can generally crank the Amount way up and achieve stunning results *(Figure 13.7)*. Avoid turning up either the Radius or the Threshold amount for reasons I've already explained (under "Small Radius").

### When to Apply Unsharp Masking

Typically you will apply unsharp masking as one of the final steps in your strategic progression toward the optimally corrected image. On occasion, however, you may be better off doing the sharpening a little earlier in the progression. Your reasoning will be something like this: for a grayscale image, scanned from a photograph, if your scanner produces a result that isn't too far off the mark in terms of overall brightness and contrast, sharpening before making final adjustments with curves might make those final adjustments slightly more accurate. This is because the Unsharp Mask filter will have a tendency to bump up the brighter highlight values a bit, depending on the intensity of your settings in its dialog box. Plus—if you apply the sharpening before adjusting the brightness and contrast, you will have more latitude with the Unsharp Mask settings. Here I am assuming that those final adjustments will be *increasing* the brightness and contrast.

If, on the other hand, your scanner creates a coal mine from a winter wonderland, you *must* correct the overall brightness and contrast first, since you'll have no clue as to what effects you are producing otherwise. In any case, you will have performed the Rotate & Crop, and Adjust Size & Resolution steps before applying unsharp masking.

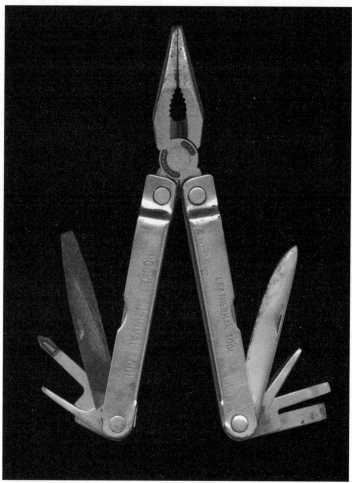

*Figure 13.7*
Most low-end scanners do a great job of scanning 3-D objects. This tool was scanned using Amount: 500, Radius: 1, Threshold: 0.

# Summary

1. Always use the Unsharp Mask filter for sharpening to take advantage of its edge detection capabilities. Do not use Sharpen or Sharpen More filters.

2. Only evaluate the results of unsharp masking at a 1:1 ratio on your monitor.

3. For files with resolutions of up to around 300 ppi, start by using an Amount of 200, Radius .5, and Threshold of 0–5 and experiment from there.

4. For files with resolutions of 350 ppi to 500 ppi, start with a Radius of from 1.5 to 2.5 pixels.

5. Threshold settings of up to 25 might be useful for images with smooth tone areas if you decide to use a high Amount setting.

6. Take a careful look at the smooth tone areas of your image and adjust the Threshold level to prevent mottling or excessive grain amplification.

7. Don't bother with applying unsharp masking to individual channels until you have considerable experience evaluating the printed results of using the filter on the composite file. The gains will be small, if any, compared with the time and effort.

8. In general, applying the Unsharp Mask filter after any resampling works best. Even if the file has already been sharpened before resampling, it can improve the image quality by applying it again after resampling.

9. You can usually use very high Amounts on scans from objects—up to 500% in some cases—with good results.

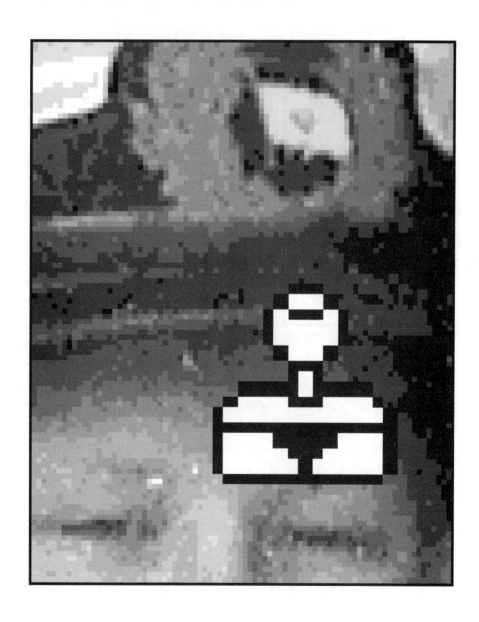

*Figure 14.1*     Kid as merchant marine.

# Cleaning Up

Your grayscale or color file is getting close to the point where you will be exporting it to a page layout program, QuarkXPress or PageMaker, if it's part of a book or brochure, or outputting it from your image editing application directly if it is a stand-alone image. If it's an element of a cover or poster, it might be headed for Adobe Illustrator where it might be combined with type and other graphic elements.

## Spots Worse?

You may have noticed that the dust, scratches, or other defects were amplified by the unsharp masking you applied, which is typically the case and an unavoidable by-product of the sharpening step. This may be especially true of an old photograph with a lot of surface abrasion from having been bumped around for years, or a contemporary print from an older negative *(Figure 14.1)*. Whether the defects were part of the original image or acquired along the way (dust or dirt on the scanner bed glass, or artifacts from the scanner itself) is irrelevant at this point—they need to be cleaned up.

## The Basic Theory

In Photoshop, the primary tool you will use for cleaning up, or spotting, is the Rubber Stamp tool. When you use the Rubber Stamp tool for spotting, you are removing a flaw by copying an immediately adjacent area with similar color and tonal characteristics and pasting it on top of the flaw. This is a very different approach from the much less effective method of painting out a spot with a flat opaque gray or color.

When you paint out a scratch or dust spot *(Figure 14.2a)* with a flat color you are not getting the benefit of using the detail or texture of the area you are spotting. If you are clumsy (perish the thought), your spotting will show up like a sore thumb *(Figure 14.2b)*.

When you use the Rubber Stamp tool to spot, you are using a similar texture, color, and grain or pixel structure to hide the flaw. Now you can be *very* clumsy before it will show *(Figure 14.2c)*. In fact, there is never a reason to

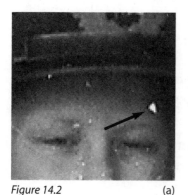 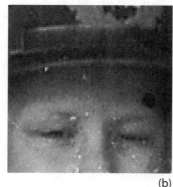 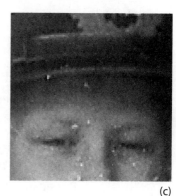

*Figure 14.2*                    (a)                                (b)                                (c)
(a) Before spotting, (b) spotted with brush tool, and (c) spotted with Rubber Stamp.

simply take a pencil or paintbrush and paint out a flaw other than not knowing about the Rubber Stamp tool or how it works.

### Getting Set

Begin by double-clicking on the icon in the toolbox *(Figure 14.3)* to show the Rubber Stamp Options Palette *(Figure 14.4)*.

Check to make sure that your Rubber Stamp Options Palette is set for:

1. **Normal mode in the pop-up.**

2. **Clone (aligned) in the Option pop-up.**

3. **100% Opacity.**

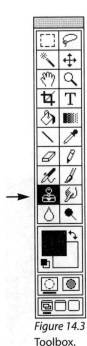

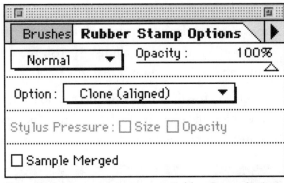

Figure 14.4                    Rubber Stamp Options.

*Figure 14.3*
Toolbox.

Next, go back and read about how to use the *Three-Finger Rule* in Chapter One: *Photoshop Essentials.* To become skillful at spotting with your computer, you *must* learn to use two hands!

Check to make sure that your Tool Cursors are set to display Brush Size and Precise in the General Preferences. Choose **File> Preferences> General...** *(Figure 14.5)*.

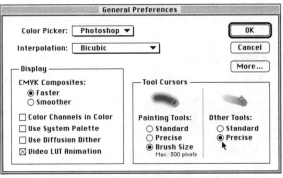

Figure 14.5                    General Preferences.

Have your Brushes Palette available. Notice that in Figure 14.4 the Brushes Palette is included in the Rubber Stamp Options Palette by default. One click on the Brushes Tab will bring the Brushes Palette to the front.

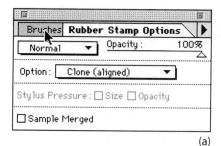

(a)

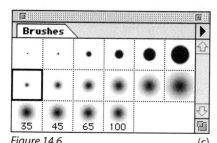

(b)

Figure 14.6                                                      (c)

(a) Drag the Brushes tab and (b) drop outside of the palette; (c) a separate Brushes Palette results.

Be aware of the option of separating and reorganizing the palettes any way that suits you. By dragging the Brushes tab out of the palette with the Rubber Stamp Options, you will give it its own new palette window *(Figure 14.6)*. To recombine palettes, drag a palette by its tab over the palette you want it to join and drop.

All of the palettes are also collapsible and resizable. When you double-click on the tab area or click once on the Zoom box (upper right hand corner of the palette window), the palette will collapse. By dragging on the Size box (lower right-hand corner of the palette window), you can resize the palette. These techniques work with all of the palettes in Photoshop.

# Using the Rubber Stamp

Using the Rubber Stamp tool is a simple two-step process. You can think of this tool as a *cloning* tool— that is, a tool that duplicates one area of your image in another area. (The Rubber Stamp tool will also clone between images or open windows, but you won't be using that feature for spotting.)

1. **Define the area you will be cloning from by Option-clicking with the Rubber Stamp tool.**

   **When you are using the Precise cursors *(Figure 14.5)*, the icon looks like ◯ (indicating your brush size). It looks like ⊕ when you Option-click to define the clone source.**

2. **Click to clone. The first time you click after defining the area to be cloned, you will also establish a fixed relationship between the two areas—that's what Clone (aligned) in the Options Palette means. Clone Non-Aligned means that the clone source point always reverts to its original position after each mouse click as you clone. It will take a little experi-**

156     Chapter Fourteen

mentation with these two options to get the idea. You will rarely be using Clone Non-Aligned for retouching, so don't worry about it if the difference between the two options isn't crystal clear.

## The Keys to Success

The keys to successful spotting with the Rubber Stamp tool are:

1. Don't squint! Zoom in to 2:1 or more. *Never* work at less than 1:1.

2. Use the appropriate brush size.

3. Define a clone source immediately adjacent to the flaw.

4. Perform frequent redefinition of the clone source.

5. Use single clicks or small strokes to retouch the flaw.

6. Be ready to Undo (⌘ Z), scroll (spacebar), and zoom in and out (⌘ spacebar, and ⌥ spacebar). In other words, employ the *Three-Finger Technique* using both hands.

## Appropriate Brush Size

When retouching, have your Brushes Palette handy. You will most likely be using one of the smaller brushes. Start with the second or third brush in the top row of the Brushes Palette. The top row has the hard-edge brushes and the lower rows have the softer edge brushes.

Note that you can define your own brush diameter, shape, and hardness by double-clicking on one of the blank spaces following the default brush sizes in the Brushes Palette. You can also modify any existing brush by double-clicking on it which will display the Brush Options dialog box *(Figure 14.7)*. Using the bracket keys [ ] will move you forward and backward in the Brushes Palette.

## Retouching Example

Here is the two-step process illustrated (zoom in on the area to a ratio of about 4:1):

1. Option-click on an area immediately adjacent to the flaw *(Figure 14.8a)*. This defines the clone source.

2. **Move your cursor to the flaw (the curved dark line just to the right in this case), then click and drag in the direction of the arrow to remove the flaw *(Figure 14.8b)*.**

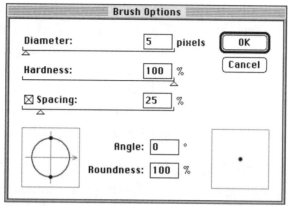

*Figure 14.7*                                    Brush Options.

In the case of single spots you would just click once on a spot, then move on to the next spot and click again, and so on. The relationship between the clone source and your brush remains fixed until you redefine the clone source by Option-clicking again.

Once you do a little spotting, you'll get the idea of how the process works very quickly. You'll understand that you are essentially copying from one point

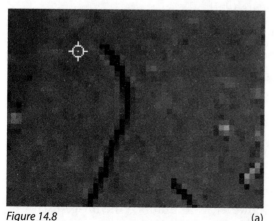

*Figure 14.8*                            (a)                                                        (b)

(a) Option-click to define source, then (b) click and drag to remove flaw.

to another on the fly, as you click or drag the cursor. To be an expert electronic retoucher you need to become proficient at choosing the optimum clone source for the particular spot at hand.

Notice that in Figure 14.8a and b the flaw is a squiggly dark dust particle. It could just as easily be a light scratch; the same technique would work. Once you have defined an appropriate clone source, you can follow along the flaw with your cursor, continually cloning from an appropriate area, since the clone source follows in a fixed relationship. This means that in tricky areas with subtle graduations—flesh tones or chrome, for example—you can easily remove the most horrendous looking scratches or dust marks perfectly.

## Dust & Scratches Filter

Wow! Why not just hit it with a filter and save myself all the time and trouble? You guessed it—there is no free lunch. While the Dust & Scratches filter will indeed live up to its name, it will do so by blurring your image, and as a consequence, blow off your carefully applied unsharp masking. If you're *very* clever, though, you might be able to use this filter to your advantage. That is, there is probably a point at which the Dust & Scratches filter will obscure some minor flaws while not completely neutralizing the effect of the Unsharp Mask filter. Then again you need to ask yourself—could I have applied the Unsharp Mask filter with a little more finesse and arrived at the same place? Anyway, it's such a cool-sounding filter, so full of promise, that it's worth a little elaboration. To activate the filter choose **Filter> Noise> Dust & Scratches...** (*Figure 14.9*).

The Radius is adjustable between 1 and 16 pixels. As with the Unsharp Mask filter, be careful about using too large a Radius, which will create gross effects. Somewhere between 1 and 3 pixels is probably the maximum useful range.

Threshold has a range of 0 to 255. This slider determines how different the pixels need to be before the filter will alter them. The higher the Threshold Level, the less effect the filter has.

You can adjust the zoom ratio of the preview window to get a better view of a sample area. More useful, however, is to examine the image itself. Remember that you can zoom in and out using the *Three-Finger Technique*

(Chapter One), even with a dialog box open.

Figure 14.10 illustrates how effective this filter can be. When applied skillfully, it can save you lots of time retouching.

To maximize the usefulness of this filter, get in the habit of selecting an area with little or no detail and *then* applying it. This technique will offer you more control in large flat areas such as skies, and you won't have to worry about blurring the areas of your image containing important detail *(Figure 14.10)*.

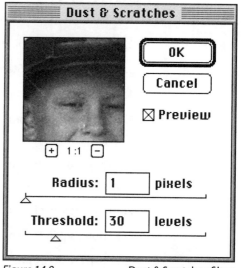

*Figure 14.9*     Dust & Scratches filter.

*Figure 14.10*                                    (a)                                                                        (b)

(a) Before Dust & Scratches filter; (b) Dust & Scratches applied using Radius 1/Threshold 30. Notice that all but the larger spots have been diminished or eliminated.

# Summary

1. Expect the spots to look a little worse after unsharp masking.

2. Always use the Rubber Stamp tool instead of trying to paint out flaws.

3. Check the Rubber Stamp Options and Tool Cursors settings.

4. Have the Brushes Palette showing.

5. Retouching takes both hands: review the Three-Finger Technique in Chapter One.

6. Using the Rubber Stamp tool is a two-step process: define clone source (Option-click) and clone.

7. Keys to retouching success:

   • Don't squint! Zoom in to 2:1 or more. *Never* work at less than 1:1.

   • Use the appropriate brush size.

   • Define a clone source immediately adjacent to the flaw.

   • Perform frequent redefinition of the clone source.

   • Use single clicks or small strokes to retouch the flaw.

   • Be ready to Undo (⌘Z), scroll (spacebar), and zoom in and out (⌘ spacebar, and ⌥ spacebar). In other words, employ the *Three-Finger Technique* using both hands.

8. Experiment with the Dust & Scratches filter but don't count on it, and know that it is counteracting the results of your unsharp masking.

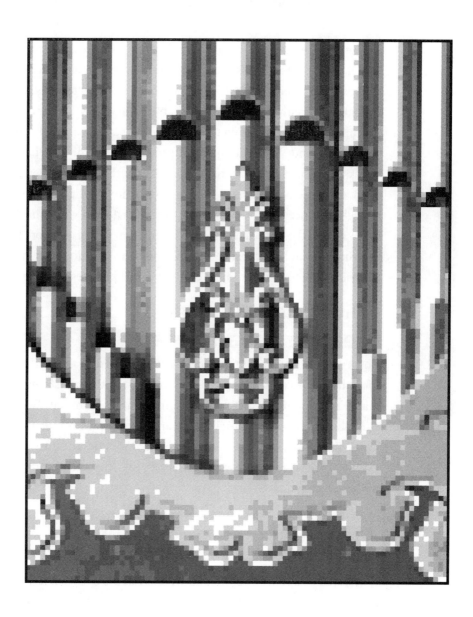

# CREATIVE ENHANCEMENTS 15

Enhancing your image by making changes that suit your artistic purpose is one of the most exciting aspects of using a powerful imaging application like Photoshop. You have a whole collection of tools and filters at your disposal. Actually, so many options are available that you will probably have to restrain yourself from using too many on the same image. The integrity of your work tends to erode in direct proportion to the number of digital "tricks" you employ for no reason other than that they're there. Certainly this syndrome is an instant giveaway of a novice digital artist. At first, though, you need to try everything to see what does what. Just be sure to throw it all in the trash and empty it. Then, when you've got more Photoshop time under your belt, consider carefully how the techniques you're using are contributing to the meaning and intent of the pictures you're making.

## Color Correction vs. Creative Enhancement

The term "color correction" means making broad overall changes to correct for undesirable color casts. The term implies that the adjustments are being made in an effort to match the original image more faithfully. Creative enhancements, on the other hand, are decisions you make to alter the image that have nothing to do with the reproduction of the original, such as altering the color of a person's shirt, or replacing a cluttered urban scene with a wheat field.

If you're using the tools for local creative enhancements described in this chapter to correct for problems left over from the scanning or *color correction* stages, a few cautions are in order.

If one area of a color or black and white image is out of kilter, the chances are *very* strong that there are other problems as well, and that the area you noticed is just the tip of the iceberg. In fact, it is a certainty that there are other problems, because if your scanning and color corrections were appropriate, the entire image would be accurate, not just parts of it. Of course there are exceptions, one being that you started with a less than wonderful or damaged original. My point is that local color or gray value adjustments should not be part of your arsenal of standard techniques for *color correction.* If you are constantly modifying the colors or grays of your image, there is something wrong with your color correction technique or calibration setup that you should look into.

Keep the difference between *color correction* and *creative enhancement* in mind as you work with this chapter, *and* keep in mind that unless the picture is your own creation from scratch or in the public domain, you'll need approval from the artist before you tamper with it.

# The Tools

In Photoshop, *selection* is the primary mechanism for making local adjustments to your image. When you need to change one area, color, or gray value of your image while leaving the other areas unaltered, you must first *select* the area to be changed. A selected area is displayed with a marquee of dancing (or marching, depending on your frame of mind) ants.

There are seven tools devoted to making selections in Photoshop:

1. **Rectangular Marquee**
2. **Elliptical Marquee**
3. **Lasso**
4. **Magic Wand**
5. **Paint Bucket**
6. **Quick Mask**
7. **Paths**

Once you have made a selection with one of these tools, you can employ any of the controls available under the **Image** menu for making alterations to the selected area, as well as load, save, or modify the size and edges of the selected area using the **Select** menu.

Exactly how to use all of the selection tools available in Photoshop is beyond the scope of this chapter, but it's important to realize that much of the program's methodology is based on the idea of selection. Selecting, by the way, is common to all image and word processing programs. In any program, to change an area or word, it must be highlighted or *selected* before you can alter it.

In addition to the seven selection tools, there are five additional tools available to help you modify specific areas or colors in your image which I'll describe in turn:

1. **Toning tools**

2. **Focus tools (Blur/Sharpen)**

3. **Smudge tool**

4. **Replace Color**

5. **Take Snapshot**

Note that the Paint tools, which include the Toning, Sharpen, Blur, and Smudge tools, cannot be used in the bitmapped or indexed color modes.

To quickly switch between tools with multiple options such as the Toning tools with Burn, Dodge, and Sponge, and the Focus tools with Blur and Sharpen, Option-click on its tool icon in the tool box.

Also, to change pressure, opacity, or exposure % for these tools, simply press the number keys: 1 = 10%, 4 = 40%, and so on.

## Tool Vectors

When using any of the paint tools to paint, sharpen, blur, rubber stamp, erase, or smudge in a straight line, you can employ the tool vector technique to move between the beginning and end points automatically. Click once at the start of a straight line, move the cursor to the end point of the line, press and hold the Shift key, and click again once. The tool will move between clicks.

## Toning Tools

Talk about cool—burning and dodging without having to go into that nasty darkroom! Like all the paint tools, this tool works in conjunction with the Brushes Palette to control the size of the area you are affecting. The Toning Tools Options Palette (double-click on the Toning Tool icon in the toolbox) is used to control the intensity of the effect, as well as options for shadows, midtones, or highlights for the Dodge and Burn tools, and saturation for the Sponge tool *(Figure 15.1)*. The palette also gives you the option of Wet Edges when using the Sponge tool. You can burn in, dodge, saturate, and desaturate localized areas. Don't get too carried away with it, since it defi-

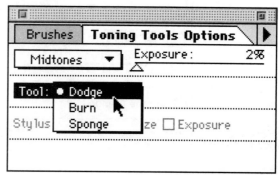

*Figure 15.1*　　　　　　　　Toning Tools Options Palette.

nitely has its limitations, and anything other than very subtle alterations will show. Too much dodging or lightening of shadow areas will tend to flatten them, and excessive dodging or burning on color images will tend to cause undesirable color shifts. There are more effective methods of enhancing the contrast and visibility of deep shadow areas in both grayscale and color images which are described in the following pages. For very subtle modifications, however, the Toning tools will do a decent job quickly and easily.

Start by setting the exposure at 5% or less and gradually, with successive strokes, alter the area you want to burn, dodge, saturate, or desaturate, little by little.

## *Blur/Sharpen Tools*

Like the Toning tools, the Focus tools are very useful for minor and quick alterations, but have distinct limitations in how much of a change you can effectively apply. With this tool set, it's the Blur tool that you will get the most use out of. You can use the Blur tool to soften the edges of selections you have pasted into a image, or local areas of an image to de-emphasize them. Frequently, when you paste one image or part of an image into another, the edges will be too hard to look believable (if that's what you're after), and you will want to soften or blur them a bit with the Blur tool.

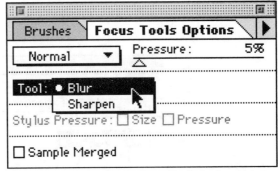

*Figure 15.2*                    Focus Tools Options Palette.

## *Blur*

Using the Blur tool is simple and straightforward:

1. **Begin by double-clicking on the Blur or Sharpen tool in the toolbox, which brings up the Focus Tools Options Palette *(Figure 15.2)*.**

2. **Select Blur from the pop-up Tool menu.**

*Figure 15.3*                    Effect of using the Blur tool.

3. As with any of the paint tools, have the Brushes Palette tab in the same palette so you can easily access the correct brush size (see "Getting Set" in Chapter Fourteen: *Retouching Defects*); and set your cursors to Brush Size and Precise in the General Preferences (choose **File> Preferences> General...**).

4. Have your left hand on the keyboard so that you can instantly Undo (⌘ Z), zoom in and out, or scroll using the *Three-Finger Technique* (Chapter One: *Photoshop Essentials*). Zoom in enough to easily see the area you are adjusting without straining.

5. Stroke the area you want to blur using short strokes and decide whether or not your pressure % is set correctly. Set the pressure using the slider in the Focus Tools Options Palette *(Figure 15.2)*, or simply press the number key corresponding to the % you want (x10). The higher the % you set, the more pronounced the effect.

6. It's better to work on an area little by little at first until you have a feel for the optimum amount of blur you are applying. See Figure 15.3 for the effect of the Blur tool.

7. Remember to view the results only at a 1:1 ratio or higher.

## *Sharpen*

1. Begin by double-clicking on the Blur or Sharpen tool in the toolbox, which brings up the Focus Tools Options Palette *(Figure 15.2)*.

2. Select Sharpen from the pop-up Tool menu.

3. Zoom way in to 4:1 or 8:1 so you can easily see what you are doing.

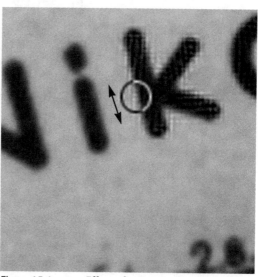

*Figure 15.4*     Effect of using the Sharpening tool.

**4. Set the the Pressure to about 40% in the Focus Tools Options Palette and stroke the area you want to sharpen** *(Figure 15.4)*.

A few words of caution about the Sharpen tool: if you've used the Unsharp Mask filter at all, you'll notice that the Sharpen tool is far less "intelligent" about locating and enhancing the edges of your detail. The limitation of the Sharpen tool is that it works very much like the Sharpen or Sharpen More filters, which lack an edge sensitivity. For this reason you'll want to use the Sharpen tool sparingly—for only a few touch-ups here and there in minor areas of your image—or better yet not at all.

When you need to sharpen a small area, use the Take Snapshot command described later in this chapter.

## Smudge Tool

This is definitely one of the coolest tools. The Smudge tool has an effect very much like pushing or pulling your finger through charcoal or wet paint. It works exactly like the other paint tools in that you can adjust the size of the

*Figure 15.5*     *Nikon Burning*: Smudge tool effect.

area you are smudging with the Brushes Palette, and the intensity of the effect with its Options Palette.

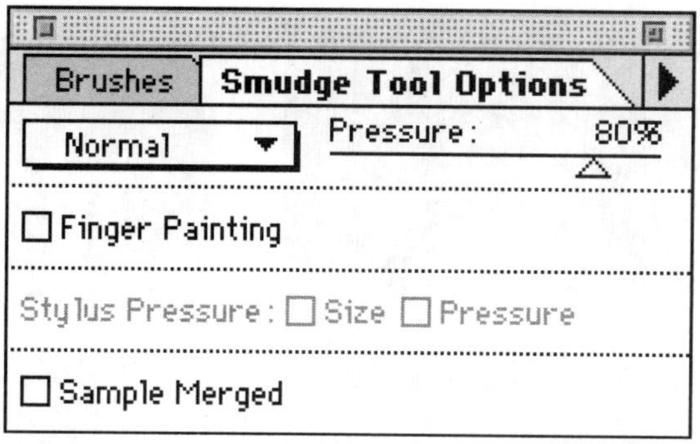

*Figure 15.6*  Smudge Tool Options Palette.

Like the Blur tool, the Smudge tool can be used very effectively for softening pasted edges as well as for more aggressive effects *(Figure 15.5)*.

The Finger Painting option allows you to continually smear through your image, while the Sample Merged option allows you to smudge between layers *(Figure 15.6)*. Trying these options once or twice is the quickest and easiest way to see how they work.

## Replace Color

The Replace Color command is a powerful tool that works very effectively to accomplish just what its name implies, and works in any of the color modes.

1. Choose **Image> Adjust> Replace Color...** to access the Replace Color dialog box *(Figure 15.7)*.

2. Begin by clicking once in the image on the color you want to replace.

3. Once you click and select a color, the Selection Preview in the Replace Color Dialog box defines the area selected with white, the black areas of the selection preview remain masked, and will be unaffected by any changes.

5. The Fuzziness slider controls the tolerance or range of colors included in

*Figure 15.7*  Replace Color.

*Figure 15.8*                                    (a)                                                    (b)
Using Replace Color: (a) Unaltered image; (b) results of settings in Figure 15.7.

the mask. Moving the slider to the right includes a wider range of colors, and moving the slider to the left narrows the color range.

6. Adjust the Hue, Saturation, and Lightness sliders to alter the color you selected, which appears in the Sample window in the lower right of the dialog box.

7. You can use the plus and minus eyedroppers to increase or narrow the color range of your mask by clicking in the image.

Although this control may seem complicated at first, and it is very sophisticated, as long as you have the Preview box checked, you see the results of your adjustments immediately and can decide whether or not you like the changes.

The beauty of the Replace Color control is that you can easily replace a specific color in one step instead of first selecting the color, and then using the Hue/Saturation control to alter the selected area. The down side is that you don't have the selection control that you have when using the other selection tools collectively to precisely select an area, and then apply Hue/Saturation, so the usefulness of Replace Color is limited. Figure 15.8 illustrates how the control can be used to isolate a particular color and replace it. In this illustration I have only used the Lightness slider for clarity in black and white.

## Take Snapshot

The Take Snapshot command is one of the most versatile methods of adjusting your image in local areas. It works by saving a "snapshot," or copy, to an invisible buffer in the same way that using the **Copy** command works, except that you can apply the snapshot image with the Rubber Stamp tool. With this command you can apply unsharp masking, make local color adjustments, enhance shadow or highlight detail, and apply any filter in a gradual and subtle manner to specific areas of your image.

## Local Unsharp Masking

In the following example using a 300 ppi grayscale file, I am satisfied with the overall sharpening but I want to enhance the sharpening on the word *Nikon* on the camera. To apply unsharp masking to a local area in a more elegant and controlled fashion than the Sharpen tool allows, follow these steps:

1. With your image open in Photoshop, choose **Filter> Sharpen> Unsharp Mask...** and apply an unsharp mask that correctly enhances the local area you are planning to adjust.

   Note that this image has already had one application of the Unsharp Mask filter, so the unsharp mask setting you're applying now will be more intense than the overall image can tolerate; but since you're only concerned with the local area, you can use an exaggerated setting *(Figure 15.9)*.

   Using the rectangular marquee tool, very roughly select the area you're

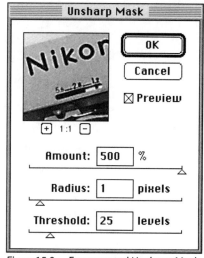

*Figure15.9*   Exaggerated Unsharp Mask.

*Figure 15.10*                    (a)                                              (b)

(a) Normal sharpening, and (b) the same image with exaggerated unsharp masking settings of Figure 15.9 applied overall. These settings are too much sharpening for the image as a whole—that's why this exaggerated unsharp masking is "undone" (after saving it as a snapshot) and used for local enhancement only with the Rubber Stamp tool.

planning to sharpen locally before applying the exaggerated unsharp mask. This way, you will only be applying the filter to a part of the image, and it will work much more quickly.

2. Choose **Edit> Take Snapshot**. This command saves the sharpened image in an invisible buffer in Photoshop *(Figure 15.10b)*.

3. Choose **Edit> Undo Unsharp Mask**, or type ⌘ Z. Now your image is back to where it started *(Figure 15.10a)*.

4. Double-click on the Rubber Stamp tool and set the option pop-up to From Snapshot. Set the Opacity to about 50% to start *(Figure 15.11)*.

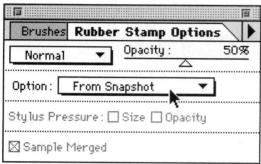

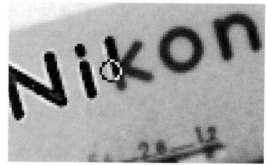

*Figure 15.11*     Set Options to From Snapshot.

*Figure 15.12*     Stroke areas you want to sharpen.

5. Zoom in on the area you are altering and stroke the detail where you want to apply additional unsharp masking *(Figure 15.12)*. Remember that you can use the Undo command and change the Opacity setting to whatever works best.

6. Zoom out to 1:1 and view the results of your work *(Figure 15.13)*.

*Figure 15.13*     (a)     (b)

(a) Normal sharpening and (b) local unsharp masking applied to "Nikon." Notice the enhanced sharpness of the Nikon label on the camera compared to the (a) image.

## Enhancing Shadow Detail

The Take Snapshot command can work wonders to enhance the shadow detail and contrast of grayscale images where detail is difficult to maintain. Shadow detail and separation is compromised by low-end scanners, which often have too limited a dynamic range or gamma to "see" into a deep shadow. This may be aggravated by a dark original and dot gain on press, making the retention of shadow detail one of the most challenging aspects of single-color offset printing.

1. With your grayscale (or color) file open in Photoshop, choose **Image> Adjust> Levels**.

2. Adjust the center (midtone) slider to the left, and the left (shadow) slider to the right *(Figure 15.14)*. These adjustments in Levels can vary considerably,

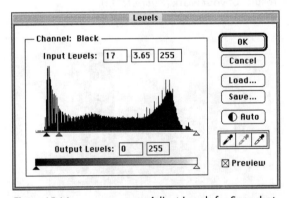

Figure 15.14          Adjust Levels for Snapshot.

Figure 15.15          Open shadows.

depending on the image at hand. The idea is to bring out all of the shadow detail and increase the darkest value a little to about 100% *(Figure 15.15)*.

3. Choose **Edit> Take Snapshot**.

4. Choose **Edit> Undo Levels** or type ⌘ Z.

5. Double-click on the Rubber Stamp tool and set the option in its Options Palette to From Snapshot.

6. Adjust the Opacity to about 20% and use a large brush to clone in the snapshot image (the one with exaggerated unsharp masking) over the original

version. Try both the Normal and the Overlay mode to see which one will work best for you.

7. In the adjusted example, the contrast in the camera lens and black parts of the body were enhanced to reveal more shadow separation and detail *(Figure 15.16)*. Compare this illustration to Figure 15.12a, before the adjustments were made.

*Figure 15.16*     Image with enhanced shadows.

Could the same effect have been achieved using the Curves command in Photoshop? Certainly—or at least something very close. But remember that had this adjustment been made using curves, everything in the file would have been correspondingly adjusted, and what if I'm happy with the stone guys at the bottom? Of course there are ways to work around that too. The bottom line is that the Take Snapshot command is very useful and quick once you have some experience.

# Summary

1. Get the artist's permission before using or altering originals that don't belong to you.

2. Use the tools in this chapter for creative enhancement rather than color correction. If you're constantly standing on your head adjusting local areas of an image in order to get it to reproduce accurately, you've got other problems.

3. Amplifying the separation and detail in the deep shadows of grayscale files is an exception to this rule, since local adjustments may be the most expedient and practical solution to combating the limitations of low-end scanners.

4. Become skillful in the techniques of creating selections, since much of the quality of your work as a digital artist depends on how well you create and manipulate selections. Pay special attention to the edges of your selections, and get to know the commands under the Select menu such as Feather.

5. Don't overdo the intensity of the Toning tools, since the effects tend to look artificial very quickly.

6. The same applies to the Focus tools, the most useful function of which may be softening the edges of selections with the Blur tool. Use the Sharpen tool very sparingly, since the effect is crude compared with that of Unsharp Mask.

7. The Smudge tool is one of the coolest—go nuts.

8. The Replace Color command can be useful in cases of distinctly segregated colors, but don't be surprised if you use it rarely. Using the other selection tools such as the Magic Wand, Quick Mask, and Paths in conjunction with Hue/Saturation will provide more control. Don't waste time or compromise results by trying to make this tool do more than it can.

9. You can do wonders with the Take Snapshot command in conjunction with the Rubber Stamp. Although important, sharpening and shadow detail are just two of many ways you can apply this command.

# SAVING YOUR FILE

# SAVING YOUR FILE 16

## File Formats

Every time you save an image file on any computer—Mac, IBM, or work-station—your file is saved in a particular file format. In essence, a file format is simply a method of arranging the information in your bitmapped or object-oriented file. A file's format will specify how it can be used once saved. There are proprietary file formats and standard file formats. Figure 16.1 illustrates a few of the more common file formats, those which Photoshop will save in and read.

### Proprietary Formats

A proprietary format is optimized for the application program that created it, such as Photoshop, Painter, QuarkXPress, PhotoStyler, Picture Publisher, Corel Draw, Freehand, or Illustrator. A proprietary format is designed to efficiently store all of the information its application needs to reopen the file and allow you to work with the data again, such as the layers in Photoshop.

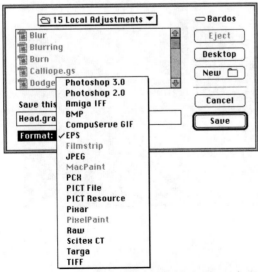

The limitation of proprietary formats is that usually only the application that created the file can read it. There are a few rare exceptions to this; for example, Painter can both save files in Photoshop format and open Photoshop files, and Illustrator 1.1 is a widely used object-oriented format that can be edited by a host of programs including Photoshop.

### Standard Formats

Industry standard file formats such as EPS (Encapsulated Postscript), TIFF

*Figure 16.1*    File formats available in Photoshop.

178

(Tagged Image File Format), and PICT can be opened by most graphic and page layout applications.

### Why Are There So Many Formats?

This is like asking why there are so many different kinds of automobiles—everybody who comes along thinks he or she has a better idea. Another reason for the number of file formats is that some were conceived of years ago and hang around like space debris. The PICT format, for example, isn't very reliable, but since there are so many PICT files floating around, new applications are designed to read and write PICT out of necessity. PICT is still the primary format for non-PostScript printers and interactive media.

# Which Format to Use and When

Happily, navigating the file format situation is fairly simple. In addition to the proprietary formats, there are only two industry standard file formats to seriously consider using for desktop publishing and printing artwork: EPS and TIFF. I'll give you some clear recommendations on how to make sound choices and point out the pros and cons of each format.

### Save In or Change to Proprietary

*Make a point of saving fresh scans in Photoshop's proprietary file format.* If your scanner has a Photoshop plug-in which opens the new scan directly in Photoshop, check the file format pop-up menu in the **Save...** dialog box the first time you save it and make sure the file is saved in the Photoshop format. If your scanner has its own application program which saves scans in a special proprietary format, the first time you open and save the file in Photoshop, make sure you choose **File> Save As...**, and save the file in Photoshop 3.0 format.

If someone gives you a file or you had a scan made by a service provider, the first time you open and save the file in Photoshop, make sure you choose **File> Save As...**, and save the file in Photoshop's format. This will probably mean changing the file format from TIFF or PICT to Photoshop 3.0 format.

## *Stay with Proprietary as Long as Possible*

*Work in the proprietary format until it is necessary to change it.* As you begin a project which may be headed for print, you'll be working in Photoshop (or another graphics program) as you move through the progression from the original scan to the corrected and sharpened finished file. The work you perform on a file may take a few minutes or a few days depending on the complexity of the image and its willingness to cooperate with you. In any case, until it's a wrap—finished and ready to be placed in a page layout program—leave it in its proprietary file format. In the case of Photoshop, using Photoshop's format is mandatory if you need to be able to save and reopen files with layers.

You want to stay with the proprietary format as long as possible because:

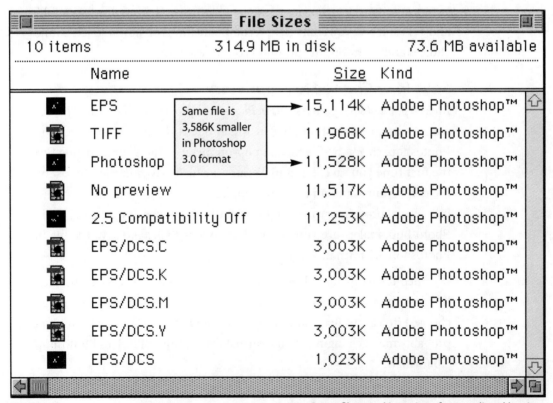

*Figure 16.2*                                      Same file saved in various formats, listed by size.

1. It's the only way to save your layers. You can save additional channels in TIFF, but not layers.

2. It's the most efficient format. The file sizes are considerably smaller than EPS or TIFF, and you'll save and open faster. Notice that the *same* file saved in EPS is more than 3.5 Mb larger than when saved in Photoshop's proprietary format *(Figure 16.2)*.

3. Photoshop compresses your files automatically when you save using a very efficient lossless compression scheme.

If your file is *not* going to be placed in a page layout program, leave it in Photoshop's format. For example, if an image is going to be output as an individual image to a desktop printer, whether color or black and white, you can print directly from Photoshop.

If you're planning to send it out to a service bureau for printing as an Iris Ink Jet, dye sublimation, or Canon Color Copier print, you'll save disk space by flattening the image if you have layers and deleting any extra channels (if you saved a selection, you created an additional channel for it).

## Save Two Versions

*Save two versions of the file.* Even after you have finished working on an image and are ready to save it in either EPS or TIFF for export to a page layout program, be sure to save the original Photoshop format file as well. Saving the file in two different file formats will dramatically increase the disk space requirements, but if you need to go back and edit the original Photoshop format file with its layers intact, you'll be thankful to have it. Saving in any format other than Photoshop 3.0 will force you to flatten the image and discard the layers.

## Saving Time and Disk Space

If you never plan to go back to version 2.5 (and why should you?), turn off the Photoshop 2.5 compatibility feature in the General Preferences. Choose **File> Preferences> General...**, then click the **More...** button. While you're there, check *Never* for Image Previews if you can live without them. You'll save considerable time when saving large files by not saving Previews.

# EPS or TIFF?

## *EPS Pros*

The EPS (Encapsulated PostScript) format is the clear first choice when saving your files for placing in any page layout program for the following reasons:

1. Reliability. What you put in is usually what you get out. It may seem strange that computers could fail in the reliability department, but only if you haven't worked with them long enough. Some other file formats, even TIFF, can produce unexpected results at the most inappropriate times, and the errors will cost you money.

2. It is the only format in which you can save screening information and transfer functions for placement in a page layout program.

3. It is the only format in which you can save duotones, tritones, or quadtones for placement in a page layout program (see Chapter Nineteen: *Duotones*).

4. It is the only format in which you can save clipping paths for placement in a page layout program.

5. It is the only format in which you can save DCS files for placement in a page layout program.

The phrase "...for placement in a page layout program" is tagged on to most of the foregoing list because Photoshop's proprietary format will do nearly everything you need, but it *cannot* be exported to a page layout program.

## *EPS Cons*

Here are two important limitations of the EPS file format:

1. You cannot edit the file in any way once it is placed in a page layout program. In QuarkXPress the contents of the **Style** menu heading are grayed out except for **Flip Horizontal** and **Flip Vertical**. (You can, however, change the file's scaling, rotation, and cropping.)

2. The preview is Quark's 36 ppi default, which looks a bit scrappy but that's all you get.

Neither of these cons presents much of a drawback when you are dealing with carefully prepared bitmapped image files, since you wouldn't be doing any color or tonal correction in Quark anyway—you've already taken great pains to make the corrections in Photoshop.

Also, since you are fast becoming a seasoned professional, you understand that the low resolution preview in Quark (or Pagemaker) bears no relationship to the way your EPS file will print unless you break the linkage to the high resolution EPS file (see Chapter Twenty: *Page Placement*).

### Saving in EPS

When saving your EPS file, by sure to set the Encoding to Binary, and the Preview to Macintosh (8 bits/pixel). If you don't need a color preview in your page layout program, you can save your EPS file with the 1 bit/pixel option, which will make the file smaller and your page layout document refresh the screen faster. Make sure you do *not* check the options for including Halftone Screen and Transfer Function unless you know what they mean and intend to override the printer's default settings *(Figure 16.3)*.

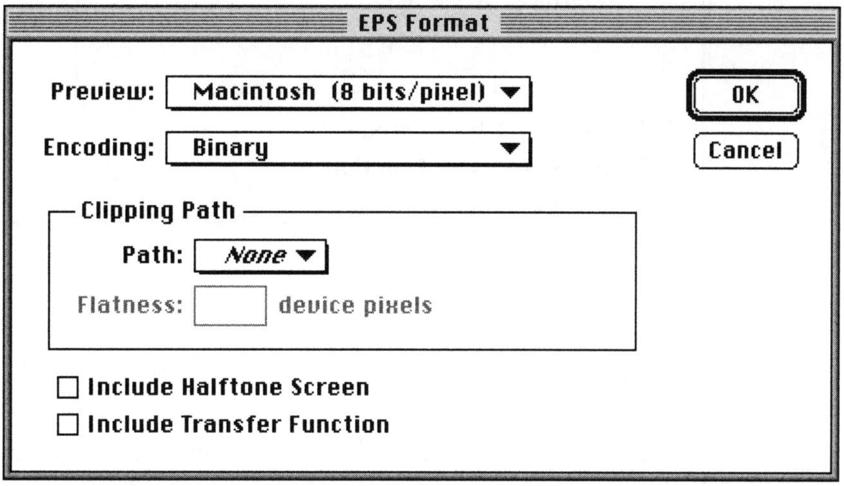

```
╔═══════════════════ EPS Format ═══════════════════╗

   Preview: [ Macintosh (8 bits/pixel) ▼ ]      ( OK )

   Encoding: [ Binary                  ▼ ]      ( Cancel )

   ┌─ Clipping Path ──────────────────────┐
   │   Path: [ None ▼ ]                    │
   │   Flatness: [    ]  device pixels     │
   └───────────────────────────────────────┘

   ☐ Include Halftone Screen
   ☐ Include Transfer Function
```

*Figure 16.3*                                                   Saving in EPS.

## EPS/DCS

The DCS (Desktop Color Separation) flavor of EPS was invented by Quark, Inc. This format saves five files as a group: a composite file, and four image files which contain the cyan, magenta, yellow, and black separations. You have the option to eliminate the composite file, or choose whether it is color or grayscale. Figure 16.2 shows a set of DCS files as the bottom five files listed. To save a file as a DCS set, choose **File> Save As...**, and use EPS for the format. A second dialog box will appear giving you the DCS option *(Figure 16.4)*.

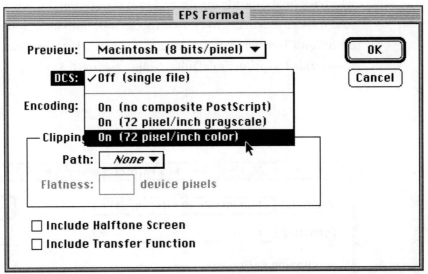

*Figure 16.4*                                                                 DCS options.

## What Good Is DCS?

There are some output devices driven by applications that require the DCS format and it may expedite the "rip time" (the time it takes an output device to prepare the file for printing) in some cases. Other than that, there is absolutely no difference in the result. A single EPS file will do the same job and has all of the same data.

## *DCS Pros*

1. DCS uses less disk space than a single EPS file when saved.

2. You can choose to use a low resolution grayscale or color preview which will automatically be used by your laser printer for proofing.

## *DCS Cons*

1. You'll have five files to manage and keep track of instead of one. Lose one and you're (goose is) cooked. If your catalog has 500 color illustrations, you will have 2,500 files to keep track of.

2. You get no performance benefit for the trouble.

3. DCS files will not work with Adobe Illustrator.

Use a single file EPS unless your service provider requests DCS, or the disk space savings is important and worth the hassle of juggling five files instead of one.

## *TIFF*

TIFF (Tagged Information Format File) is your second choice file format for placing bitmapped graphics into a page layout program. The one and only reason to use it is to be able to edit the file once placed in a page layout program.

## *TIFF Pros*

1. Once a file is placed in Quark you can edit with all of the controls under the Style menu. These include color, shade, contrast, and screens.

2. You can set Quark's Preferences to display a 256-level grayscale preview, and a 32-bit color preview. This means that the previews in Quark will look as good as they do in Photoshop.

While you might have occasion to use this feature when presenting your work to clients using your monitor, you should switch the file format back to EPS after the presentation for the sake of printing reliability.

3. As a standard format TIFF can be read by a wide variety of application programs.

4. TIFF images can be placed in a page layout program as RGB and then converted to CMYK.

## TIFF Cons

1. TIFF is not as reliable as EPS. I've seen weird things happen to the edges of placed images, and strange streaks which appeared on film from the image-setter. These problems were cured when exactly the same file was changed to EPS format and placed back in the same Quark file.

2. QuarkXPress will automatically sample down TIFF files that have a resolution of more than two times the lpi you are using.

   This can be disastrous when quality counts (and when doesn't it?), because Quark's down-sampling routine is less than wonderful and will degrade the image quality. Worst of all, Quark will do this without warning you.

3. The TIFF format won't save screens, transfer functions, clipping paths, or duo-tones, but we already knew that.

# Saving Files in Photoshop

One handy feature of Photoshop 3.0 is the **Save a Copy...** File item. Using this command can save you a lot of frustration at 4:00 A.M. when you can't figure out why a file won't save in EPS format and it has to be at the service bureau at 8:00 A.M. Frequently, the answer to the save dilemma is that the file contains layers or channels which cannot be saved in the EPS format. The differences between **Save As...** and **Save a Copy...** follow.

### Save As...

When you use the **Save As...** command (not an illogical decision, after all) to save a file you have worked on with layers, the EPS format option will *not* be available in the format pop-up menu of the **Save As...** dialog box. In fact, the only option available will be Photoshop 3.0 (*Figure 16.5*). You will have to

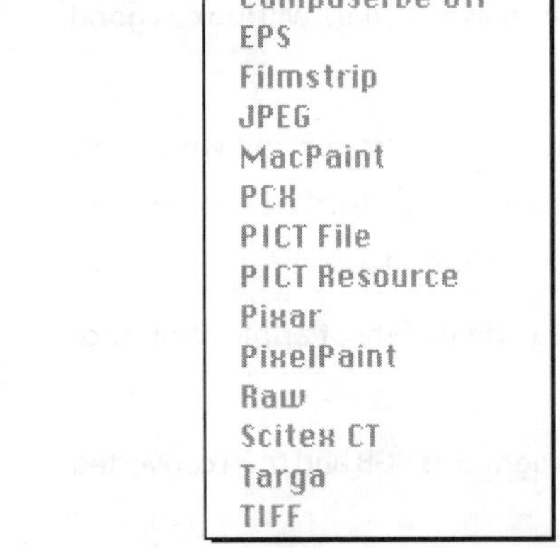

Save this document as:

Custom

Format: ✓Photoshop 3.0
        Photoshop 2.0
Image Pr  Amiga IFF
        BMP
        CompuServe GIF
        EPS
        Filmstrip
        JPEG
        MacPaint
        PCH
        PICT File
        PICT Resource
        Pixar
        PixelPaint
        Raw
        Scitex CT
        Targa
        TIFF

*Figure 16.5*
When you use the **Save As...** command under the File menu to save a file with layers, you're dead in the water except for Photoshop's proprietary format.

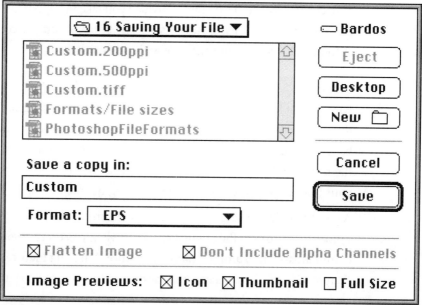

*Figure 16.6*
When you use the **Save a Copy...** command under the File menu, EPS is available even for a file with layers and channels. The file will be flattened automatically when you choose the EPS format.

cancel the **Save As...** procedure and go back to the Layers Palette Options to flatten the file before saving.

## Save a Copy...

In contrast, using **Save a Copy...** will be a little friendlier by providing two checkboxes asking if you want to dump the layers and channels. You don't even have to bother to check them because the EPS format *is* available, and when you choose it, the *Flatten Image* and *Don't Include Alpha Channels* checkboxes automatically get checked and your file is saved in EPS *(Figure 16.6)*.

Another difference between **Save As...** and **Save a Copy...** is that when you use the former, the file that you are saving becomes the currently open file, closing the file you were working on (provided you change the file name). When you choose **Save a Copy...** the file that you are saving a copy of remains the currently open file, but now you have a copy on the disk you selected and in the file format you chose. Both options have their uses, and both create a second file on disk, provided you take the opportunity to change the file name when using **Save As...**. The **Save a Copy...** command will automatically suffix your new file with the word *copy*.

## Save

Last but not least is the old standard **Save**. The **Save** command overwrites the previously saved data *without asking*, so make certain you mean it. If you have any doubts, here is where to use the **Save As...** command, using a new file name, and continue working with the assurance that your work up to your last save is saved intact under the original file name.

A good practice for saving progressive revisions of your file is to simply add numerical suffixes to the original file name when you execute your **Save As...** commands—for example, Amazing Picture, Amazing Picture 01, Amazing Picture 02, and so on. Later, when the dust settles, you can go back and dump any unnecessary versions.

# Summary

1. When you work with any computer, you are employing file formats, so you might as well pay close attention to the formats you're using and why.

2. There are generally two categories of file formats: proprietary and standard.

3. When you begin working on an image, starting from saving the scan, use the program's proprietary format.

4. If you acquire a file from another source that is not in your program's proprietary format, change it right away before you work with it.

5. Photoshop's proprietary format is the only format that will save it's layers.

6. Stay in the proprietary format until you have to change it.

7. Proprietary formats such as Photoshop 3.0 cannot be placed in page layout programs, so that's when you will have to change your file format to either EPS or TIFF.

8. When you change formats for placement in a page layout program, retain the proprietary format file with its layers in case you need to go back and make changes. Use the **Save a Copy...** command.

9. Always use the EPS format to export to your page layout program. It is the most dependable, and offers the most options. It is the only standard format that will save screening instructions, duotones, and clipping paths. Even if you won't be using those options, use EPS anyway for its reliability.

10. When saving your EPS file, by sure to set the Encoding to Binary, and the Preview to Macintosh (8 bits/pixel). Make sure you do not check the options for including Halftone Screen and Transfer Function unless you know what they mean and intend to override the printer's default settings.

11. Use TIFF only when you need to alter the color and/or shade of a grayscale image in your page layout program or when you have many RGB files to place and plan to convert to CMYK in the page layout program.

12. Don't use the DCS format unless your service bureau or printer insists. The disk space savings don't offset the trouble of managing five files instead of the single file you get with EPS.

13. You cannot save layers or channels in EPS, so get familiar with Photoshop's **Save a Copy...** command, which makes it easy to change formats even if your file has layers and channels.

14. Save progressive copies of your files as you work in case you change your mind. Use file names you can easily identify and go back later to get rid of any files you don't need.

## Color Models

Although in the introduction I promised to keep it simple and limited as much as possible to what you need to know to function, the material in this chapter is essential to your being able to function in an informed manner. That's not to suggest that this chapter is terribly complex, but if your background is not in photography or if you don't have an inkling of scientific methods lurking somewhere, the material presented here may be a little hard to grasp at first.

If you really have a hard time with the concept of color modeling or color separation, I suggest reading as much other writing on the subject as you can stomach rather than giving up on it.

### RGB (Additive)

RGB (red, blue, green) is an additive color model (it's also a color space on your computer), since it's made up of light emitted from energy sources such as the sun, light bulbs, and cathode ray tubes like your computer's monitor and your television set. RGB is white light (daylight for example), which can be broken into three approximately equal thirds—red, blue, and green. When red, blue, and green light are projected individually to superimpose, the result is white. Just about every book on color theory or desktop color management has an illustration like the one in Figure C.14, which shows red, green, and blue colored circles overlapping to create white in the center. What's always somewhat hard to grasp about these illustrations is that although the illustration *itself* is ink on paper, the intention is to show what happens when you project colored *light*, from three slide projectors, for example, each with a colored filter over the lens, onto a wall. Thus you are *adding* the colors together to create white light. Keep the three approximately equal thirds aspect in mind as you read about CMYK.

### *CMY and K (Subtractive)*

When you look at Figure C.15 illustrating the CMY (cyan, magenta, yellow) color model you're seeing the real thing, not a simulation as in Figure C.14. CMY is known as a subtractive system because each color works to *subtract* a portion of the visible spectrum from the white light reflected from the paper. The white light is being absorbed by the cyan, magenta, and yellow ink printed on the paper's surface. The ink acts exactly like a color filter to subtract part of the light that is passing through it.

Theoretically, when cyan, magenta, and yellow ink are superimposed on paper, the result is a total absence of light: black. In practice, what you end up with is a murky brown *(Figure C.15)*. That's because the inks aren't as perfectly efficient in real life as they are in theory, and the offset lithographic medium prints a microscopically thin film of ink which has its limitations. To make up for this deficiency, black ink has been added to the mix to beef up the murky brown and create a rich black where there is supposed to be one. The black ink actually does much more than beef up the murky browns, and how you use it can make or break a color separation (Chapter Eighteen: *Managing Color*).

### *How Black Became K*

Once upon a time, in the good old days of color printing when process color was still in its infancy, the tradespeople in the shops had a natural tendency to call cyan ink "blue." In fact, referring to cyan as blue is still almost irresistible. To make a short story shorter, there are several places in the work flow of a printing plant where the separation films that go on the printing press, of which there are four to make the four printing plates, sometimes needed to be inscribed with the appropriate color designation. Now following the natural human tendency to economize when in a hurry (and printers are always in a hurry), people would often abbreviate a color by using only the first letter of the color, and, well you can just imagine—blue, black—B, B. When the cyan plate is printed with black ink and the black plate is printed with cyan ink, the results are not pretty. The confusion was serious enough for the powers that be to come up with the solution: henceforth throughout the graphic kingdom black shall be abbreviated with its last letter—the noble and unconfusable "K."

## The Interesting Part

While descriptions of color models in themselves may seem a bit dry, the interesting part of this discussion is how RGB and CMY work together, and which is the crux of understanding how color separations are made. There is an elegant symmetrical relationship between these two color models.

The key to understanding the relationship between these two color models is that they both divide their composite colors by approximate equal thirds. RGB divides white light, which includes all colors, into red, green, and blue, while CMY divides black, the sum of all printed pigments, into cyan, magenta, and yellow.

To explain this process, I am going to use the conventional approach to making color separations as a model. This is the method which used a process camera and colored filters before separations were made using either electronic or digital technology, and upon which these later systems are based.

## Conventional Separations

The first step is to place a color original of any kind in the copyboard of a process camera. The copyboard of a process camera is evenly illuminated by lights that are attached to it. A red filter is placed in front of the lens so that the image of the color original passes through the red filter. The filter used in this process is very specially designed to effectively pass only light the color of the filter, and to absorb, or prevent from passing through the filter, all other colors of light. So in this case, only red light passes through the filter, and green and blue are absorbed.

Curiously, black and white rather than color film is placed in the camera and is exposed with the light passing through the red filter. Although the film is black and white, it is sensitive to all colors (panchromatic), just like the typical black and white film you would use for taking a photograph today.

The exposed and processed film is a record of the green and blue parts of the color original. Why—when the red filter was in front of the lens? Because when the color original, which is a positive image, exposes the film in the camera, the resulting image is a negative just like when you expose film in your 35mm camera.

As in all photography, the generations alternate orientation between negative and positive. To use your 35mm camera again as an illustration—when you take a snapshot of the subject in front of your camera, which is a positive image, the film in the camera records the subject as a negative. When you make a print from that negative you get a positive print to show to your friends.

Okay, that's why it's negative, but why is the film in the process camera a record of the blue and green light when a red filter was in front of the lens? When the red light exposes the film, the film records the red light striking it as density or dark areas. This means that these dark areas of the film represent the red part of the spectrum and the unexposed areas of the film represent the green and blue parts of the spectrum, that is, everything other than red. When a positive print is made from this negative, the dark areas of the print represent the green and blue of the original in the camera *(Figure C.13)*.

The next steps are to follow exactly the same procedure but using a green filter, and then a blue filter, resulting in three separate negatives, each a record of two thirds of the spectrum.

Now for the interesting part. While the three color filters pass (or transmit) one third of the white light and *absorb two thirds*, the inks, on the other hand, pass (or reflect) two thirds of the white light and *absorb one third (Figure 17.1)*.

Thus when the red filter separation (which is a record of the blue/green light) is printed in cyan ink (which reflects blue/green light), you have a perfect representation of the blue/green areas of the original color image. The same perfect symmetry holds true for the green and blue filter separations which are printed in magenta and yellow ink, respectively, and it is this symmetry that forms the basis of the process color separation system.

Compare the charts in Figure 17.1 and notice the symmetrical relationship between the filters and the inks.

| Red filter | absorbs green/blue | transmits red |
|---|---|---|
| Green filter | absorbs red/blue | transmits green |
| Blue filter | absorbs red/green | transmits blue |

| Cyan ink | absorbs red | reflects green/blue |
|---|---|---|
| Magenta ink | absorbs green | reflects red/blue |
| Yellow ink | absorbs blue | reflects red/green |

*Figure 17.1*     Symmetrical relationship between RGB and CMYK color spaces.

This is a good time to point out that when you're working on your computer in the CMYK mode, it's really just simulated. Your monitor is an RGB device—it can't show you ink on paper, but it can *fake* it pretty well if you are careful about calibrating.

# Other Color Models

## *HSB*

In addition to RGB and CMYK, there are three other color models you will find important to your work. HSB (hue, saturation, and brightness) is an option in Photoshop's color picker. Working with the HSB color model is fairly intuitive. Hue, or color (such as green, purple, yellow), is the color as it occurs around a standard color wheel *(Figure C.10)*, and is measured in degrees from 0 to 360. Saturation is the purity of the color from gray and is measured from 0% (equal amounts of red, green, and blue) to 100% (absence of one or two of the RGB primaries). Brightness is a measure of the lightness or darkness of a color expressed in % from 0% (black or *no* brightness) to 100% (white).

## CIEL*a*b

CIEL*a*b, shortened to LAB in Photoshop, is a significant (though for the most part invisible) color model for desktop color. It is emerging as a standard for color description on the desktop. The LAB color model's importance is that it uses a *device independent* description of color, not dependent upon the monitor, scanner, or any other component of the desktop environment.

Note that using the LAB model does not mean that a color will actually *look* the same on a variety of monitors and output devices (life should be so simple). It means that in spite of the fact that it may look different on various monitors and printers, the *description* of it will remain the same. What does this buy me, you're asking yourself? Just this: when the CIEL*a*b color description is coupled with an accurate device profile, there is at least some chance of having colors come out the same on various devices.

This model is based on the research performed by a group of color scientists, la Commission Internationale de l'Eclairage (CIE), who in 1931 proposed it as an international standard for color measurement. The model was overhauled in 1976 and given its current name: CIEL*a*b.

LAB is composed of three components: luminance, or lightness, an *a* component ranging from green to red, and a *b* component ranging from blue to yellow.

The LAB color model is at the heart of Photoshop, which uses it as a reference whenever you change modes, and most color management systems, which use it as a basic standard of reference. As a mode in Photoshop, LAB is not very intuitive to actually work in and is best left for what it was conceived for—a behind-the-scenes internal reference that Photoshop uses to execute color space conversions.

## YCC

Developed by Kodak, the YCC color model is the basis of its Photo CD system. It works by separating the luminance data from the color data and is faster than the CIEL*a*b model, allowing the compression of the Photo CD to be a workable reality.

# Gamut

Gamut is the entire range of colors that a particular color model is capable of displaying or printing. The largest gamut is the color range perceived by the human eye in nature. The CIEL*a*b color space can map the entire visible spectrum. The color space with the next largest gamut is RGB, and CMYK is the smallest *(Figure C.11)*. Gamut is an important consideration when working with color on your monitor since some colors that can be displayed in the RGB color space of your monitor cannot be printed. And while it may seem strange, even though the CMYK gamut is smaller than the RGB gamut of a monitor, there are some colors that can be printed but not shown on your monitor, such as 100% cyan.

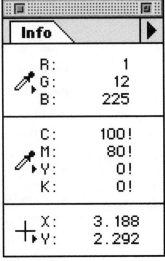

Figure 17.2    Info gamut warning.

## *Exclamation Point!*

When working in the RGB, Indexed Color, or LAB modes, Photoshop has incorporated a couple of tools to help you identify which colors are printable in CMYK and which are not. To begin with, the Info Palette will display exclamation points after CMYK colors that are not printable or are out of gamut *(Figure 17.2)*. The Picker Palette and the larger Color Picker dialog box also display exclamation points after out-of-gamut colors *(Figures 17.3 and 17.4)*. In the Color Picker's dialog boxes, you are shown an example next to the warning triangle of what the closest printable color is. If you click once on the small sample color, Photoshop will change your current out-of-gamut color choice to the closest printable color.

## *Gamut Warning*

In addition to these tools the Gamut Warning mode will temporarily replace any out-of-gamut colors of your image

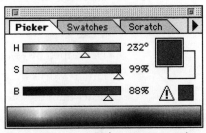

Figure 17.3         Picker gamut warning.

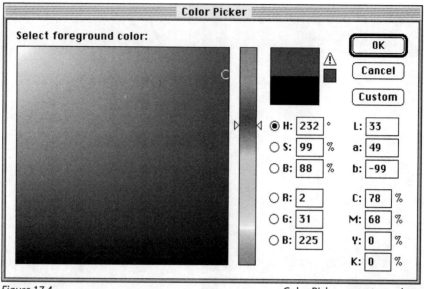

*Figure 17.4*                                    Color Picker gamut warning.

with an indicator color so that you can
identify them. To change the out of
gamut warning color, choose **File>**
**Preferences> Gamut Warning...**
*(Figure 17.5)*. Click once on the color
patch to open the Color Picker and

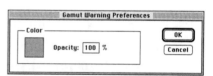

*Figure 17.5*   Gamut Warning Preferences.

select a new color. Figure 17.6a and b show an image with and without the
gamut warning mode invoked. The white areas in Figure 17.6b indicate out-
of-gamut or unprintable colors.

## CMYK Preview

Lastly, there is the CMYK Preview mode, which will convert the entire image
to a preview of the CMYK color you will end up (choose **Mode> CMYK**
**Preview**. The CMYK Preview option allows you to stay in RGB and get an
accurate preview of what the color will look like once you convert your file
to CMYK. If you are not familiar with the differences between RGB and CMYK
gamuts, this feature can be very useful. The closer you stay to the CMYK gamut
while you're working in RGB, the less dramatic (and disappointing) the
conversion to CMYK will be when you take the plunge. To turn off either the
Gamut Warning or the CMYK Preview, simply choose them again.

 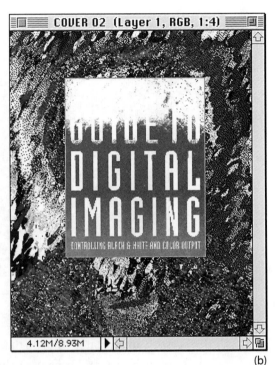

*Figure 17.6*                    (a)                                    (b)

Image shown without (a) and with (b) gamut warning on.

## *Warning About Gamut Warning!*

Before using the Gamut Warning or the CMYK Preview option, or worrying about exclamation points popping up here and there, you must first set up the Preferences submenu items Monitor Setup, Printing Inks Setup, and Separation Setup, according to the your particular monitor and the target output device's color profile. Photoshop uses the data you enter into these three preferences dialog boxes to determine which colors are out of gamut and which colors are printable. Without relevant data in these preferences, all of the out-of-gamut warning devices are meaningless, so don't even bother with them. You'll find details on setting up the preferences submenu items in Chapter Eighteen: *Managing Color.*

## It's a CMYK World

Before printing your file you'll want to make the color separations that have been the subject of much of this chapter. You need to make the conversion from RGB to CMYK because *all color output devices, including offset presses, reproduce color using cyan, magenta, yellow, and black ink, toner, or dye.* Actually, some printers leave out the black, but only for economic reasons—the results are usually better with all four colors, so the elimination of black is a compromise of quality to make the device more affordable. See Figure C.17 for a progressive proof (colors building up one at a time) of the *process colors*, which is another term for CMYK inks, and notice that the CMY version, without the black, definitely lacks contrast and density compared to the CMYK version.

Even though you may have had dye sublimation, Iris, or other types of digital prints made from your RGB files in the past, someone, somewhere, made the conversion to CMYK for you. Usually the device driver will have conversion software built in to perform this task. But now that you have turned over a new leaf and decided to take control of your color files yourself (that's why you bought this book, remember?), you'll achieve more consistent results, and color that matches your monitor more closely, when you make your own color separations based on the printer profiles you'll create. There are some CMY-based dye sublimation printer drivers that won't accept a CMYK file, in which case Photoshop's color management system won't work.

## It's a Big Step

As you can see from the foregoing discussion of color models, changing modes from RGB to CMYK is actually a significant transition involving some remarkable and well established technologies. When you change modes in Photoshop, which is as simple as choosing **Mode> CMYK**, you are making a *color separation*. In the printing world *color separating* (or the resulting film) is also called *process color separation, four-color process, four-color separation,* or simply *process color*.

With the push of a button you are accomplishing a feat that, prior to electronic systems, required hours of working in a darkroom using a graphic arts (or *process*) camera, manipulating colored filters and several generations of film. No, I didn't have to walk barefoot ten miles to a one-room schoolhouse and back, but the magnitude of the transition is important to keep in mind, and one that you shouldn't undertake until all your marbles are in place—that is, until your monitor setup, printing ink setup, and separation setup are adjusted to provide the results you want. You can make as many kinds of color separations as there are spots on a dalmatian, and most will not produce optimum results.

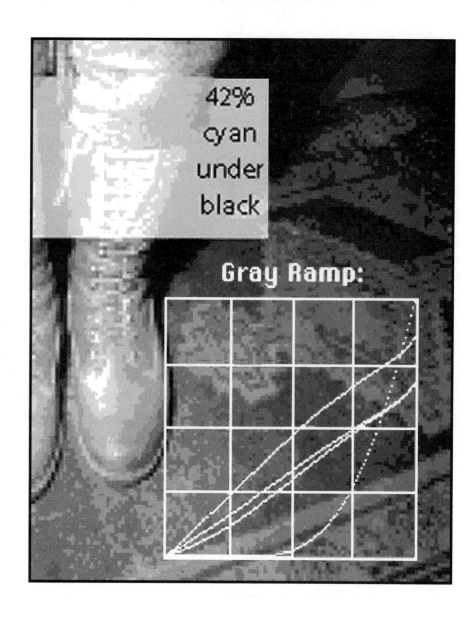

## CMS—The Basics

Color management systems (CMSs) are turning up everywhere you look these days. Currently, there are at least a dozen systems to choose from, including Apple's ColorSync, Monaco Systems' MonacoColor, Kodak's Precision Color Management System, DayStar's Color Match, Agfa's FotoTune, Electronics For Imaging's EFIColor Works, Radius's ColorComposer, Ofoto Color, and Sonnetech's Colorific.

### *You Need a System*

You definitely need a system of some sort in order to manage color on your desktop. Without one, you have absolutely no hope of consistent results, no hope of being able to predict how color will change as you move from one color space to another, from scanner to monitor to printer.

In professional prepress environments, workers get a handle on color by extrapolating from years of experience and seeing thousands of files through the production cycle. More often than not, they will rely in large part on the densitometric readings of particular colors for appraising their accuracy, totally ignoring how the color looks on a monitor. In addition, they usually have the luxury of making several generations of digital proofs before committing the file to film output and final proof. Specialized as this approach is, it works, and it is, in fact, a color management system. It is not, however, a system that can be put in a can and sold to you for use on your own equipment.

Color management for a wider market is still in its infancy, with the major players jostling for position at the starting gate. There is no doubt that, despite the difficulty of the challenge, eventually systems will emerge that are completely reliable and functional.

## How CMSs Work

Many of these systems work through Photoshop, and they generally follow a similar scenario to try to give you a match between your original and final output. First, the scanner is characterized by scanning an industry standard reference target called IT8, available in both reflective and transmission versions. The IT8 contains 264 patches of color and grays *(Figure C.16)*. Once the IT8 is scanned, the CMS compares each patch to CIE LAB descriptions of the IT8 reference which are the result of very accurate readings with a spectrophotometer. In Photoshop the scanned IT8 file's CIE LAB readings are compared to the CIE LAB descriptions of the original target and any discrepancies are noted in a device-specific profile or tag.

Output devices are *characterized* by printing an expanded IT8 reference and reading the results with a spectrophotometer. These readings are are compared to the CIE LAB color description of the original target. As with the input characterization, any deviation from the standard is noted in a device-specific profile.

With the input and output characterizations in hand, the CMS identifies any variation from the CIE LAB readings of the original IT8 target, and then creates a correction strategy, theoretically resulting in the closest match possible.

Notice that the monitor has nothing to do with getting an accurate color match. The monitor can be characterized and added to the system as an *option* in order to make color corrections for less than perfect originals.

## Getting Real

The packaged CMS systems promise push-button, effortless control of your color. The reality of the situation is that none of the CMS systems currently available work perfectly in every situation, and understandably so, considering the immense complexity of the DTP (desktop publishing) environment. There are literally thousands of scanners, monitors, printers, and proofing systems to choose from, each with unique *profiles* (responses to the same digital information). A particular make and model of one device will respond differently depending on its age, and calculating the response as the device ages leads to a vast variation of profiles. When offset printing with all of its variables, such as type of press, brand of ink, paper stock, and operator temperament, is added to the mix, the number of variables that need to be accounted for becomes truly astronomical.

# Mission Impossible (Your Own CMS)

Now that you know how impossible color matching from original to reproduction really is, you're going to build your own system using Photoshop's very sophisticated color management tools. Your personal system will have the advantage of being unique to the equipment you use, as opposed to most of the out-of-the-box solutions which, of necessity, are based on generic characterizations (or at best, averages) of the output devices involved.

## The Advantages

Two bonuses of this build-your-own approach are that if you have Photoshop there is little additional expense, and that developing it is not much more difficult or time consuming than getting a packaged solution up and running. A third advantage is that in developing your own CMS, you'll be better informed about what's going on, and even if you use a packaged version, you'll be in a better position to tailor it to fit your needs and recognize any weak points.

## Not System-Based

There is an important distinction between the system you are about to create and packaged versions which are based on system-level transformations between color spaces, and which work by comparing scanned data with stored IT8 readings and device profiles. Your personal CMS is dependent upon device profiles that you create within Photoshop and are applied in Photoshop as you make the conversion from RGB to CMYK. The goal of this chapter is to produce color images in Photoshop that will reproduce what you see on your monitor as accurately as possible when printed on various output devices. I am taking the position that how these same files are displayed in QuarkXPress or Pagemaker is irrelevant, and that they are only *placed* in these page layout programs for positioning on the page in relation to other graphic elements.

If the way your color is previewed in QuarkXPress is important to you, you can install the mini-version of EFIColor that ships with it. This will give you a better (though not perfect) idea of the way spot colors will look when printed, and may improve the preview of images saved in the TIFF format that you import from Photoshop. The most accurate color for a preview is likely to be from Photoshop files saved in the EPS format, though there is nothing you can do about the low resolution (36 ppi).

Many design professionals are content with the poor quality preview of their images in page layout programs, secure in the knowledge that the files are in fact fine, and will print the way they looked in Photoshop. In the case of spot colors, PMS, Toyo, or process mixes, many design professionals and (all) printers will refer to books of actual printed color combinations for an accurate prediction of the way an on-screen color mix will print.

# Making Color Separations

The first step in the process of making color separations is building a *printer profile*. The goal is to modify the image's color and gamut to conform to what is actually printable by the target printer, and by building a printer profile you will have the opportunity to preview the printed results. For this stage of the process, use a proof created by the medium you are planning to use to print your separations.

# Printing Inks Setup

This dialog box *(Figure 18.4)* is where you will adjust for ink colors, dot gain, and gray balance. Along with the Separation Setup dialog box discussed later in this chapter, it is one of the primary tools for defining precisely how your color separations are going to be made by Photoshop.

## Ink Colors

With your proof in your viewing box, and the Olé No Moiré file open in Photoshop, you are going to compensate for the particular ink characteristics used by the printer or press that made your proof. In other words, if the MY (red) patch in the Olé No Moiré file on your monitor is different from the MY patch in your proof, you can change the way that Photoshop displays MY to more closely match the proof.

In cases where the final print will be produced in a medium where the ink colors may depart widely from standard offset colors, such as screen printing, some ink jet printers, or the Canon Color Laser Printer, this adjustment to compensate for the peculiar ink colors is crucial. In addition to having the proof be from the target device, it is important to have a proof on the type of paper you plan to use. In any medium, including offset, variations in paper will have a huge impact on the appearance of colors. To alter your color patches:

1. Choose **File**> **Preferences**> **Printing Ink Setup.**

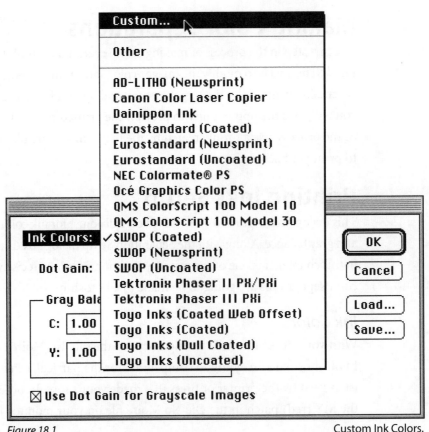

Figure 18.1                                                        Custom Ink Colors.

2. Put the pointer on the Ink Colors pop-up menu and select **Custom...** from the very top of the menu *(Figure 18.1)*.

3. When the Ink Colors Dialog box appears *(Figure 18.2)*, click once on the color patch you want to adjust and the Color Picker will appear *(Figure 18.3)*, allowing you to adjust the color to more closely match the corresponding patch in your proof.

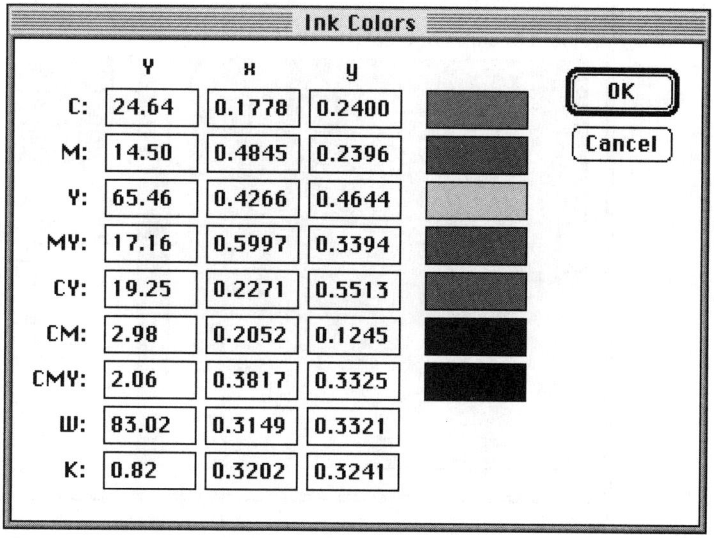

| Ink Colors | | | | |
|---|---|---|---|---|
| | Y | x | y | |
| C: | 24.64 | 0.1778 | 0.2400 | |
| M: | 14.50 | 0.4845 | 0.2396 | |
| Y: | 65.46 | 0.4266 | 0.4644 | |
| MY: | 17.16 | 0.5997 | 0.3394 | |
| CY: | 19.25 | 0.2271 | 0.5513 | |
| CM: | 2.98 | 0.2052 | 0.1245 | |
| CMY: | 2.06 | 0.3817 | 0.3325 | |
| W: | 83.02 | 0.3149 | 0.3321 | |
| K: | 0.82 | 0.3202 | 0.3241 | |

OK       Cancel

*Figure 18.2*                                    Ink Colors.

The tables on the left of the color patches in the Ink Colors dialog box *(Figure 18.2)* are coordinates where you plug in the correct color descriptions as measured with a colorimeter or a spectrophotometer. Unless you have one of these devices, ignore these numbers. If you are going for standard offset, adjusting these patches can be a hugely subtle adjustment which will impact how Photoshop converts RGB to CMYK. If you can't readily see a difference, don't make any changes. For offset, the red patch can typically stand to be a little brighter and more yellow. Make the change and notice if it improves your monitor's display of the reds compared to the proof, especially in the turban Chiquita wears on her head in your Olé No Moiré proof. You can adjust each of the colors one at a time. Note that pure cyan cannot be accurately displayed on a monitor, so don't drive yourself crazy, just come as close as you can or leave it alone. The adjustments you make here will affect how Photoshop thinks about the CMYK gamut. By making changes you will be expanding or contracting your gamut, which will be reflected in the gamut warnings.

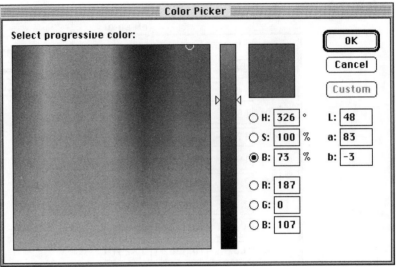

*Figure 18.3*                                                        Color Picker.

If your medium is silkscreen on imported rag paper, the ink color shift from the SWOP set you are starting with will be more obvious.

*Remember that to make this adjustment to ink color, you must have a proof in the actual medium, using the same ink set and the same paper that you plan to use.*

## Dot Gain

Traditionally, dot gain refers to the increase in size of a halftone dot between the film and the printed press sheet. Halftone dots tend to increase in size due to a variety of factors (see Chapter Ten: *Adjust Gray Values* for a discussion of variables). Usually, dot gain percentages refer to a *relative* (rather than absolute) increase in halftone dot size. For example, a 10% dot gain for a

50% halftone dot means that it becomes a 55% halftone dot, not a 60% halftone dot. Fortunately, it isn't necessary for you know what the calculations at the bottom of this designation are, because you will be using the Dot Gain field in the Printing Inks Setup dialog box *(Figure 18.4)* in an intuitive manner, making adjustments based on visual assessment of the variance between your proof and your monitor display.

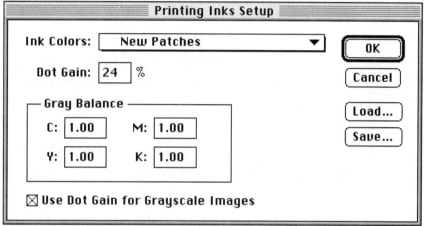

*Figure 18.4*                                          Printing Inks Setup.

In Photoshop, with your proof in your viewing box, if your monitor is lighter than the proof, simply increase the dot gain % in the Printing Inks Setup dialog box and the monitor will respond by displaying a darker image. If your monitor is darker than the proof, decrease the dot gain %. Adjust the dot gain % until your monitor matches your proof in overall brightness. Working in this way to create a printer profile, you really don't need to know what the printer's dot gain is as a numerical designation—you've got the proof of the pudding in front of you in your viewing box.

## When You Don't Have a Proof

In cases where you are preparing files for a press from which you have no physical proof, you should ask your printer how much dot gain he expects from film to press. While asking your printer is the only prudent approach, there are a couple of serious wrinkles in this well-worn advice.

The first is that, believe it or not, many printers will have absolutely no clue about what their dot gain is. When you "ask your printer," you can get responses ranging from 2% to 60%. Obviously, we're not all in the same reality plane. Just be mindful of the fact that not all printers are EDP (Electronic Document Preparation) or Photoshop savvy yet, and if you deal with one who isn't, don't expect any sort of useful responses to the question of how to set up the Printing Inks Setup dialog box.

Second, even when your printer is all over dot gain and other technical aspects of his craft, the question of exactly what you *do* with the information you are provided with remains open. The following guidelines will give you a reasonable chance of success.

If a printer tells you that his dot gain is about 6% for a high quality sheetfed press, simply add that number to Photoshop's default 20% to yield a dot gain of 26% in your Printing Inks Setup dialog box. Likewise, if a printer tells you that his dot gain is about 12% for a web press, add it to 20% to yield a total dot gain of 32%.

*Do not, under any circumstances, use the dot gain % your printer provides by itself in the Dot Gain field of the Printing Inks Setup dialog box!* The one exception to this is when a printer is way into Photoshop, and knows exactly what you're talking about. Otherwise, a dot gain of 5%–15% in this field would create a disastrously dark set of separations.

Where a printer provides a number in the 40%–60% range, *ignore it completely* rather than trying to figure out where he's coming from. In this case, and when you have no dot gain % at all to work from, use 24% for sheetfed presses running coated stock, to 28% for sheetfed presses running low quality uncoated stock. Elevate these numbers by 6% for web presses. Remember that these are only guidelines, and that for any kind of reliable profile of a press, you must have a *printed* proof (ink on paper) *and* the exact file that was used to make the film. Without such concrete evidence from a printer, you're shooting in the dark.

## Gray Balance

The Gray Balance boxes in the Printing Inks Setup dialog box allow you to adjust for color casts which may occur as a natural part of the printing process. Factors such as screen angles and frequency, the printing sequence of colors, different dot gain characteristics between colors, and various pigment characteristics of the inks themselves can all contribute to color casts. To adjust for color casts in your proof:

1. **With your proof in your viewing box and the Olé No Moiré file open in Photoshop, choose Image> Adjust> Levels.**

2. **Put the pointer on the Channel pop-up menu** *(Figure 18.5)* **and select one color at a time, adjusting the center input slider only, to try to match your proof.** *Do not adjust the CMYK channel.*

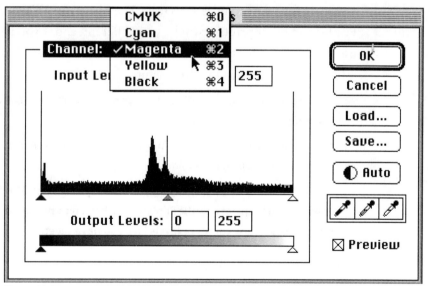

*Figure 18.5*                                                Levels Channel pop-up menu.

3. **As you adjust each color, write down the gamma value (center Input Levels text box) before going to the next color.**

4. **Do not adjust any other sliders. Click on Cancel when you are finished. Do** *not* **apply the adjustments to the image.**

5. Choose **File**> **Preferences**> **Printing Inks Setup** and type in the gamma values you recorded from the Levels dialog box in the appropriate color's Gray Balance text box and click OK.

Your monitor should match your proof very closely. If necessary, make an adjustment to the dot gain % to fine-tune your settings after adjusting the gray balance. You have now created a printer profile for the printer or press that created your proof.

## Save Your Settings

You will eventually have printer profiles for a variety of different devices which will all have different settings. Save the Printing Inks Setup information, giving the file a title that connects it with the particular job or printer who made the proof. When you save the Printing Inks Setup you will also be saving the custom ink patches you created. Be careful not to mix up the custom patches of the printer profiles you create. The patches for a Canon Color Laser Printer and offset printing will be very different, and if you inadvertently use the Canon profile to make separations for offset, the results could be disastrous. To save the Printing Inks Setup:

1. With the Printing Inks Setup dialog box open, click on the Save box on the lower right (*Figure 18.4*).

2. You will get a Save dialog box giving you the opportunity to name the file and direct it to the appropriate folder.

3. Create a folder dedicated to saving your CMS-related data. This folder could be where you keep not only the Printing Inks Setup files, but also the Separation Setup files, and any curves or levels files you have saved.

## Very Pertinent Tidbits

There are several aspects of using the Printing Inks Setup preferences you just created that are crucial to their correct implementation.

- To use the Printing Inks Setup preferences you must start with an RGB file and change mode to CMYK with the appropriate preferences loaded. Photoshop will then use the information in your Printing Inks Setup preferences (as well as the Monitor and Separation Setup preferences) to create color separations optimized for the printer for which you created the settings.

- Opening a CMYK file that was created with a different set of preferences and then loading your new preferences will have *absolutely no effect* on the CMYK values even though its display changes. You *must* change modes from RGB to CMYK to apply the information in the Printing Inks Setup dialog box.

- Because of the way this system works, you should always retain a copy of the RGB file from which you made the CMYK separations. This way, you will be able to make a new set of CMYK separations for different output devices.

For example, if you have an file named *Wonderful Picture* that is destined to be printed in offset by a particular printer, you may want to make a Canon Color Laser proof, or a proof from a desktop color printer you may have, just as a rough check for size, color, position, and before having the film and contact proof made. This will require making two different sets of color separations, because the printer profile (Printing Inks Preferences) that is designed for getting best results from the Canon Color Laser printer is going to be radically different from the profile you will use to make the offset separations.

Starting from the RGB version of your file *Wonderful Picture*:

1. **Load the Printing Inks Preferences you created for the Canon and change the mode from RGB to CMYK. Save this file (use Save a Copy) with the file name** *Wonderful Picture.Canon.*

2. **When you are ready to go to film, starting from the same RGB file, load the Printing Inks Preferences you created for the offset press, and change the mode from RGB to CMYK. Save this file (again using Save a Copy) as** *Wonderful Picture.offset.*

You now have three files which is where you want to be:

- **Your original RGB file intact**
- **A CMYK file for the Canon Color Laser printer**
- **A CMYK file for the service bureau or offset printer from which to make film**

*You must save the original RGB version of the file because you cannot go back to RGB from CMYK without degrading the quality of your image.* Actually, you can go back in a pinch—if you didn't retain the RGB version—but it's something you want to avoid. If you find you must go backwards, make absolutely certain that exactly the same Monitor, Printing Inks Setup, and Separation Setup preferences are loaded as when you made the conversion from RGB to CMYK initially. This leads to the final tidbit:

- Exactly the same Monitor and Printing Inks Setup preferences you used to create a CMYK file must be loaded in order to display that file as it appeared when you created it.

The monitor display of CMYK files responds to your preferences (without changing the saved file data). Using the previous example, if you have Wonderful Picture.Canon open with the preferences for your offset press loaded, the Wonderful Picture will look less than wonderful. Simply load the preferences that were used to create Wonderful Picture.Canon, and Wonderful will again live up to its name.

## Separation Setup

Once you have determined what the settings are for your Printing Inks Setup, you will need to adjust the Separation Setup dialog box (choose **File> Preference> Separation Setup**) before making the transition from RGB to CMYK. The Separation Setup dialog box *(Figure 18.6)* gives you the option of selecting either the GCR (gray component replacement) or UCR (undercolor removal) type of separation, and allows you to customize how your black plate is generated. Both types of color separations are designed to remove some of the cyan, magenta, and yellow in neutral tones and replace them with black ink. This replacement reduces the total amount of ink in dark tones which is necessary for printing on high-speed, multicolor presses; these presses can't tolerate solids of all four inks (400% total ink coverage) in dark shadow area. Multicolor presses require that the total ink coverage be no more than approximately 300%. With less ink printing on the paper, dot gain is constrained, registration is improved, and the potential for setoff (wet ink accidentally transferring to the next sheet of paper

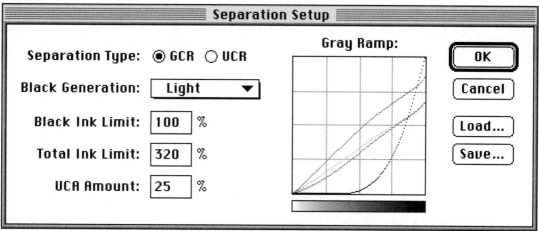

<table>
</table>

*Figure18.6*                                                  Separation Setup dialog box.

delivered in a stack) is reduced. In addition, employing either method cuts down on the amount of the more expensive color inks used, thus reducing the overall cost of printing.

## Gray Ramp

The Gray Ramp gives you a visual indication of how the settings you use are affecting the relationship between CMY and black. It's a great tool for learning about color separations, and for getting an idea of the how much GCR is being applied. For example, you'll see how Photoshop reduces the CMY to compensate for the increased amount of black if you set the Black Generation to Heavy, and how it increases the CMY if you set the Black Generation to Light.

Get in the habit of trying to visualize what kind of separations any given set of settings will produce. As an exercise, make separations with a variety settings and view the results of each channel individually, noting the correspondence between the Gray Ramp and the amount of color and black in each channel. To best evaluate the channels, turn off the Color Channels in Color checkbox in the General Preferences dialog box (choose **File> Preferences> General**), and have your Info Palette open to measure the differences in dot %. Choose **Window> Show Channels**, and click on the eye icon at the left of each channel to see it by itself; or you can type ⌘

1 through 4 to select the individual channels, and ⌘0 to return to the composite CMYK preview.

## GCR

GCR (gray component replacement) is Photoshop's default separation type and is the more recently developed strategy. Any color made up of cyan, magenta, and yellow has some neutral or gray component which can be replaced by black ink. In a color that has a high percentage of all three inks, one of the inks is only *graying* the color as more of it is added. This is the part, the *gray component*, that can be *replaced* with black with little impact on the appearance of the color. GCR works on any color, even light colors, containing cyan, magenta, and yellow, not just in the shadows.

GCR can help to maintain gray balance on press because of the stabilizing effect of the black in any given color. For example, a chocolate brown color which contains high amounts of CMY is highly susceptible to shifting with any variation of the cyan (graying) component, but becomes more stable as cyan is replaced with black. In fact, the stabilizing effect of large amounts of GCR can be a limitation on press in circumstances where the flexibility to subtly shift the balance of key colors is desirable. Too much GCR can also result in weak blacks in images with large amounts of neutral dark areas.

## UCR

Undercolor removal is the traditional method of controlling the total ink coverage of the image. This method works mainly in the shadows, with the UCR effect decreasing toward the highlights. Using the UCR method of generating your black plate will result in more saturated separations, especially in the shadows, with none of the obvious gray component replacement in other areas that is typical of the GCR method.

## GCR or UCR?

Stick with GCR unless you know exactly what the difference is and why you think that UCR is going to work better for you. You'll find that, in general, the GCR method of separation offers much more control and if you set it up right, you can do just about the same thing with it as you can with the

UCR method. Do a little experimenting and separate the same RGB image with both methods, comparing the results by placing individual channels side by side to get a feel for how they act differently. If you have little experience with going to press with color separations, you won't have a reference to determine which produces better results, but you will be able to see how very differently the two methods create separations for you, and that's a start.

## Setting Up Your Separation Setup

There really isn't one magic setup to use that is going to be ideal for all of your images, so in using this dialog box, stay flexible and fine-tune your setup from one printed result to the next, correcting what you don't like as you go along. The settings you use here will have a *dramatic* impact on the results you get on a press sheet, with less impact on the results from digital proofs. Here are a few guidelines that will ensure reasonable results from most images.

## Black Generation

Figure 18.7 shows a pop-up menu which offers you None, Light, Medium, Heavy, Maximum, and Custom.

Always use Light for the Black Generation. Too much black (which is usually what happens with the Medium setting) will tend to produce separations with dirtier colors and wimpy dark shadows. You'd think that more black

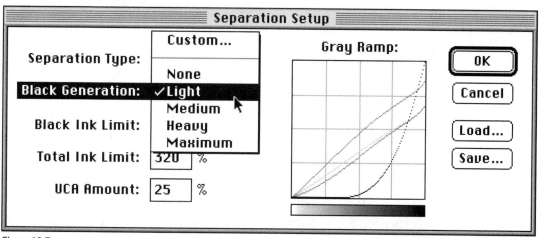

*Figure18.7*

Black Generation pop-up menu.

would give you more saturated shadows, but that's not the way it works. The shadows get wimpy because as you set the Black Generation higher, more CMY is removed from the shadows, leaving more of the black by itself, which doesn't cut it *(Figure C.18)*.

None will live up to its name, and you won't be using it except for special effects. A color separation for offset must have a black plate for normal results.

Medium, Heavy, and Maximum will produce too much black and as a result, too little of everything else to compensate. Maximum has some value when you want to reproduce a monotone or black and white photograph in four-color process.

## Black Ink Limit

This option allows you to specify the maximum amount of black. SWOP standards disallow 100% density of any color including black, and you usually don't want any more than about 90% black anywhere in a separation. Use your Info Palette to check the black's maximum density after you make the mode conversion. Even with this option set to 100% the black plate probably won't print 100% density anywhere in the image, with the Total Ink Limit set to 300%–320%, and the Black Generation set to Light. How your separations respond to this setting depend on all of the settings in this dialog box *and* the RGB values of the image you are about to convert to CMYK. For your standard starting point, leave the Black Ink Limit set to 100% (which doesn't mean you'll actually get 100% black).

## Total Ink Limit

This option specifies the maximum allowable density of all four colors combined. How you set this option varies with the type of press used to print the separations. SWOP standards call for a maximum of 300%. Like the Black Ink Limit, however, how this setting reacts depends upon all the other settings *and* the maximum RGB values of the image before conversion to CMYK. Remember that for best results, your RGB image shouldn't have dot % readings of 0, which would indicate clipping of the vital shadow data. With the Separation Setup illustrated in Figure 18.6, even though the Total Ink

Limit is set to 320%, the resulting separations never exceed a total ink saturation of more than 290%, which will work for sheetfed as well as web presses. Note that the RGB values before the CMYK conversion were higher than 0–0–0. Set the Total Ink Limit option to between 300% and 320% and check your results after the conversion with your Info Palette to make sure you don't exceed your printer's recommendations. If your printer can't give you a Total Ink Limit to shoot for, limit your actual total density to 300%.

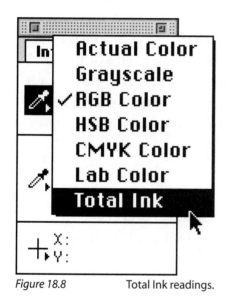

*Figure 18.8*      Total Ink readings.

To check the actual total ink density of the CMYK file after you've made the conversion, put the pointer on the options triangle next to the eyedropper in the Info Palette and drag down to Total Inks *(Figure 18.8)*. Now when you move the cursor over your image, the Info Palette will read off the total ink density. For the correct Total Ink Limit to set for any specific press, ask your printer and provide him with separations that conform to his specifications. Note that different types of printing presses can tolerate varying amounts of total ink densities. Also, the total ink density specifications will vary between printers using the same type of press. Web presses without dryers between color units can tolerate the least amount of total ink, from 280% to 320% depending on the printer's preferences, the paper

stock, and the screen frequency (lpi). Web presses with dryers can tolerate a much higher total ink density. Process color is sometimes printed on two-color equipment, which also might allow a higher total ink density. There are even places (though rare) where four-color printing is still done on single-color presses, which could print total ink densities up to 400% if desired, because the inks have the opportunity to set between colors, alleviating many of the technical issues which mandate a limit.

## UCA Amount

The UCA (undercolor addition) option is used to moderate the amount of gray component replacement specified by the other settings in this dialog box. The default is 0%, adjustable up to 100%. Put another way, the higher the UCA Amount, the less undercolor removal is allowed to occur. It sounds like a silly option to have, since you would think you could simply set the dialog box for less undercolor removal in the first place, but you really can't in the GCR mode. In fact, this option is quite an important one for preventing the GCR from getting out of hand. You use this option to prevent too much GCR from occurring in images with heavy shadows covering a large area which might look too weak from lack of ink otherwise. There are instances where setting the UCA Amount to 100% works well—for example, pictures with large black areas lacking in detail, which need to look fully saturated when printed. Using a high % in this field causes the GCR mode to act very much like the UCR mode. Not being a fan of excessive GCR, I usually set this option anywhere from 25% to 50% for typical photographic images. Save your Separation Setup settings in the folder you created for this purpose.

# Overview:
# Making CMYK Color Separations

Assuming that you are going to print in offset lithography and starting with your RGB color-corrected, sharpened, and otherwise adjusted file:

1. Choose **File> Preferences> Printing Inks Setup...**.

2. Enter the data you generated for this dialog box based on the proof you referred to, or choose **Load...** and open the Printing Inks Setup file you saved.

   If you haven't generated your own settings, see "When You Don't Have a Proof," earlier in this chapter, for dot gain recommendations. Leave Ink Colors at the default SWOP (Coated), and the Gray Balance at 1.00 for all colors.

3. It's better to use Save and Load, since these options will input not only the Dot Gain % and Gray Balance settings, but also the Ink Colors you generated.

4. Choose **File> Preferences> Separation Setup...** and load the settings you saved for this dialog box. If you haven't created any custom settings of your own, use those illustrated in Figure 18.6 for images that are more or less "normal" in color, contrast, and brightness.

5. Choose **Mode**> **CMYK**.

6. Check your total ink limit to make sure it conforms to your printer's specifications (see "Total Ink Limit").

7. Make any final color corrections which might be required, since changing from RGB to CMYK may have altered the appearance of some colors due to CMYK's compressed gamut.

8. Save your CMYK file in Photoshop's EPS format without saving screening or transfer function information. Use Save a Copy and make sure you retain your original RGB version intact.

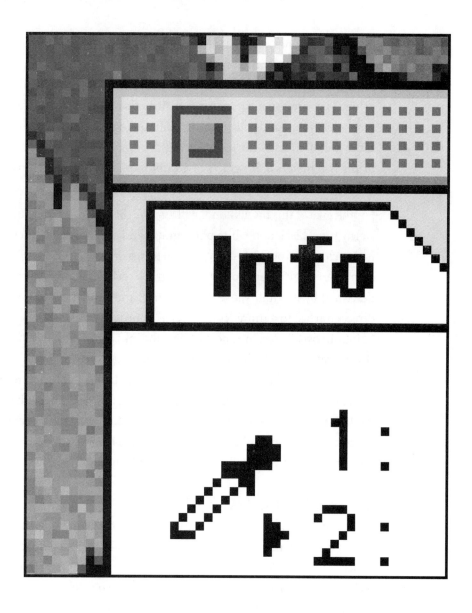

Duotones, tritones, and Quadtones are used to add dimension and dynamic range to pictures printed in offset lithography. Most typically, these techniques are used to reproduce monochrome photographic silver gelatin prints. They are also great for reproducing other types of photographic prints such as platinum and palladium. In addition to photographic originals, duotones are often used for reproducing drawings. Frequently, photographic prints will be *toned*, in which case duotones can be used to closely match the color of the original.

For the sake of this discussion, I will assume that you are reproducing a fine, warm-tone, black and white photograph and are trying to match the original as closely as possible—not only in terms of tone reproduction as might be measured by a densitometer, but in the feel of the original as might be described by its vitality, overall brilliance, and subtlety of color. This is in direct contrast to a more "commercial" approach of using a photograph to fit into an overall design concept where the inks are already specified by other considerations, and where respect for the original print is less important. Of necessity, this latter approach often uses bizarre color combinations, including CMYK, which might be appropriate for the design at hand. There are 137 examples of duotone curves in the **Goodies> Duotone Presets** folder of your Photoshop application, most of which fall into the second category, and if that's what you need you'll undoubtedly find something suitable there.

## What Is a Duotone?

A duotone is created by printing two impressions from two plates to reproduce a monochrome original. Notice that I didn't say two different colors, which is what the name *duotone* ("two tones") implies. While a duotone is usually black and a gray or color, it can also be two blacks. In the typical case of black and gray, for example, each plate will use different curves so that the shadow detail is somewhat enhanced by the black plate and the more delicate highlight areas are enhanced by the gray or lighter color plate.

A tritone and quadtone is the same concept extended to three and four colors. Typically, at least one of the "colors" is black with the others being delicately tinted grays. A quadtone is not the same as a four-color process separation and usually doesn't use process color inks (cyan, magenta, yellow, and black). Even in cases where process color inks are used to create quadtones, the result is still not a color separation.

## Why Is Duotone Used?

Even in cases where the original is a very neutral silver gelatin print with no obvious color toning, if the printing medium is offset lithography, there is a distinct limit to the ink density that can be printed. Offset presses print a very thin film of ink, and a single impression—one printing—cannot reproduce the maximum black density of a good silver gelatin print while maintaining favorable printing characteristics in the rest of the grayscale.

While a printer might, by running a high density of ink, come close to a believable black, other aspects of the printing would be seriously compromised. Dot gain would soar and the dot quality would suffer producing a grainy appearance. Delicate shifts in the tonal range would be compressed or disappear, and the technical aspects of handling and drying the over-inked press sheet would become a serious problem.

The solution to this technical limitation is to print two, three, or four colors to achieve a believable maximum density and optimize the tone reproduction throughout the rest of the grayscale.

## About Reproduction Quality

While the concept of multicolor printing of monochrome originals is a proven success, the results aren't always or automatically better than printing a single color. In cases where the film is prepared (either conventionally or electronically) by inexperienced operators, a duotone can look worse than a good single impression halftone. Producing a fine set of duotone, tritone, or quadtone films is a highly skilled art form that can elude even the most sophisticated printers. All the latest high-end equipment for color measurement, monitoring, and printing are no substitute for the the sensitive and trained photographic eye. This is why most of the best books featuring reproduction of fine photographic prints are still produced with conventionally made duotone films (film shot in a graphic arts camera rather than scanned). If you look at the colophon of a book in which photographs are reproduced beautifully, you'll often see the name of the person who shot the film listed as separate from the printer. Individuals such as Richard Benson, Michael Becotte, Robert Hennesy, and Robert Palmer have made the film for many fine books and are renowned for their ability in this area.

## Process Color Reproduction of Black and White

This approach is taken frequently, especially in magazines but the quality is far from rivaling the potential of a real duotone, tritone, or quadtone. Process color is wonderful for reproducing color originals, and you would think that the same process would be great for monochromatic originals, but there is something subtle missing. The richness and vitality of carefully balanced black and grays can't be matched by process color techniques. The challenges are partially due to the lower screen frequencies of process color printing which produce moiré patterns that are often visible and disturbing. Duotone, tritone, and quadtone printing, on the other hand, often employ screen frequencies of 200 to 300 lpi. In addition to the minimizing of screen moiré or rosette patterns (see Chapter Four: *Pixels, Dots, & Spots*) by the finer screen frequencies, the combination of black and various lighter grays tends to reduce any visible rosettes, since moiré patterning is most obvious between strong colors.

## Digital Duotones

Can digital duotones rival the quality of conventional duotones? Unquestionably. We are still in a transitional stage of moving from conventional to digital where duotones are concerned. This means that there is a wealth of fine, conventionally produced books on photography, including all of the classics of the photographic book genre, and relatively few fine examples of the digitally produced books featuring fine photography. Time will change the balance, however, and the potential of stochastic screening (see Chapter Four: *Pixels, Dots & Spots*) for fine reproduction of monochrome photography is far from realized.

# Doing It

As with color separations, there are more ways to make a duotone than there are spines on a porcupine's backside. This example will illustrate one typical, time-tested approach. A duotone's black plate has more contrast than its gray or color plate, which reveals more shadow separation and prints lighter in the midtones and highlights. As you will see, the black plate stops short of printing the very brightest highlights—those that have a tone but are without detail.

The gray plate has less contrast than the black, and prints fuller throughout the tonal range, including in the highlights. Essentially, the gray ink has little ability to carry the important detail but does a good job of defining delicate tonal variations in the lightest values. These two plates, when printed gray over black, create the enhanced shadow density, richness, and delicate highlight brilliance that results in a print more like a good gelatin silver print than a single impression could ever hope to achieve.

To use the Duotone mode in Photoshop you must start with a grayscale file. If the image you want to use is in any other mode such as RGB, you must first change it to Grayscale before changing it to Duotone.

The Duotone mode in Photoshop is really quite extraordinary in that it offers you a great deal of control over how your image will reproduce, including a preview in the colors you select.

Be aware of the fact that the dot gain % you enter in the Printing Inks Preferences dialog box will affect the display of your duotones when the **Use Dot Gain for Grayscale Images** checkbox is checked. Also note that you can improve the accuracy of your duotone preview by comparing the on-screen color to a printed swatch (such as a Pantone guide) and making adjustments to the color patch if necessary. To adjust the display of a Pantone color, click on the Picker button in the Custom Colors dialog box after selecting your color *(Figure 19.2)*.

### Start with a Full Range Grayscale

Make sure you start with a grayscale file that has close to a full density range from about 95% in the shadows to about 5% in the highlights (unless you are working with an image that has an intentionally limited tonal range). Doing this will make your life easier, because when you bring a grayscale image into the Duotone mode, Photoshop maps your file with a *null curve* (straight line across the grid) from 100% to 0% of ink values relative to the pixel values you start with. In other words, if you start with a grayscale file with a maximum pixel value of 70%, in the duotone mode that 70% will be assigned to the 100% field of the ink curve. If you enter 95% in the 100% field following the instructions given here, you end up with 95% of 70%, which is 66%. While Photoshop is happy to do this, you will not end up with the results you might be expecting and certainly not the results intended by this example. Figuring out what is happening in the highlights will be similarly confusing. To avoid this potential confusion, simply start with a grayscale file that has a range from about 95% to 5%. To avoid clipping (see Chapter Six: *Scanning*), don't change your file to range from 100% to 0%.

## Specify inks

With your image in Grayscale mode:

1. Choose **Mode**> **Duotone...** *(Figure 19.1)*.

2. If you're using the Duotone mode for the first time, the Duotone Options dialog box will open set for Monotone. Select Duotone from the Type pop-up option.

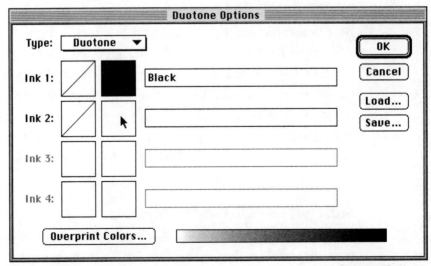

*Figure 19.1*                                    Duotone Options.

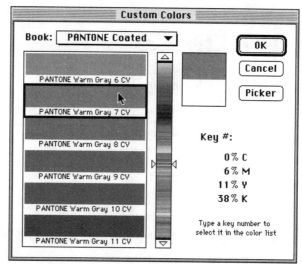

*Figure 19.2*                              Custom Colors.

3. Ink 1 will be Black by default. Make sure that the name in the ink color field is listed as Black with no spaces or other words before or after. If it is listed as Pantone Process Black CV, eliminate everything but the word Black.

   To specify Ink 2, click once on the square to the right of the Ink 2 curve box *(Figure 19.1)*.

4. If the Color Picker appears, click once on the Custom button and select Pantone Coated from the Book pop-up option. The Pantone Coated book will open by default if this is your first use of the Duotone mode.

5. Scroll to Warm Gray 7. You can substitute Cool Gray 7 if you prefer a more neutral result. (The Grays are located just after Pantone 447, so if you type 447 and click twice on the scroll down arrow you will see Warm Gray 7.) Click once on the Warm Gray 7 CV color swatch and click OK or press Return *(Figure 19.2)*.

## Adjust Ink 1 (black) curve

6. Adjust the black curve by clicking once on the black curve box *(Figure 19.3)*.

7. When the black Duotone Curve dialog box opens, enter 95 in the 100% field and 1 in the 5% field and click OK *(Figure 19.4)*.

The concept behind this adjustment is to "open up" the black plate by increasing the contrast and lowering the density throughout the tonal

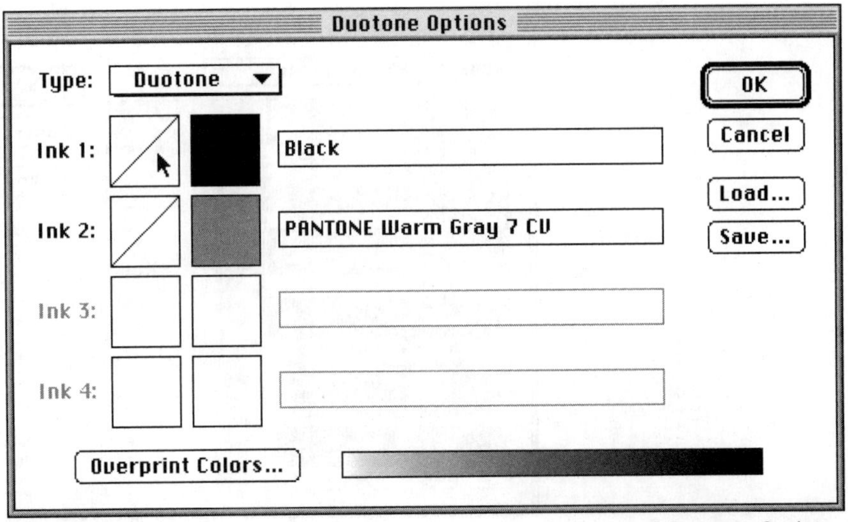

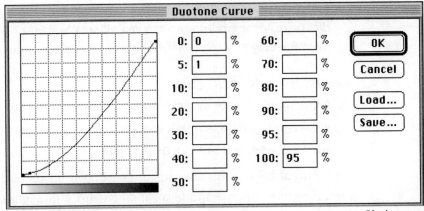

*Figure 19.3*                                                    Duotone Options.

range. This will reveal more separation and detail in the shadow areas. Refer to Figure 19.9 to see the results of this adjustment compared to the grayscale file before the change to the Duotone mode. The overall lightness of the black duotone plate will allow for the addition of the gray plate.

## Where the Black Breaks

A *critical* aspect of adjusting the black plate curve is carefully measuring the density (using the Info Palette) of the highlights to determine exactly where the black "breaks," or goes below 2%. Don't count on the imagesetter, print-

*Figure 19.4*                                                    Black curve.

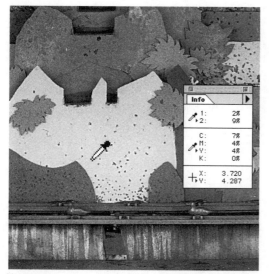

*Figure 19.5*                    Black /gray densities.

ing plates, or press to hold a 1% dot (assume that 1% means the same as 0%, that is, that it will not print).

The goal is to allow the black plate to carry or print the lightest important detail in your highlights. You will need to make this assessment and adjustment of every image you print in duotone. *This means that you will need to adjust the value you entered in the 5% and 0% fields of the Black Duotone Curve dialog box for each image.* If the black plate breaks too soon and fails to print some important detail, the detail will disappear in the final printing. The reason for this is that the gray ink is usually is too light a pigment to render the highlight information legible. See Figure 19.5 for an illustration of the black just holding the brightest whites with detail.

Note that the Info Palette displays both the black and gray color of your duotone as 1 and 2, provided you have it set to read Actual Color (*Figure 19.6*).

## More Bad Breaks

Another potential hazard is allowing the black to break at an awkward point in an area of the image that graduates from light gray to white. This

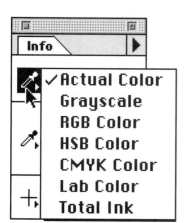

*Figure 19.6*          Actual Color.

is an aspect to watch for *in addition* to the black carrying detail. Avoid allowing the black plate to break in a critical graduated tone even if there is no important detail. Where the black changes from where it prints to where it does not print, an obvious tonal shift occurs. Figure 19.7 illustrates an image where the black breaks badly (a), and the same image with black prevented from breaking (b). The color plate will not hide the effects of a bad black break point even though the color prints in these areas.

(a)                                  (b)

*Figure 19.7*
Where the black plate "breaks" causes an obvious tonal shift and should not be allowed to go to 0% in a critical area such as in the face (a). The black plate is prevented from "breaking" and prints at least a 2% halftone dot even in the brightest highlights (b).

## Adjust Ink 2 curve

8. Click once on the Ink 2 curve box to adjust it. When the Warm Gray 7 Duotone Curve dialog box opens, enter 90 in the 100% field, 50 in the 50% field, and 2 in the 0% field, and click OK *(Figure 19.8)* and OK again at the Duotone Options dialog box.

9. Use the Save button to save your settings, and the Load button to apply them to other grayscale files *(Figure 19.3)*.

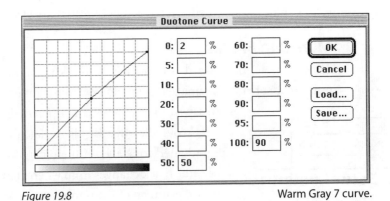

*Figure 19.8*                                      Warm Gray 7 curve.

## Final Results

Figure 19.9 illustrates the results of the curves applied in the step-by-step process outlined above. The gray plate in this figure would of course be printed in the Warm Gray 7 Pantone ink, not the black ink used to print this page,

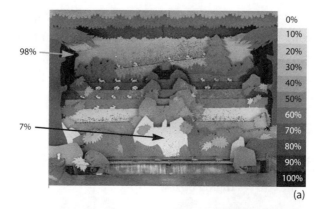

(a)

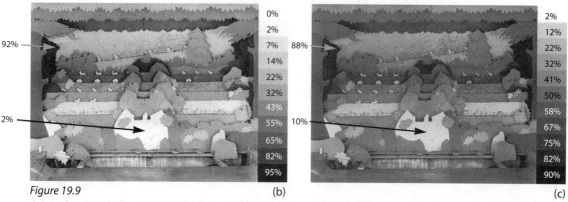

*Figure 19.9* (b) (c)
Original grayscale file (a), black duotone plate (b), and gray duotone plate.

and would have much less contrast and show far less definition of detail than it does here. These two plates will print superimposed, black printing first. Compared to the original grayscale file, notice the way the Warm Gray 7 plate increases in density toward the highlights, and the Black plate decreases toward the highlights. Note also that the black was not allowed to "break" in the highlight area in the center of the image, but holds a 2% dot.

# Viewing Individual Channels

Save your duotone file before you attempt this for the first time, so that you can Revert to the saved file (choose: **File> Revert**) if things don't go well. To see the results of the curves you drew in the Duotone Options dialog boxes as individual channels, choose **Mode> Multichannel**. The single duotone channel containing the two plates will separate into its composite channels, allowing you to see them *one at a time*. The multichannel mode will open showing channel 1. To see channel 2, type ⌘ 2. If you are working with tritones or quadtones, type ⌘ 3 and ⌘ 4 to view the other channels. When you have finished looking at the channels, type ⌘ Z to Undo the mode change and return to the Duotone mode.

*If you make any changes to the channels, the file will not come back together as a Duotone.* All you can do is look at the channels, and type ⌘ 1, ⌘ 2, and ⌘ Z. You cannot edit the individual channels of a duotone except with the Duotone Curves dialog boxes.

# Proofing Duotones

If possible, press proof any job of critical importance, especially if you don't know exactly how reliably your monitor is calibrated to the printing press that the duotone is destined to be printed on.

Digital proofs of your duotone are not possible, since almost all proofing systems use a CMYK ink system, not the two-color combination of your duotone; making a digital proof would require converting the two-color file into CMYK and the result would only be a vague simulation of the actual printed image, practically no use at all except for checking other aspects of the page such as type.

# Printing from Photoshop

If you are printing your duotone files directly out of Photoshop instead of placing them in a page layout application, you will need to set your screens before you print. Choose **File> Page Setup...**. When the Page Setup dialog box opens, check the Calibration Bars, Registration Marks, Crop Marks, and Labels checkboxes and click once on the **Screens...** button *(Figure 19.10)*. When the Halftone Screens dialog box opens, click once on the **Auto...** button *(Figure 19.11)*. Check the Use Accurate Screens checkbox in the Auto Screens dialog box *(Figure*

*Figure 19.10*      Page Setup....

*Figure 19.11*      Halftone Screens.

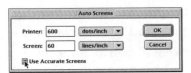

*Figure 19.12*      Auto Screens.

*Figure 19.13*      Halftone Screens.

*19.12)* and click OK. You will be returned to the Halftone Screens dialog box where you will see that the Use Printer's Default Screens checkbox has become unchecked, which is what you want *(Figure 19.13)*. Photoshop has set your screen angles to 45° for black and 105° for Ink 2. If you are a traditionalist, you can change the angle of Ink 2 to 75° by putting your pointer on the Ink pop-up menu and changing to Ink 2. Then enter 75 in the Angle field and click OK. After you are returned to the Page Setup dialog box, click OK again.

# Saving Duotone Files

You must save your duotone in either Photoshop or EPS format. If you are planning to place it in a page layout application such as QuarkXPress you have one option: EPS.

You need to know what type of imagesetter is going to be used to output the film, because Scitex systems will not read Photoshop's duotone EPS files. If your document is going to be output on Scitex equipment you will have to convert your duotone file to a CMYK file and save it in the Scitex CT format. Begin by saving a copy of your duotone file in Photoshop's format so you can start this process again if you crash and burn.

New Channel icon

*Figure 19.14*    Click Cyan channel.

## *Saving for Scitex*

1. **Open the Channels Palette by choosing Uieш> Shoш Channels.**

2. **Choose Mode> Multichannel to split your duotone file into two separate channels.**

3. **If you have any selections saved in alpha channels, delete them.**

4. **Add additional channels by clicking on the New Channel icon at the bottom of the Channels Palette *(Figure 19.14)* until you**

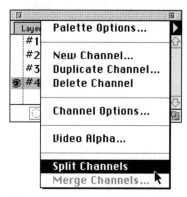

*Figure 19.15*         Split Channels.

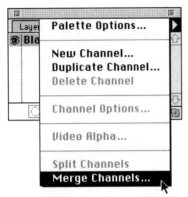

*Figure 19.16*    Merge Channels.

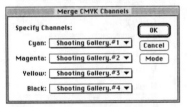

*Figure 19.17*    Mode: CMYK.

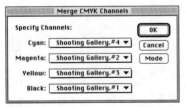

*Figure 19.18*  Merge CMYK Channels.

*Figure 19.19*    Specify channels.

*Figure 19.20*    EPS Format options.

have a total of four. Click OK at the New Channels dialog box that will appear.

5. Choose Split Channels from the Channels Palette options *(Figure 19.15)*.

6. Choose Merge Channels from the Channels Palette options *(Figure 19.16)*.

7. When the Merge Channels dialog box opens, select CMYK from the Mode pop-up menu and click OK *(Figure 19.17)*.

8. When the Merge CMYK Channels dialog box opens *(Figure 19.18)*, use the pop-up menus to put #1 in the Black channel and #4 in the Cyan channel *(Figure 19.19)* and click OK.

You moved your #1 file to the Black channel so that it will print with the correct screen angle: 45°. Your original gray plate, which was file #2, stays in the Magenta channel so that it will print with the correct 75° (sometimes expressed as 165°) screen angle, since that is the normal angle for magenta. The Cyan and Yellow channels will be blank. Once you have completed this process your file will look totally weird, but it will print as it should provided you have consulted with your service provider and you're all on the same wavelength. The Scitex system will ignore the blank channels you created, but it needs the four channels in CMYK format to feel like it's doing its job. Be sure to follow these steps exactly—simply changing the mode from Duotone to CMYK will definitely *not* do the trick.

## Placing Duotones in QuarkXPress

For a duotone you have converted to CMYK and saved in the Scitex CT format, simply place the file in a picture box as you would any other CMYK file. Your previews in QuarkXPress will look wrong, but they should print correctly provided that your printer uses the magenta film to make the plate for your second color.

*Note that if you are using the gray or color of your duotone as a spot color some-where else in the Quark document, for type for example, you will have to specify the color of that element as magenta.*

As you can see, convincing Scitex to print your duotone file is a giant pain. If you have the option, use a service provider with equipment that is clever enough to read Photoshop's duotone files (Agfa's Selectset, Linotronic, etc.).

In the latter case, save your duotone file in the EPS format using the Macintosh (8 bits/pixel) Preview and Binary Encoding options. Leave the Include Halftone Screen and Include Transfer Function checkboxes unchecked *(Figure 19.20)*. Indicate your printer's preference for screen fre-quency (lpi) and the screen angles you want on the order form you send with your file to the service provider. Give instructions for duotones for black at 45° and gray or color at 75° screen angles.

If you have some compelling reason to save the screens with the file such as the need to specify that the duotones have a different screen frequency from other screened elements in the same Quark document, you can spec-ify and save screens with the file in Photoshop (see "Printing from Photoshop" above). The Include Halftone Screen checkbox in this case should be checked *(Figure 19.20)*.

# Naming Names

This is a detail you need to check on before sending off your Quark docu-ment to the service provider. The names of all your ink colors (two in the case of a duotone) saved with the Photoshop EPS file must exactly match the names as they occur in the QuarkXPress document into which they were placed. One of the annoying little quirks of computers is that they do pre-cisely as you instruct it, and this very same specificity could cause problems. This is not an issue with duotone files you have converted to CMYK and saved in Scitex CT format as long as you remember to use magenta as your sec-ond color. To check your colors for consistency:

1. **In Photoshop with your duotone file open, choose Mode> Duotone.**

2. **When the Duotone Options dialog box opens, write down the color names exactly as listed** *(Figure 19.3)*.

As I mentioned earlier, it is important that Black be listed as just that: *Black*, with a capital B and no spaces, periods, or other embellishments.

3. In QuarkXPress, choose Edit> Colors... .

4. The Pantone Warm Gray 7 CV color used in this example should show up in the list of the Colors *(Figure 19.21)*.

5. Click on Edit to check the full name as listed in QuarkXPress *(Figure 19.21)*. The name should match, provided your General Preferences in Photoshop is set for Short PANTONE Names *(Figure 19.22)*. If the ink color name in Quark does not match the name exactly as you noted it from the Photoshop Duotone Options dialog box, enter Warm Gray 7 in the PANTONE No. field *(Figure 19.23)*.

6. While you are checking the color name in the Edit Color dialog box of QuarkXPress, put your pointer on the Screen Values pop-up menu and change the selection to Magenta *(Figure 19.23)*.

    This will ensure that the screen angle for your duotone color comes out as the 75° you want. Changing this item isn't absolutely necessary, since you will have specified on the order form to your service provider that 75° is what you want for this color. But—in the unlikely event they overlook that instruction, the screen angle could come out wrong, at 45° for example, which would require new film being made. Technically this would be your service provider's mistake and it wouldn't cost you extra, but it could cost you time. Think of this change as insurance.

5. Make sure that the Process Separation checkbox in the Edit Color dialog box is unchecked and click OK *(Figure 19.23)*.

## If Your Duotone Color Name Is Not on the List...

When you place your duotone image in QuarkXPress, your duotone color name will automatically turn up on the color list provided you are using a recent version of the program. In the event that your duotone color did not end up on Quark's list of colors, you will need to add it as follows:

1. Choose Edit> Colors... .

2. When the Colors dialog box opens, click on the New button *(Figure 19.21)*.

3. In the Edit Colors dialog box, type Warm Gray 7 in the lower right corner field for PANTONE No. *(Figure 19.23)*.

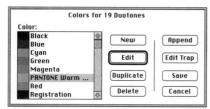

*Figure 19.21* Colors list.

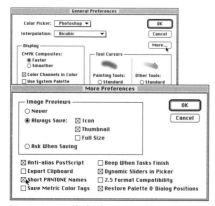

*Figure 19.22* Click Short PANTONE Names.

4. Change the color to Magenta in the **Screen Values** pop-up menu to designate a 75° screen angle for this color and click OK or press Return.

## Why All the Fuss over Color Names?

Seems like an awful lot of trouble, but the reason to be concerned has to do with your purse strings. If your Photoshop Black ink color name is **PANTONE Process Black CV** and you are using just plain old **Black** as a QuarkXPress color, you would get two black films, which is not what you want—it's especially not what you want when you have to pay extra for it.

Likewise, if your Quark document uses the Warm Gray 7 as a spot color somewhere in addition to the duotone second color, you will get two Warm Gray 7 films if there is the slightest variation in names.

Be sure that this checkbox remains unchecked.

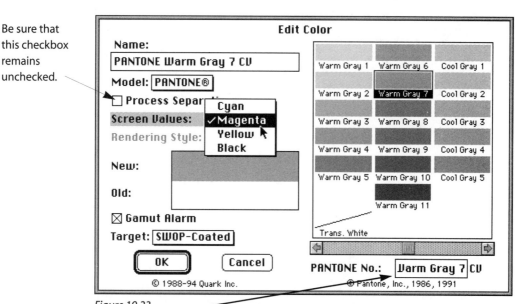

*Figure 19.23*
Enter Warm Gray 7, and change Screen Values to Magenta.

## *Insurance*

No matter how careful you are, there's always the chance that you might over-look something as you prepare your files to send to the service provider. As an insurance measure, it's a good idea to specify exactly what films you are expecting in the "Special Instructions" area of your service provider's order form. This way your service provider will have the opportunity to correct for any error or oversight you may have made before running the job.

# PAGE PLACEMENT 20

If you're planning to combine your images with text, create a layout with multiple images, and have more than a single page, you will want to import your files into a page layout program such as QuarkXPress for printing.

The goal of this chapter is to get you up and running with a simple Quark document containing both text and pictures, and to run through a few basic techniques with a nuts-and-bolts mini-tutorial covering:

- **Creating a new document**
- **Selection tools**
- **Creating text and picture boxes**
- **Deleting boxes**
- **Adding and deleting pages**
- **Moving around in your document**
- **Making your pictures behave**
- **Runaround text**
- **Colors**
- **Text over a picture**
- **White text on black background**
- **Text inset**
- **Alignment**
- **Printing**
- **Trapping**
- **Getting Bonged**

QuarkXPress is a very capable and complex application requiring years of experience to become aware of all its intricacies. Even to begin to use it, you should buy a couple of books on the subject to use as a reference in addition to the documentation that came with it. If you are new to the program and serious about EDP (Electronic Document Preparation), don't try to figure it out by noodling around—you'll never get to the bottom of it.

# When to Use QuarkXPress

You should use QuarkXPress if:

- **Your work has multiple individual images to be arranged together.**

- **Your document is more than a single page.**

- **You use type that is not imbedded in the image.**

If you are a digital or electronic artist who exhibits individual images or exports images to multimedia applications, much of your work may fall outside of these three conditions. If, on the other hand, you do any kind of graphic design, professionally or otherwise, you won't get very far without learning a program like QuarkXPress.

## *Why Can't Photoshop Handle It?*

Clearly Photoshop does a great job of processing images, but the minute any more than a few words are involved you bump into the limitations of a bitmapped or raster type of program which renders typographic characters with a grid of pixels instead of using an object-oriented or vector approach (see Chapter Two: *Resolution & File Size*). Programs like Quark excel at managing huge quantities of text in an object-oriented format, creating crisp, clean typographic characters at any size. Photoshop has almost no word processing, few typographic controls, and doesn't know from more than one page. When your work exceeds the single page, it's time to move to Quark, which was conceived just for the purpose of managing many pages with lots of text and graphics. Most books, magazines, brochures, and pamphlets are put together using QuarkXPress.

# Mini-Tutorial

The best way to begin and run through a few of the basics is to create a new document in Quark and combine some text and a few pictures as an exercise. For this mini-tutorial you'll need some sample text and at least one picture file saved in EPS, TIFF, or PICT format.

## *Open a New Document*

With QuarkXPress running:

1. Create a new document by choosing **File**> **New**, or type ⌘ N. In the New Document dialog box you have the opportunity to specify page size, margins, and facing pages *(Figure 20.1)*.

2. Click on the U.S. Letter radio button, and enter margins of 1 in. all around.

3. The Column Guides area in the upper right of the New Document dialog box is for creating text boxes with multiple columns. The gutter width field sets the space between columns and is irrelevant unless you enter a number greater than 1 in the Columns field. For now, just leave the default 1 in the Columns field.

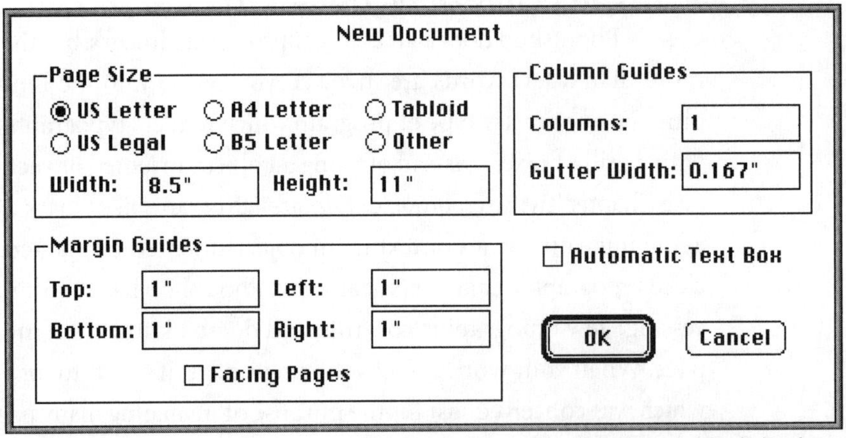

```
┌──────────────────────────────────────────────────────────────┐
│                         New Document                           │
│  ┌─Page Size────────────────────────┐ ┌─Column Guides────────┐ │
│  │ ◉ US Letter  ○ A4 Letter ○ Tabloid│ │                      │ │
│  │ ○ US Legal   ○ B5 Letter ○ Other  │ │ Columns:    [  1  ]  │ │
│  │ Width: [ 8.5" ]  Height: [ 11" ]  │ │ Gutter Width:[0.167"]│ │
│  └───────────────────────────────────┘ └──────────────────────┘ │
│  ┌─Margin Guides──────────────────┐    ☐ Automatic Text Box     │
│  │ Top:    [ 1" ]  Left:  [ 1" ]  │                             │
│  │ Bottom: [ 1" ]  Right: [ 1" ]  │    ┌────────┐  ┌────────┐   │
│  │        ☐ Facing Pages          │    │   OK   │  │ Cancel │   │
│  └────────────────────────────────┘    └────────┘  └────────┘   │
└──────────────────────────────────────────────────────────────┘
```

*Figure 20.1*                                    New Document dialog box.

4. The Facing Pages checkbox is for creating documents with a left and right page for printing on both sides. Leave this box unchecked for the purposes of this exercise.

5. The Automatic Text Box checkbox will place a text box inside the margin guides you specified. Leave this box unchecked for now.

6. Click OK, or press Return.

A new document will open at 100% view, and if your monitor is 17 in. or smaller, you won't see the entire page. Type ⌘ 0 (fit in window) to see the entire page.

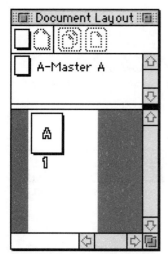

Figure 20.2
Document Layout Palette.

QuarkXPress like Photoshop, uses floating palettes for the tool box and to adjust important attributes of files such as color and document layout. Make sure that you have a Tools, Document Layout, and Measurements Palette open *(Figures 20.2, 20.3, 20.4)*. If these three palettes don't appear with your new document choose **View> Show Tools, Document Layout,** and **Measurements**.

## Tools

I'll describe only the four tools of the Tools Palette *(Figure 20.3)* you'll be using for this exercise, one at a time.

The top tool is the Item tool ⊕. It is used for selecting items (boxes) and moving them around on the page. You need to have this tool selected to select more than one box at a time (by holding the Shift key and clicking on boxes one at at time). With multiple boxes selected you can group (⌘G) and ungroup (⌘U) them using the Item menu. You can also move boxes all the way to the front or back (or forward and backward only one layer if the Option key is depressed) of all other items by selecting an item (click once on it) and using the Item menu. With this tool selected you can't edit the content of either a text box or a picture box—you can only move it around.

The second tool from the top is the Content tool ✋. The Content tool is used for editing text or graphics *inside* the boxes. You can't move the boxes on the page with this tool selected.`

You use the Text Box tool 𝐀 to create text boxes and the Picture Box tools ⊠ to create picture boxes (no surprises here).

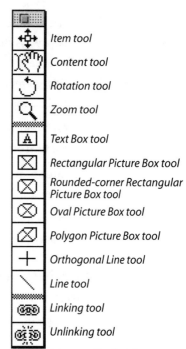

Figure 20.3        Tools Palette.

| | |
|---|---|
| ⊕ | Item tool |
| ✋ | Content tool |
| ↻ | Rotation tool |
| 🔍 | Zoom tool |
| 𝐀 | Text Box tool |
| ⊠ | Rectangular Picture Box tool |
| ⊗ | Rounded-corner Rectangular Picture Box tool |
| ⊗ | Oval Picture Box tool |
| ⊠ | Polygon Picture Box tool |
| + | Orthogonal Line tool |
| ╲ | Line tool |
| ⊙⊙⊙ | Linking tool |
| ⊙⊙⊙ | Unlinking tool |

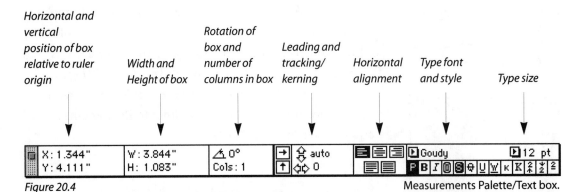

*Horizontal and vertical position of box relative to ruler origin*   *Width and Height of box*   *Rotation of box and number of columns in box*   *Leading and tracking/ kerning*   *Horizontal alignment*   *Type font and style*   *Type size*

*Figure 20.4*                                                    Measurements Palette/Text box.

## Create a Text Box

In order to get text into QuarkXPress, you must first create an empty text box and then either type in text or copy it from somewhere else and paste it in. You can also copy and paste boxes with text already in them from other Quark documents using the Item tool. To create a text box:

1. Select the Text Box tool in the Tools Palette.

2. Move your cursor to the document window and click and drag out a text box that is 6.5 in. wide and 9 in. high. Don't worry about getting the size exact; you can always change the size of either text or picture boxes later. Once you draw your text box you can select either the height or width field in the Measurements Palette *(Figure 20.4)*, enter an exact number, and press Return or click once anywhere on the page.

   You'll notice that your new box will snap to your margin guides—a feature you can turn off in the **View** menu.

3. Enter some *greeking* (sample) or other text in your text box so you have some words to work with.

   Take a good look at the Measurements Palette *(Figure 20.4)* and notice that much of what you need to control text is available there.

## Create a Picture Box

Create a picture box anywhere on your page on top of your text box:

1. Select the rectangular Picture Box tool in the Tools palette.

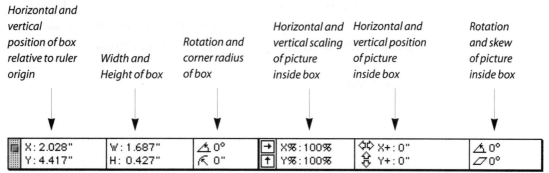

*Horizontal and vertical position of box relative to ruler origin*

*Width and Height of box*

*Rotation and corner radius of box*

*Horizontal and vertical scaling of picture inside box*

*Horizontal and vertical position of picture inside box*

*Rotation and skew of picture inside box*

*Figure 20.5*            Measurements Palette/Picture box.

2. Move your cursor to the document window and click and drag out a picture box that is 4 in. wide and 5 in. high. Again, don't worry about getting the size exact; you can always change the size of the box after you draw it. If you need to, select either the height or width field in the Measurements Palette *(Figure 20.5)*, enter an exact number, and press Return or click once anywhere on the page. Note that the Measurements Palette changes depending on whether you have a text or a picture box selected.

3. To put a picture in the box you just created, with the box selected (click once on it) and the Content tool selected, choose **File**> **Get Picture** or type ⌘E.

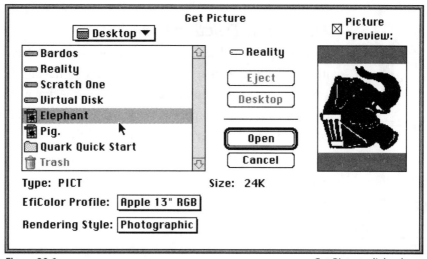

*Figure 20.6*            Get Picture dialog box.

You will get a dialog box asking you what picture you want to place in the box *(Figure 20.6)*. Locate the EPS, TIFF, or PICT image file you want to place and either click once on it to select it, then click Open, or double-click on it.

## Deleting Boxes

To delete either a text box or a picture box, with the box selected, type ⌘K if you're in either the Item or the Content tool. The Delete key will only work with the Item tool selected. If you're bored and want to see and hear a little space man 🏃 march across your screen and blast the box to smithereens, type ⌘ ⌦ ⇧ K with either the Item or Content tool selected.

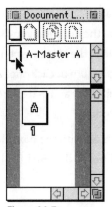
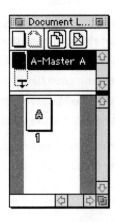
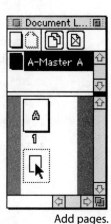

*Figure 20.7*                                        Add pages.

## Adding and Deleting Pages

*Figure 20.8*
Delete pages.

To add pages or delete existing pages, choose **Page> Insert** or **Page> Delete**. It's easier to add individual pages by having the Document Layout Palette open and dragging a master page down to the page layout area in the bottom part of the palette *(Figure 20.7)*. If you need to add ten pages, it's easier to use the Page menu.

To delete pages with the Document Layout Palette, click once on the page you want to delete (shift click on multiple pages) and click on the delete page icon in the top portion of the palette *(Figure 20.8)*.

You can also use the Document Layout Palette to rearrange the pages in your document by dragging a page to a new location within the page sequence.

## Moving Around in Your Document

To get from one place to another, from page 2 to page 6, for example, just double-click on the page you want to go to in the Document Layout palette, page 6 in this case. If you have hundreds of pages in your document, it's easier to choose **Page: Go to...**, or type ⌘J, and enter the page number you want to go to *(Figure 20.9)*, rather than scrolling to a distant page in the Document Layout Palette.

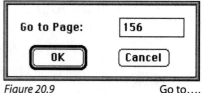

*Figure 20.9*                    Go to....

## Making Your Picture Behave

When your picture opens, it may be cropped in a way you didn't intend, or look a bit scrappy since it is only a low resolution preview. Don't despair—Quark will do just about anything you need to do in terms of managing size, shape, or proportion.

Here are a few pointers:

If your picture is 8 x 10 in. and the box you made is 4 x 5 in., guess what—it won't fit. To cure this mismatch you have three options:

1. **Change your box to the size you want either by dragging on any of its handles and watching the Width and Height fields of the Measurements Palette *(Figure 20.10)*, or by entering the correct size in the Width and Height fields of the Measurements Palette *(Figure 20.5)* and pressing Return.**

2a. **Tell Quark to fit the picture into the box you made by typing ⌘ ⌥ ⇧ F. Note that this command instructs Quark to make the picture as large as possible within the box without distorting it (assuming a shape discrepancy between box and picture). This is usually what you want to have happen *(Figure 20.11)*.**

2b. **If you want your picture to conform to the box shape and become distorted from its original shape type, ⌘ ⇧ F *(Figure 20.12)*.**

You can rotate or skew your picture *(Figures 20.13 and 20.14)* using the Measurements Palette (far right fields), or with the Picture Box Specifications

dialog box by choosing **Item>
Modify...** (*Figure 20.15*). The Picture
Box Specifications dialog box gives you
other options such as altering the *box*
angle, skew, corner radius, and color.
You can also use the Rotation tool (third
from top) in the Tool Palette.

*Figure 20.10*          Drag box handles.

## Runaround

When you created your picture box on
top of the text box, your picture box
pushed the text aside. This is called the
Runaround function in Quark, and it
happens by default because it's usually
what you want to happen (instead of the
picture covering up the text). However,
it usually doesn't look very good to have
the text right up to the edge of the box
with only the 1 point default space. You
can control how close the text gets to the
sides of the picture box with the
Runaround dialog box *(Figure 20.16)*.
Choose **Item> Runaround...** or type
⌘T to access this dialog box.

*Figure 20.11*          Fit picture to box—
not distortion: ⌘⇧ F.

*Figure 20.12*          Fit picture to box—
distort: ⌘⇧ F.

To see how this works, select the Item
tool and drag your picture box to the
right side of your page. Switch to the
Content tool, type ⌘T, enter 20 in the
Top, Left, and Bottom fields and click
OK. The text will now stay 20 points
away from the edges of the picture box.

QuarkXPress will not run around both
sides of a box.

*Figure 20.13*          Rotate.

*Figure 20.14*          Picture skew.0

**Picture Box Specifications**

| | | | |
|---|---|---|---|
| Origin Across: | 1.118" | Scale Across: | 66.8% |
| Origin Down: | 7.357" | Scale Down: | 66.8% |
| Width: | 2.125" | Offset Across: | 0.028" |
| Height: | 0.937" | Offset Down: | 0" |
| Box Angle: | 0° | Picture Angle: | 0° |
| Box Skew: | 0° | Picture Skew: | 0° |
| Corner Radius: | 0" | | |

─Background─
Color: [White]
Shade: ▶ 100%

☐ Suppress Picture Printout
☐ Suppress Printout

[ OK ]  [ Cancel ]

*Figure 20.15*　　Picture Box Specifications.

You can also allow the picture box to cover up the text without pushing it aside by changing the Runaround mode from Item to None in the Mode pop-up option *(Figure 20.17)*.

## Colors

You can change the color of your type, the text box background, a box frame (choose **Item> Frame** or type ⌘B) if you made one, or the picture if it was saved in TIFF or Pict format. Choose **Style> Colors,** or choose **View> Show Colors** to display the Colors Palette *(Figure 20.18)*.

With a box selected, to change the color of frame, text, or background, first select the appropriate icon in the top section of the Colors Palette, and then click once on the name of the color you want (click on the *word*, not the color swatch). Alternatively, you can drag the color swatch to the box you want to alter and drop it (release the mouse button).

To create new colors or use a color matching system such as PANTONE, Command-click on the currently selected color *name* in the Colors Palette and the Colors dialog box will open.

### Text over a Picture

One of the most important "colors" in the Colors Palette is None. When you want to have text over a picture and not show the text box itself:

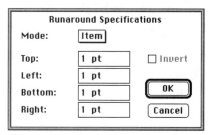

**Runaround Specifications**
Mode: [Item]
Top: 1 pt      ☐ Invert
Left: 1 pt
Bottom: 1 pt   [ OK ]
Right: 1 pt    [ Cancel ]

*Figure 20.16*　　Runaround Item.

**Runaround Specifications**
Mode: [None]
Top:        ☐ Invert
Left:
Bottom:    [ OK ]
Right:     [ Cancel ]

*Figure 20.17*　　Runaround None.

*Select frame color*     *Select text color*     *Select back- ground color*

Figure 20.18          Colors Palette.

1. Create a small text box on top of your picture and type a word or two into it *(Figure 20.19)*.

2. With your text box selected, click once on the background icon at the top of the Colors Palette, then click once on the word *None* in the Colors Palette *(Figure 20.20)*.

3. You won't see the result until you deselect your text box by clicking once anywhere on the page, preferably in the border so that you don't unintentionally select another box.

4. To see the full effect of your efforts, hide the Guides by choosing **View**> **Hide Guides** or type F7 if you have an extended keyboard *(Figure 20.21)*.

## White Text on Black Background

There are many occasions when you may want to change the color of your text to white (or any other color) over a black (or any other color) background as in the typical *knockout* type. To accomplish this:

1. In your sample document, create a small text box and type a few words into it, or use the box on top of your picture. Select your text box *and* select the text within the text box by typing ⌘A (select all). You can also select the text by dragging the I-beam cursor over it *(Figure 20.22)*.

2. With the Text icon in the top portion of the Colors Palette selected, click once on the word White. Don't panic when the text disappears—it should, since you will now have white text on a white background *(Figure 20.23)*.

3. In the top portion of the Colors Palette change the selected icon to Background and click once on the word Black *(Figure 20.24)*.

Figure 20.19                              Hungry Pig.

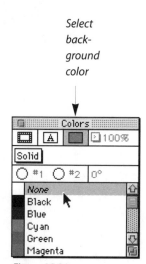

*Select back-ground color*

Figure 20.20

Figure 20.21                      Hungry Pig: final version.

4. Deselect the box by clicking once in the border of your document, step back, and admire your work *(Figure 20.25)*.

## *Text Inset*

In the likely event that you don't want your text hugging the edges of your text box as in Figure 20.25, you have two options. The first is to use the text inset control.

1. With your white-text-on-black-background box selected, choose **Item> Modify...** (or type ⌘M) to display the Text Box Specifications dialog box *(Figure 20.26)*.

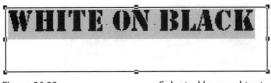

*Figure 20.22*                    Selected box and text.

*Select text
color*

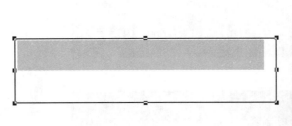

*Figure 20.23*                    Change text color to white.

*Select back-
ground color*

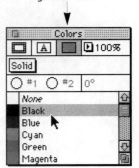

*Figure 20.24*                    Change background
color to black.

*Figure 20.25*                    Completed change.

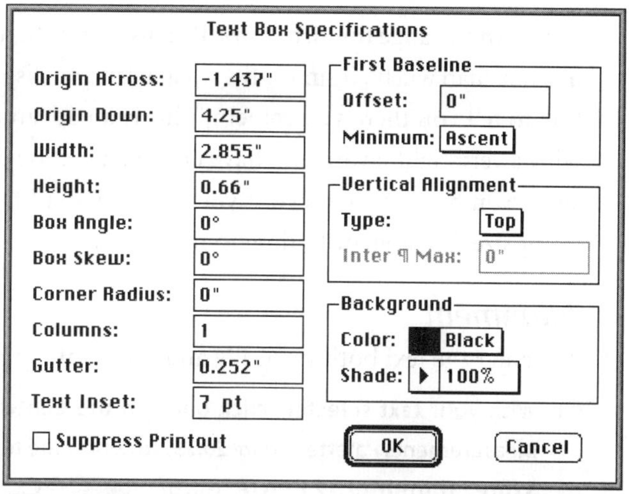

*Figure 20.26*                                    Text Box Specifications.

2. Enter 7 in the Text Inset field. You don't have to type in pt or points.

3. Click OK or press Return, and all text will stay at least 7 points away from all four inside edges of your text box *(Figure 20.27)*.

Okay, the result in Figure 20.27 isn't really what you had in mind—you want the text centered perfectly in the box. Keep the Text Inset embedded somewhere in your memory banks, since there are many occasions such as this box, where it's just the thing. Horizontally centered alignment wouldn't work here because this paragraph is already set for justified alignment.

*Figure 20.27*                    7 pt text inset.

*Figure 20.28*                    Overflow indicator.

If instead of a result like the one in Figure 20.27, you are left with only a portion of your type and the overflow indicator (small checkbox) in the lower right of your text box *(Figure 20.28)*, it means that for the amount of Text Inset you entered, the type will no longer fit in the box. This illustrates one of the beauties of QuarkXPress: it will not change the size of your boxes unless you change the size yourself. This means that if you try to put more in a box than will fit, it simply fits what it can and displays the overflow check-box to tell you there's a problem. This is an advantage if you are working with a very tight layout and have created a text box that occupies the only space you have for the text. If your text doesn't fit, you'll have to alter the point size, kerning, or leading to make it fit.

## Alignment

To center the text both vertically and horizontally, proceed as follows:

1. **With your text selected, click once on the Center Alignment icon in the Measurements Palette *(Figure 20.29)* to center the text horizontally, or choose**
   **Style> Alignment> Centered, or type ⌘ ⇧ C.**

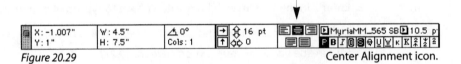

*Figure 20.29*                                                                        Center Alignment icon.

2. **Type ⌘ M to display the Text Box Specifications dialog box, and select Centered from the Vertical Alignment Type pop-up *(Figure 20.30)*. While you're there, change the Text Inset field to 0 so it doesn't conflict with your new instruc-tions. Click OK or press Return. The result should resemble the illustration in Figure 20.31.**

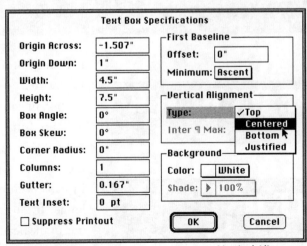

*Figure 20.30*                                                                        Vertical Alignment.

If your text is too high or low in the box, use the Baseline shift control under the Style menu to adjust it.

*Figure 20.31*   Horizontally and vertically centered text.

# Printing from QuarkXPress

Printing files combining complex text and graphics can be a struggle for any application, especially if the files have dozens or hundreds of pages and contain high resolution bitmapped files. I don't mean to be making excuses for when things go wrong, but they often do, which brings me to the next topic: backup.

## *Back Up Your Backup*

There's an old joke about computing that goes something like: "There are only two kinds of computer users: those who have lost files due to corruption or crashes and those who are about to." Like most jokes, this one contains more than a little truth.

Before you even think of sending off your only copy of a document to a printer or service bureau, back it up. The list of possible tragedies that could befall a disk you allow to leave your immediate possession is too long and obvious to even begin. Having a copy on your hard drive really isn't good enough—you should back it up on some type of removable media in addition to having a copy on your hard drive (and in addition to the copy you are sending to the service provider).

First of all, hard drives go soft. Every now and then, not that often, but enough to make you nervous, hard drives simply quit. Be especially cautious for the first few weeks of using a new drive—it can fail in a way that makes the data irretrievable even for wizards with sophisticated tools.

Second, your computer could get damaged or one of your precocious children could decide to reformat it for you at 4:30 A.M. (by accident, of course). The more important the document, the more urgent the need to back it up (a couple of times). Remember the celestial law governing the likelihood of a failure: the chances increase in direct proportion to the importance and urgency of a document.

If a file is totally unimportant, you can be confident that it will never fail. Even though you saved it on a damaged disk and ran it through a metal detector that ruined 12 rolls of film (kept in a lead-lined pouch)—the unimportant file will be fine. You'll probably find extra copies of it years after you thought you finally disposed of it.

## Linkage

The sooner you get a hold of this concept the happier you'll be working with any page layout program. When you import any picture file into QuarkXPress using the Get Picture command described earlier, Quark doesn't suck up the file and swallow it whole (except for PICT files, which is a good reason not to use large PICT files, since they will bloat your Quark document). It's too smart for that. It only takes a low resolution preview that is part of the bitmapped image file and creates a *link* to the parent high resolution file.

This link tells Quark where the parent file is located, last date of modification, file format, size and shape of the picture, color information, and other details. When you work with the placed picture—the preview you see in your picture box—Quark is only manipulating the low resolution preview and taking notes (to itself) about what you are doing. When you change the scale, cropping, shape, or anything else about the preview you see on your monitor, Quark the note taker is there. It knows exactly what page you placed it on, in exactly what position, and what its relationship is to all the other elements on the page, and it leaves it at that—until the time comes when you press ⌘P to print the document.

When you print, Quark gets out its notebook and runs down the list of pictures you placed in the document. If any of the original parent pictures files got thrown away, or moved, or if you opened one again in Photoshop and

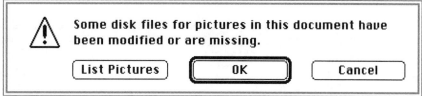

*Figure 20.32*                                                        Missing alert.

made a change, instead of printing you will get a bong and a box alerting you to the fact that there is something missing or modified *(Figure 20.32)*.

Now you have three choices: **Cancel**, to go get a cup of coffee and consider your next move; **OK**, to ignore Quark's concern and print anyway (this option will use the low resolution previews in place of the missing pictures); and **List Pictures**.

If you choose *List Pictures*, Quark will show you a list of the problem pictures *(Figure 20.33)*. Click on any item in the list to select it (or hold the Shift key down and drag over the entire list to select all) and click on Update. Next

| Name | Page | Type | Status | Print |
|------|------|------|--------|-------|
| Bardos : Illustrations :Head.grayscale | 1 | EPS | Missing | √ |
| Bardos : Illustrations :Head.grayscale | 2 | EPS | Missing | √ |
| Bardos :20 Page Placement :Document Layout | 4 | PICT | Modified | √ |
| Bardos :20 Page Placement :New document | 4 | PICT | Modified | √ |

**Missing/Modified Pictures**

Update    Show Me    OK    Cancel

*Figure 20.33*                                List of Missing/Modified Pictures.

you will get a dialog box with the problem picture noted at the top, and essentially saying, "Okay, you lost the picture, now show me where it went so we can get on with this printing" *(Figure 20.34)*.

You will then proceed to locate the missing file so that it shows up in the list. Once you find it, you either double-click on it, or click once on it to select it and then click Open. If you selected all the problem pictures in the previous dialog box, Quark will automatically give you a new "Find…" dialog box asking you to locate the next missing picture. If more than one of the

Missing picture

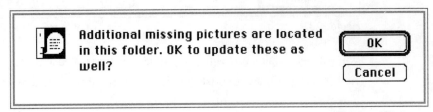

Find "Head.grayscale"

⊟ Picture
  Preview:

▦ Desktop ▼

◻ Bardos
◉ PCD2287
◻ Reality
◻ Scratch One
◻ Virtual Disk
▣ Head.grayscale
▢ Quark Quick Start
🗑 Trash

◻ Reality

[ Eject ]

[ Desktop ]

( Open )

( Cancel )

Type: EPS                    Size: 122K

EfiColor Profile: –

Rendering Style: –

Figure 20.34                                            Find....

missing pictures happens to be in the same folder as the first one you identified, Quark will notice that and give you a dialog box asking you if it's Okay to update all of them *(Figure 20.35)*. Click OK if it is, and the print operation will proceed. Save the file after printing to avoid repeating the exercise of locating your missing pictures.

To check picture linkage before printing, you can look at the Picture Usage utility (choose **Utility> Picture Usage...** ) which works the same way as the missing picture dialogs you get when you print *(Figure 20.36)*. Click on the

**Additional missing pictures are located in this folder. OK to update these as well?**

( OK )

[ Cancel ]

Figure 20.35                                     Additional Pictures.

Close box in the upper left of the Picture Usage dialog box when you have located all the problem files.

As you can see from all of this, Quark is quite serious about linkage, and if you fail to locate a missing picture, Quark will print the low resolution preview. This can be an expensive mistake, unless you are just printing a proof from your laser printer, since the low resolution preview is a long way from reproduction quality. Needless to say, the film, if that's what you had made, will be useless. Usually, your service provider will not go forward if pictures

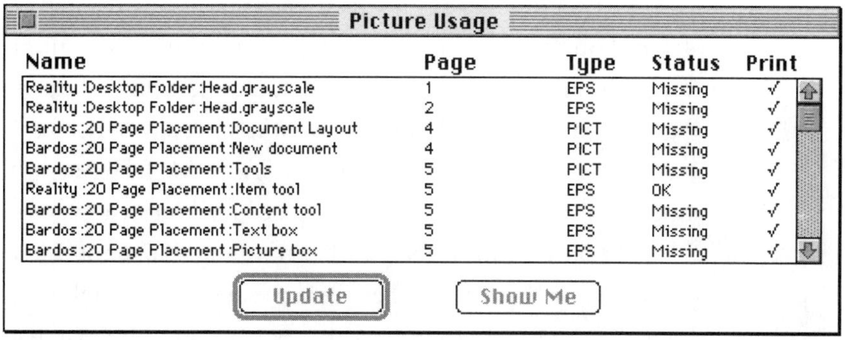

| Name | Page | Type | Status | Print |
|------|------|------|--------|-------|
| Reality :Desktop Folder :Head.grayscale | 1 | EPS | Missing | √ |
| Reality :Desktop Folder :Head.grayscale | 2 | EPS | Missing | √ |
| Bardos :20 Page Placement :Document Layout | 4 | PICT | Missing | √ |
| Bardos :20 Page Placement :New document | 4 | PICT | Missing | √ |
| Bardos :20 Page Placement :Tools | 5 | PICT | Missing | √ |
| Reality :20 Page Placement :Item tool | 5 | EPS | OK | √ |
| Bardos :20 Page Placement :Content tool | 5 | EPS | Missing | √ |
| Bardos :20 Page Placement :Text box | 5 | EPS | Missing | √ |
| Bardos :20 Page Placement :Picture box | 5 | EPS | Missing | √ |

Picture Usage. Update. Show Me.

*Figure 20.36*                                                    Picture Usage.

are missing and will give you the opportunity to repair the problem. This still represents time and expense in coming up with the little orphans and getting them to the service provider where they belong.

As a safeguard against broken linkages, you should always print out a proof copy of your file on your laser printer to make sure everything is set to go. Most service providers require hard copy of the file to help them keep everything straight, and to check against in case of questions they might have about position and other details.

## *Trapping*

Trapping is a term used to describe what happens when one ink is printed on top of another. In the graphic arts it has two related definitions. First, it describes an aspect of presswork where printing on a multicolor press requires wet ink to print on top of wet ink as the paper travels through the press with only fractions of a second between impressions. This is known as *wet trapping* and the issues related to this include maintaining a decreasing *ink tack* (stickiness) so that the ink printed first will have a higher tack allowing subsequent inks to stick to it, or be *trapped* by it.

Second, the word *trapping* is used to describe the amount of overlap between two adjacent colors, and this is the definition important to designers and the one we will discuss here. To understand why some overlap is necessary, it is important to realize that with the exception of black, the inks generally used in offset lithography are transparent. This means that you can't simply print one color on top of another without the colors interacting. When you print blue ink on top of red, for example, you end up with purple. If you want to end up with blue *surrounded by* red, you need to knock a hole in the red where the blue will print *(Figure C.19)*. Here is where trapping issues come into play: it is the size of the knockout relative to the size of the element that fits into it that is what trapping is all about. One color must *spread* over or *choke* under the other so that there is a slight overlap between them. This *trap* is necessary because paper is not dimensionally stable and its size is susceptible to change relative to the humidity of the pressroom and the slight amount of moisture and "squeeze" it encounters while traveling through the press. This means that an absolutely perfect fit between two graphic elements on the press sheet that should match up is almost impossible to achieve. Other factors such as the press's ability to register between colors also affect the degree of precision with which colors fit together.

With some notable limitations, QuarkXPress will automatically trap the colors in your document very effectively *(Figure C.24)*. When sending a document to a service provider to be imaged, be sure to specify that you want to retain your trap preferences. This is important since some service providers will turn off the trap preferences you set (leaving you with no trap) unless you specify that you want to keep them. Quark's default trap setting is a weeny .144 point which I usually change to .2 point for multicolor presses. I use a larger trap of about .25 point for single color presses printing documents with more than one color and where trapping is an issue. Because trapping requirements will vary from press to press and paper stocks, check with your printer before setting the trap preferences to find out what she prefers for the particular job at hand.

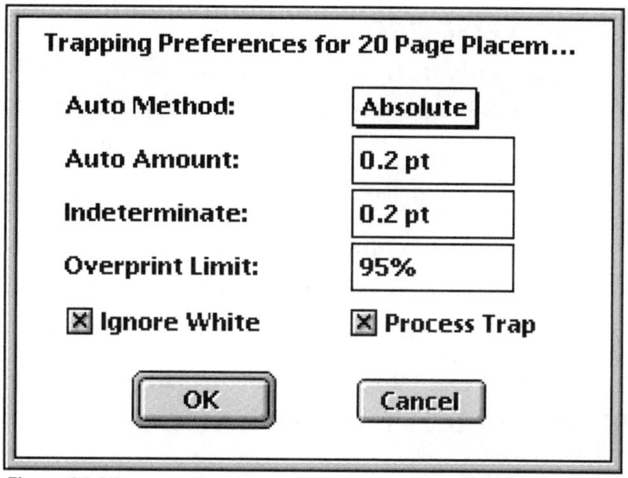

**Trapping Preferences for 20 Page Placem...**

| | |
|---|---|
| Auto Method: | Absolute |
| Auto Amount: | 0.2 pt |
| Indeterminate: | 0.2 pt |
| Overprint Limit: | 95% |

☒ Ignore White    ☒ Process Trap

[ OK ]    [ Cancel ]

*Figure 20.37*                              Trapping Preferences.

To set your trapping preferences choose **Edit> Preferences> Trapping...**. When the Trapping Preferences dialog box opens enter your preference in the Auto Amount and Indeterminate fields *(Figure 20.37)*. You can also set trapping for specific color pairs in the Edit Color dialog box. To understand more fully how this and the Trapping Preferences dialog box works, refer to your QuarkXPress documentation or other reference material. Trapping is a very esoteric subject and you will need to spend some time with it in order to get comfortable.

## What to Give Your Service Provider

When zero hour arrives and it's time to put everything together to send to your printer or service provider, you need to collect three categories of files:

1. Your QuarkXPress documents.

2. All files you have placed in QuarkXPress. This includes any Photoshop picture files in their EPS or TIFF format, and any files from other applications such as Illustrator or Freehand. Remember that PICT files get absorbed entirely, so you don't need to include those.

3. Any strange or unusual type fonts you used in any of the QuarkXPress documents. Most service providers will have the complete Adobe library of fonts, so you usually don't have to worry about including them. For fonts from other foundries, however, check with the service provider to see if you need to include them on your disk.

## Fonts (Typefaces)

Type 1 fonts are two-part affairs. The first part is the *bitmapped* file which lives in the *suitcase* and contains the image of the font that your computer needs to draw the face on your monitor. You *can't print* successfully to a PostScript printer using only this part of the font pair.

The second part of the pair is the *outline* or PostScript file. Your laser printer, imagesetter, or any PostScript printer needs the outline file to create the type you used. If you fail to send the outline file, your job will bounce.

If you use a font that you need to include with your files, make sure that you send *both* the bitmapped file and the outline file (Figure 20.38).

GALLIARD     GalliBol     GalliBollta     Gallilta     GalliRom

*Figure 20.38*     Suitcase (bitmap) and (outline) PostScript files.

## TrueType Fonts

TrueType fonts were developed jointly by Microsoft and Apple and consist of only the outline description. The monitor image for a TrueType font is created by reading the outline file and converting it to whatever bitmapped point size is called for by the monitor. Most professionals agree that the results from TrueType fonts are not as reliable for printing as those from Type 1 PostScript fonts. You will run into enough other hassles on the road to getting your work printed, so my advice is to avoid the unnecessary risk of using TrueType fonts. Also, for peace of mind and to avoid confusing your computer, never have the same font running in both TrueType and Type 1 versions at the same time.

## City Named Fonts

*Do not use city named fonts for PostScript printing —period.*

These fonts were designed to be more legible on screen and print better from low resolution QuickDraw printers. Aside from that, the fonts called New York, Geneva, and Monaco are poor cousins of the fonts Times, Helvetica, and Courier. When you print from a PostScript printer using the city named versions of these fonts, the results look terrible, since they lack the sophisticated kerning of the real thing, and half the time, the printed results vary widely from what you saw on screen.

If you are new to graphic design, typography, and EDP (Electronic Document Preparation), go to the bookstore right now (or after finishing this chapter) and buy *The Mac Is Not a Typewriter*, by Robin Williams.

## Collect for Output

There is a handy little item under the File menu called Collect for Output *(Figure 20.39)*, which will gather up all your odds and ends (except for your fonts) and put them together for you in a new folder *(Figure 20.40)*. If you

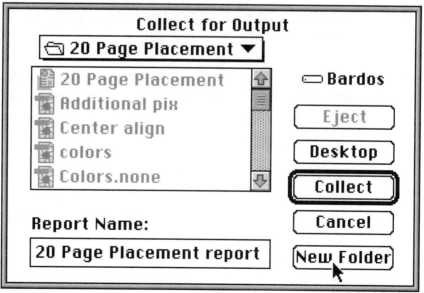

*Figure 20.39*                                                    Collect for Output.

are nervous about getting all your image files together in the same place for shipping to your service provider, this could be just the thing for you.

Collect for Output will produce a report that will list all the fonts you used in a document. It will even list the fonts that won't show up in the Font Usage utility such as the ones you used in EPS files imported from another appli-

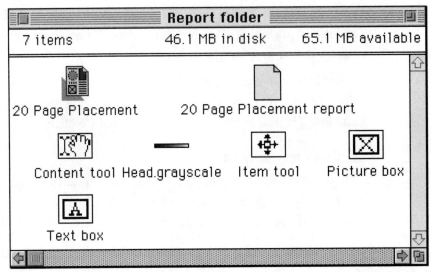

*Figure 20.40*                                Report folder.

cation or created in Quark itself. In addition to font usage, the report will detail every aspect of picture usage, which extensions you had running, as well as a host of other pertinent information for your service provider. Make an extra copy of the report and include it with your disk.

## Watch Out for Spot Colors

If you have created new colors in your document, make sure you know if they are going to be output as individual plates in addition your other plates or embedded in the four CMYK films. If your document contains pictures in CMYK format and you plan to print the job in four colors *only*, check your Colors dialog box to make certain that the Process Separation box is checked *(Figure 20.41)*. If it is not checked, Quark will output the color as

*This item can have a significant impact on your checkbook.*

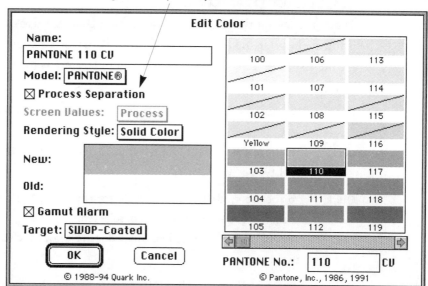

*Figure 20.41*                                                              Spot color.

an additional plate (film). This can be a very costly mistake, since it would mean remaking the film.

## Get Organized!

However you put together your files for your service provider, whether you manually collect them or use Collect for Output, make sure you keep all the picture files in the same folder with your Quark document.

Don't send off a cartridge with a whole collection of files that are not used in the particular job and that will make it unnecessarily difficult to decipher what's what. If you have other files on the disk, create a new folder and put them all into it. Name the folder something like *Not for Output*, or *Ignore This*. You should only have folders on the top level of your directory. That way it's easier to see what's going on, and the service provider doesn't have to sort through a bunch of single files.

Best yet—send a disk with *only* the material required to do the job.

# Getting Bonged

There are a few quirks in Quark that are almost guaranteed to drive you nuts if you are just starting to use the application. You won't actually get bonged for the last three, but they'll still drive you nuts. Here is the very short list along with the cures:

**Quirk:**  You get bonged when you try to delete a selected box using the Delete key.

**Cure:**  You have the Content tool selected. To delete a box with the Content tool, type ⌘K.

**Quirk:**  You get bonged when you try to delete a box using the Delete key and you *know* you have the Item tool selected.

**Cure:**  There is no box selected and Quark doesn't know which box you want to delete.

**Quirk:**  You created a picture box but you get bonged when you type ⌘E for Get Picture, or the Get Picture option is grayed out and not available.

**Cure:**  You have the wrong tool selected. Change to the Content tool and try again.

**Quirk:**  You created a picture box and when you go to the folder to open your picture it doesn't show up even though you know it's there.

**Cure:**  You saved it in the wrong format. A picture must be in EPS, TIFF, or PICT to import into QuarkXPress. Open the picture again in Photoshop and choose **File> Save a copy** and change the format in the pop-up menu before you click OK.

**Quirk:**  You created a text box on top of a picture and changed the background to None in the Colors Palette but nothing happened.

**Cure:**  Deselect the box by clicking in the border of your document and the picture box background will disappear.

**Quirk:**  You created a picture box, placed a picture, and want to move the box, but instead of the box moving the picture slides around inside the box.

**Cure:**  Wrong tool. Change to the Item tool (or hold down the Command key to temporarily access the Item tool) and the whole box will move.

## *The Importance of Selection*

QuarkXPress will follow your instructions precisely, but to implement many instructions or commands, there must be a selected box or selected text so that Quark will know where and how to apply your command. You will very quickly develop the habit of noticing what is selected and what isn't.

In the case of text, Quark works like most applications: the text is selected when it is highlighted.

In the case of either text boxes or picture boxes, the box is selected when its handles are visible *(Figure 20.42)*.

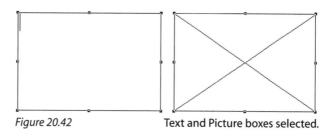

*Figure 20.42*                 Text and Picture boxes selected.

Making CMYK color separations for processes other than offset lithography, such as photo-etching, photo-collagraph *(Figure C.20)*, photo-woodblock, and photo-silkscreen printing *(Figure C.21)*, requires a distinctly different setup for the Printing Inks and Separation Setup Preferences. The amount of ink the sheet will hold, the ink colors, and the shape and frequency of "dot" you print will vary from the requirements of offset. Using Photoshop's diffusion dither bitmap mode is a very effective method of imaging your separations for these processes. A resolution of between 60 and 100 ppi is usually the maximum you will be able to print.

You can get good results using separations on paper directly from your laser printer. Once you have the four separations on ordinary laser printer paper, you can use them to expose the photo-emulsion in silkscreen as though they were transparent positives. If you need enlargements, you can have your separations blown up by giant size copiers available in some copy shops. Another option for bigness is to print from your laser printer but tile your separations using QuarkXPress, which will produce multiple prints that you can put together to form one larger print. Separations on paper may suffer from imprecise fit due to the dimensional instability of the paper, which will be aggravated with increasing size. If you need perfect fit, you can have positive films made by an imagesetter.

## Printing Inks Setup

Before making the conversion from RGB to CMYK, you should obtain samples of the inks you are planning to use to make the prints. If you don't have printed samples of the inks you'll be using, a simple draw-down or tap-out (ink from the can spread thinly with an ink knife or tapped out with your finger to a thin film) on the paper you plan to print on will do for the purposes of adjusting the ink patches in the Ink Colors dialog box. The inks used for printmaking may vary significantly from those used in offset printing, so the step of customizing your ink colors is an important one (see Chapter Eighteen: *Managing Color*).

After adjusting the ink patches, you may want to consider using a dot gain of about 30% for these printmaking processes, but you'll really need to have a proof (an image you have separated and printed using the paper, ink, and printing process you intend to use) to compare to your monitor before you can make an informed decision.

## Separation Setup

Since your separations will not be printed on multicolor presses, there is no need to be concerned with having too much ink on the sheet. This means that you can turn off the undercolor removal or gray component replacement in the Separation Setup Preferences by entering 100% in the UCA Amount field and crank up the Total Ink Limit to the maximum of 400% (*Figure 21.2*).

## Making Separations

1. Choose **File> Preferences> Printing Inks Setup...** and set it up to conform to Figure 21.1. Click OK.

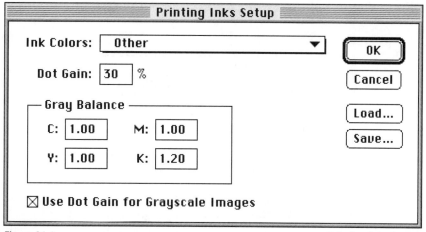

Figure 21.1                                        Printing Inks Setup.

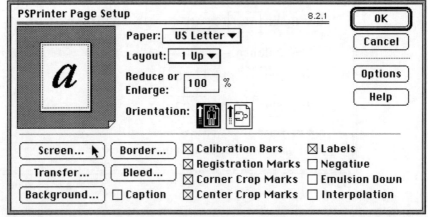

*Figure 21.2*                                                                    Separation Setup.

2. Choose **File**> **Preferences**> **Separation Setup...** and set it up to conform to Figure 21.2.

   You don't need GCR (Gray Component Replacement) for printmaking processes, and setting the UCA (Under Color Addition) Amount to 100% will turn it off. Click OK.

3. Choose **Mode**> **CMYK**.

4. At this point it would be a good idea to save your file, so choose **File**> **Save As...** and suffix the existing file name with *.CMYK*. This way you know it's the CMYK version of the RGB file.

*Be sure to choose **Save As...**, not **Save**, which will replace your original RGB file.*

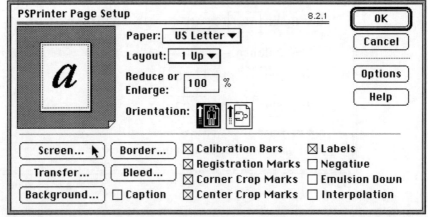

*Figure 21.3*                                                                    Page Setup.

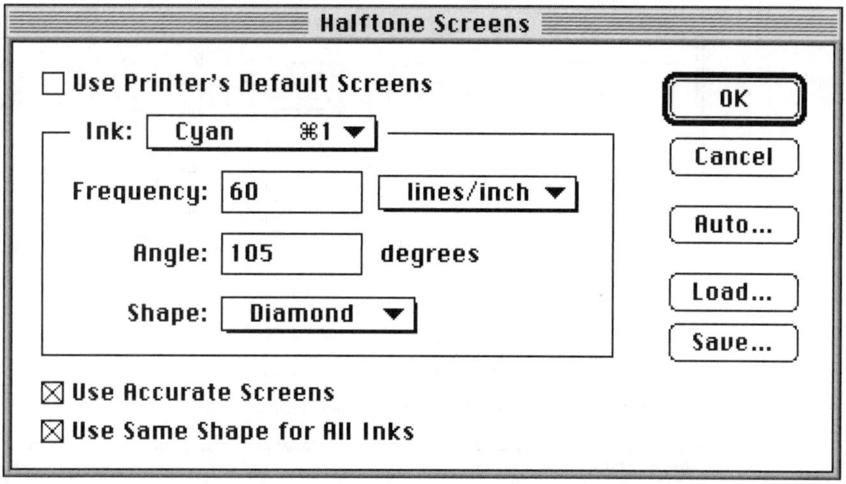

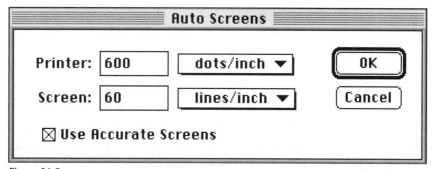

*Figure 21.4*                                                    Halftone Screens.

# Halftone Separations

You could print your separations now as halftones, or convert the files to diffusion dither bitmaps. Skip to the next section to print as diffusion dithered bitmaps. To print as halftone separations:

1. Choose **File> Page Setup...** .

2. When the Page Setup dialog box *(Figure 21.3)* opens, click on the Calibration Bars, Registration Marks, Corner Crop Marks, Center Crop Marks, and Labels checkboxes.

3. Click on the **Screen...** box. When the Halftone Screens dialog box *(Figure 21.4)* opens, click on the Auto box.

*Figure 21.5*                                                    Auto Screens.

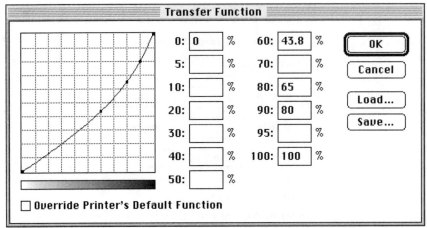

*Figure 21.6*                                                    Transfer Function.

4. When the Auto Screens dialog box opens, click on the Use Accurate Screens checkbox. Enter 600 in the Printer field and 60 in the Screen field, or whatever lpi you prefer, and click OK *(Figure 21.5)*.

   Keep in mind that if you are going to enlarge these separations 200%, the 60 lpi will become 30 lpi.

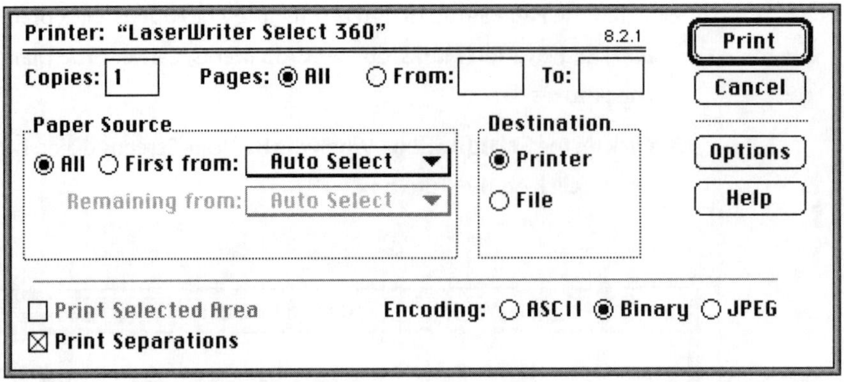

*Figure 21.7*                                                    Print Separations.

You won't get good results with an lpi over 80 unless you use a transfer function to correct for the tone compression in the shadow range. To use transfer functions, click on the **Transfer...** button in the Page Setup dialog box *(Figure 21.3)* and enter the values shown in Figure 21.6 as a starting point.

Your Halftone Screens dialog box should look like Figure 21.4. Click OK.

5. choose **File> Print** and click on the Print Separations checkbox *(Figure 21.7)*. Click Print.

# Diffusion Dither Bitmap

Starting with your CMYK file open in Photoshop, to print your separations as diffusion dither bitmaps:

1. If your Channels Palette is not open choose **Windows> Palettes> Show Channels.**

2. When the Channels Palette opens, put the pointer on the options triangle and select **Split Channels** *(Figure 21.8)*.

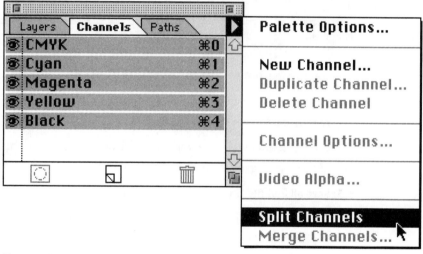

*Figure 21.8*                                                              Split Channels.

3. Your CMYK file will split into four grayscale files, one for each channel. Choose **Mode> Bitmap.** When the Bitmap dialog box opens, click on the Diffusion Dither radio button and enter the Output resolution you want. Use about 60 for images that you are not planning to reduce or enlarge. If you are planning to enlarge the image, for example, if you are enlarging 200%, use a resolution of 120 in this dialog box *(Figure 21.9)*. Calculate the appropriate resolution so you end up with about 60 ppi .

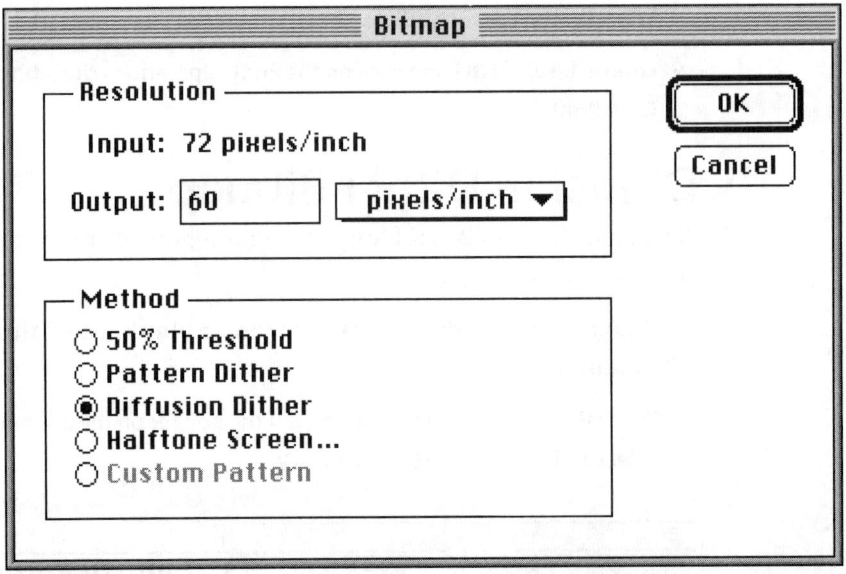

*Figure 21.9*                                    Bitmap.

Transfer functions are not relevant to this approach. Click OK.

4. Click once on the other three grayscale files and convert them to Bitmap in exactly the same way as in step 3.

*Note that your image on the monitor will look scrambled at any ratio lower than 1:1, but this has no effect on the printed quality.*

5. Save all four files in the Photoshop 3.0 format.

6. Choose **File**> **Page Setup** *(Figure 21.3)* and click on the Calibration Bars, Registration Marks, Corner Crop Marks, Center Crop Marks, and Labels checkboxes. Screens are not relevant here. Click OK.

7. Choose **Print** and print your files one at a time.

# Viewing the Dithered Image in Color

If you want to preview what your separations might look like when printed, you will need to merge the CMYK channels back into one composite CMYK file. This composite file is useful only for previewing—not for printing.

1. With your four bitmapped files open in Photoshop, click once on any one of them and choose **Mode**> **Grayscale**. When the Grayscale dialog box opens it should be set for 1 in the Size Ratio field *(Figure 21.10)*. Click OK.

2. Convert the remaining three bitmap files to grayscale as in step 1.

3. Put the pointer on the Channels Options triangle and select **Merge Channels** (Figure 21.11).

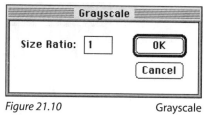

*Figure 21.10*        Grayscale

4. Click OK at the next dialog box which should be set up with CMYK in the Mode field and 4 in the Channels field *(Figure 21.12)*. Click OK.

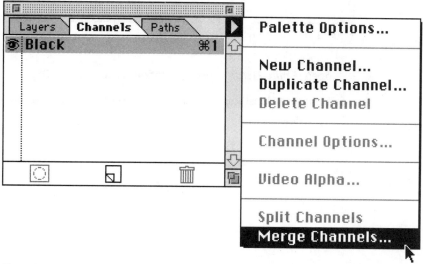

*Figure 21.11*        Merge Channels....

5. The Specify Channels dialog box will open next and will have the correct information unless you have more than one file with exactly the same attributes

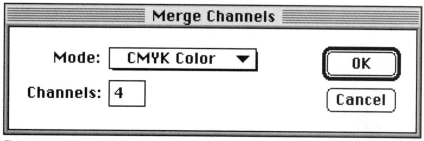

*Figure 21.12*        Merge Channels

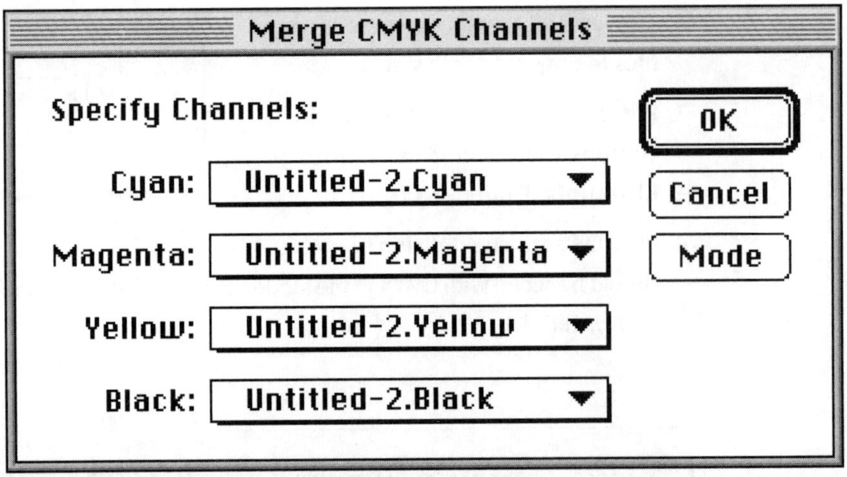

```
╔══════════════ Merge CMYK Channels ══════════════╗
║                                                  ║
║  Specify Channels:              ┌──────────────┐ ║
║                                 │      OK      │ ║
║    Cyan:  [ Untitled-2.Cyan    ▼]└──────────────┘║
║                                 ┌──────────────┐ ║
║  Magenta: [ Untitled-2.Magenta ▼] │   Cancel   │ ║
║                                 └──────────────┘ ║
║  Yellow:  [ Untitled-2.Yellow  ▼] ┌──────────┐   ║
║                                   │   Mode   │   ║
║   Black:  [ Untitled-2.Black   ▼] └──────────┘   ║
║                                                  ║
╚══════════════════════════════════════════════════╝
```

*Figure 21.13*                         Merge CMYK Channels.

open *(Figure 21.13)*. If the information is correct, click OK.

6. Congratulations! You have succeeded in putting your image back together for a preview.

# INDEX

# Colophon

The typeface used for the body text of this book is Minion. The heads are set in Myriad multiple master.

QuarkXPress was used for composition and page layout, and Photoshop and Illustrator were used to prepare all of the illustrations.

The book was produced using a Macintosh IIci with a DayStar Turbo 601/100 MHz accelerator card and a Radius IntelliColor Display/20e with a Radius PrecisionColor Pro 24x video card.

The author can be contacted at: smfa_sesto@flo.org

## *Picture Credits*

All illustrations are by the author with the exception of Figure C.6 by Virginia Beahan and Laura McPhee, Figure C.20, by Pat Kellogg Friedman, Figure C.21 by Rand Borden. Figures 20.19 and 20.21 are sample images from CMCD, Inc., and Figure C.4, Olé No Moiré, are both bundled with the deluxe CD-ROM version of Photoshop.